THE UNIVERSAL BUSINESS KN(

ESSENTIALS
OF
PRACTICAL BUSINESS KNOWLEDGE

SELECTIVE GUIDES

By
Mielu Rabinovici, B.A. (Soc. Sc.), B. Educ. (Business)
Diploma School of Commerce (Business)
Advanced studies in Educational Science

This book is dedicated
to my wonderful mother

Published
By
International R & D Business Education Limited

Copyright © Mielu Rabinovici, 1992

ISBN: 973-0-00073-5

CONTENTS

INTRODUCTION..5

PART ONE: A BUSINESS AT ITS START...............................7
General Considerations

PART TWO: BASIC BOOKKEEPING-ACCOUNTING............................23
A practical study guide

PART THREE: SELECTIVE EXERCISES AND SELF-TESTING
QUESTIONS IN THE FIELD OF BASIC
BOOKKEEPING-ACCOUNTING STUDY............................107

PART FOUR: THE PAYROLL WORK: ITS IMPORTANCE.......................153
A practical study guide

PART FIVE: A SIMPLIFIED GUIDE FOR INVENTORIES
CONTROL AND MANAGEMENT..219

PART SIX: BUDGETING AND CASH FLOW PROJECTIONS.............251
(Including Selective Illustrations)

PART SEVEN: BUSINESS WRITING SKILLS...............................291
A selective guide

PART EIGHT: THE 'KNOW-HOW' TO PREPARE AND
OBTAIN A BUSINESS LOAN...325
Certain useful guides

PART NINE: OTHER RELEVANT ISSUES..............................373

Anyone in the position of an owner-manager or in a managerial position, should "opt" for the best combination of the much needed essential management attributes.

It also has to be noted that effective management of any type of business enterprise, at any level, is not always an easy or simple function to perform.

Academic training alone, no matter its achievement, is not a valid and exclusive yardstick to employ in measuring a managerial prospective capability or a predicament for success.

It is rather one's proven record in his daily business life that counts best.

It is also through perseverance, diligence, hard work and good experience on the job, primarily, in a healthy interrelationship milieu, that one can stand the test of time and overcome the unexpected circumstances

INTRODUCTION

There are numerous individuals of various occupational backgrounds and from different industries around the world who may take interest in the present selective subject matters and their relevant aspects. Many of such interested readers may find the present manual an interesting and useful one, with immediate and practical applications. Indeed, it is written in a simple, clear and concise way in order to satisfy the needs of a certain category of individuals like managers and their assistants, small-business owners, students of business education and many others.

The various facets presented in this Manual will, undoubtedly, assist the interested learner to make a noticeable progress on the road to success, based on one's own abilities and potential capabilities of development in the specific and chosen field.

The descriptive material that follows in the subsequent pages should be seen as merely a guide and not as a substitute for one's need to acquire the needed knowledge through proper, practical and theoretical training and adequate and sufficient experience at work while seeking assistance, in the form of advices and consultations, from a professional in the field. This, each and every time the actual problems which may arise at work will signal the need for it.

The practical and selective guides that comprise this Manual are designed to be used for self-instruction on one hand, and for teaching-learning situations, on the other.

Certain useful tools like dictionaries of business terminology, accounting and financial notions should always be on hand for better understanding of their meanings. This, in turn, will enhance one's level of business communication skills in general, and the work performance in the chosen field of occupation in particular.

One of the interesting paradoxes of modern times may be the fact that even the best known schools of management cannot constitute a substitute for the much needed practical experience to be gained on the "battlefield" of work

It is only through "trial-and-error" that one can constantly hope and reach higher levels on the road to success. This, especially, when the growing pace of modern technology and the existing complexities of life are ahead of our simpler minds...

As there is not a royal road to reach the sea of knowledge it is my strong belief that with perseverence, strong will, determination and consideration for other people's good experience, one may hope to reach its splendid shores.

PART ONE

A BUSINESS AT ITS START

General Considerations

CONTENTS

Introduction 9

You as an Entrepreneur...10

The Professional Assistance
- Financing...11

Evaluating your Business Potential, your Product
Strength and State of Existing Competition...13

Choosing the Legal Form of Business
- Sole Proprietorship...14
- General Partnership 15
- Limited Partnership 16
- The Corporation 16

The Law, the Rules and the various Regulations regarding Licences and Permits 18

The Name Search 19

Your Business Records and Accounts..19

The State of your Business Records: A Questionnaire...20

Introduction

Anyone interested in managing successfully a business enterprise on his own, should try and gain certain useful and relevant knowledge on the various business matters one may come across during the daily business life. A tentative outline or directions of learning is presented below:

- Basic bookkeeping-accounting operations and related knowledge of recording of various categories of business transactions like sales, purchases, cash receipts, cash disbursements, etc;

- Familiarity with the payroll procedures and the requirements based on the law, the rules and various regulations in force;

- Oral and written business communications skills, namely the degree and extent to which one should be versatile in communicating with others at different levels. The art of writing business letters, once learned, may exercise a tremendous impact on a certain business result;

- The Know-How to prepare a business plan;

- The Know-How to prepare a cash flow projection plan and the art of budgeting wisely;

- Familiarity with the various business and recording forms in the particular field of occupation, in particular, and with the outside forms used by the financial, governmental institutions, in general;

- Familiarity with the various terminology in use, along the business, financial and accounting lines;

- The Know-How to read the economic charts and interpret the various data presented by the newspapers, magazines, research and economic and financial institutions, on a regular and periodical basis;

- Permanent contacts with the trading fairs, trade associations, various specific conferences and seminars on various topics related to one's field of operations.

- Knowledge of the availability of funds and assistance from various sources and authorities in the area, and how to obtain such help;

- Knowledge of the social and business environment, the state of competition, the existing diversity of the product lines, the marketing forces at work in the specific area of business occupation;

- Learning how to obtain the best professional services and how to handle the relationships with the banker, the accountant and others, like the insurance agent, the brokers, etc.

YOU AS AN ENTREPRENEUR

In managing your business, the art of record-keeping is one of the most important parts of your needed knowledge along with buying, pricing, selling and managing personnel.

A series of questions regarding your capabilities and the extent of your knowledge, both general and specific, may be rightly asked, namely:

– What are your general management capabilities?

– What is your background in business in general, and in your chosen field of occupation in particular?

– Do you know how your business is doing?

– Do you know how to interpret your financial statements?

– Do you have a firm programme of financing or a proposed plan?

– Will such a plan favorably affect your business?

– Are you aware of the risk(s) you are taking? What is your degree of feeling of security?

– What is the extent of your market knowledge with respect to cycles, product and competition?

– How strong is your cash flow standing and your working capital?

– Is your business strong enough to cope with eventual economic cycles?

– Are you doing forecasting to know where you are going?

– But, above all, what are your attributes or essential characteristics related to your business, prospective growth and developent, like the following:

  – Drive: responsibility, acting, taking risks, etc.

  – Thinking ability: both creative and analytical

  – Human relations: ability gained through good and wide experience in dealing with people of various occupations and different backgrounds

  – Communications ability: both verbal and written

  – Technical knowledge of business, etc.

– Are you self-motivated?
– To what extent are you independent in knowing what to do?
– What are your feelings about other people?
– To what extent are you able to get along with them?
– Are you capable of undertaking responsibility?
– Would you rather delegate tasks to others?
– How good are you at organizing?
– Do you like planning in advance?
– How good are you as a worker?
– Would you rather be a manager?

THE PROFESSIONAL ASSISTANCE

A public professional accountant can serve a useful function in the organizational structure of a small business. This, especially when a small enterprise is limited by a reduced staff and does not have the needed knowledge of organizational guidelines and managerial skills.

In its capacity, the accountant can make important and detailed recommendations concerning the organizational structure. This will make possible to prevent many administrative problems.

Certain expected administrative problems may take place even in an already established enterprise still controlled by the founder-owner. The owner having the decision-making powers but still occupied with the details of administration, may lack the understanding of the importance of delegation of authority. Sooner, he may find himself facing the need to make all kinds of decisions while being overloaded with work. In such a framework, the owner will not have any longer the cooperation from his employees and will face their incompetency.

The usefulness of a professional accountant lies in his ability to discover the causes and sources of such problems when the business faces the deterioration of its administrative machinery and declining of efficiency. Such a professional accountant will more likely conduct an elaborate analysis of the company's business and offer sound solutions to the problems. Such deficiences may be within the various departments like accounting, purchasing, sales, inventory control, etc.

The recommendations made to the owner may be along the following lines of thought:

– Owner may be asked to review his involvement in the business operations;

– Emphasis on ability;

– A clear-cut delineation of the responsibilities outlined, and

– Managers 'trained' how to handle staff.

FINANCING

The professional accountant can play an important role as an advisor as well as an auditor, offering special useful services like tax advice, systems analysis and consultations on a variety of important business matters. But most of all, is his ability in dealing with business financing matters. In this respect, the professional accountant can make plans for establishing the business debt and capital structure, advice on the possible contribution by the various leading institutions, with needed information as to their terms for loans and the related interest rates, restrictions, and other important matters.

It can be emphasized that for current working capital requirements, banks will be recommended for term loans. Another source of financing can be considered as been represented, under certain conditions, by the existing government agencies.

Finally, a noticeable source of medium- to long-term capital financing is that of specialized financial institutions dealing especially with small and medium sized enterprises.

In selecting one of these sources over the others, the professional accountant will analyze the degree of intervention in many decisions, by outside institutions, their rate of interest, terms of repayment, and the guarantees sought.

Funds for growth can be procured basically from two sources: internally, from cash profits, and outside, from banks and other lending institutions.

In support to the needed working capital growth, the professional accountant, together with the firm's management, will prepare forecasts in respect to sales expected figures and the cash-flow projections, as part of the required presentation to be made to the lending institutions.

The related security may involve accounts receivable and inventories, personal guarantees of the owners, etc.

The cash flow originating from receivables can be directed into productive ways of investment in the form of expended facilities or other possibilities of generating other income.

A business course of action along its financial wisdom, can be its decision to grow more slowly by being contempt of living within the firm's means, while succeeding to save income taxes that will help future financial growth.

A good professional or expert on taxes should, whenever possible, be used together with judicious planning.

It has to be stressed that many decisions made in the early stages of the business development, may have an enormous impact on the future course of business events. The professional accountant will try and assist the firm, from its start, to evaluate the nature, value and feasibility of new facilities.

In order to reach a satisfactorily level of success, the following conditions should be met:

– Owner is ready to reinvest all cash profits;

– loans obtained were used as they become approved and needed to be used;

– owner initiative and ability prevailing before considering sharing the equity with outsiders;

– owner does not hesitate to devote the needed length of time, energy, efforts and perseverance required by the business operations;

– owner and management recognize the advantages offered or coming from the outside expertise on financial matters.

EVALUATING YOUR BUSINESS POTENTIAL, YOUR PRODUCT STRENGTH AND STATE OF THE EXISTING COMPETITION

Certain essentials for 'fitness' of your business potential must be analysed. This prior to the actual start and setting-up of your business enterprise.

It is known by many, that certain small companies like yours, perhaps, are responding to market needs more quickly than larger enterprises. You should assess, first of all, your firm's prospective potential of development in the area. In this respect, market research or market investigation is of essential. It will tell you as to whether or not you have a good or viable product or service to offer and stand the test of time, while facing the existing competition. Any realistic approach to a carefully planned research should be based on good experience and good analytical skill. If you can afford, you should entrust a marketing research agency in performing such a task and present to you the results of their work.

You must reach a point of satisfactory information presentation on which basis you will be able to ponder the eventual benefits against the costs and risks involved in having and managing a business of your own.

Assuming you know certain factors well enough regarding the product(s) or service(s) your business can provide, the related price(s), the promotion and distribution and organizational skills and efforts involved, you have to further assess, in the light of the existing state of competition, what should be the sales value and volume, the prices and profit margins you can or should reach, if good results are to be attained.

A thorough analysis or investigation of the existing environment or the area in which you will operate is needed. Also at the place of your business and in the general framework of the country's economic and financial outlook, certain useful questions should be asked.

What are your sources of financing and the strength of your capital, expressed in terms of money, manpower and equipment and machinery, to carry on your business plan vis-a-vis the competition with the same industry, and based on the prospective consumers' needs and/or requirements?

What are your skills and level of knowledge regarding the product quality, design, price, specific features, terms of sale, seasons, and the like?

To what extent you are ready to be flexible and make the necessary adjustments during the business life, especially, during the first period of business operations, the so-called trial-and-error period of work.

It is paramount that one will realistically perform a self-assessment picture before embarking or launching himself in the venture of a chosen business. One should always bear in mind that a good combination of sufficient capital and specific trading skills, in a healthy business environment, and based on good country's economics trends, can ensure a certain level of success and form the basis of encouragement a business needs in order to succeed.

CHOOSING THE LEGAL FORM OF BUSINESS

There is a noticeable and growing trend of new firms been formed by independent people around the world, eager to prove themselves of their attributes and capabilities of running their own business and making their own decisions. Such business owners are aspiring to reach personal satisfaction that arises from the successful operation and management of the business they founded. There are certain types or forms of business organization one may choose and get involved with, namely the following:

- Sole proprietorship;

- General Partnership;

- Limited Partnership;

- Corporation.

The legal form of business one may select, has to do with certain considerations, like the ones listed below:

- The available or existing funds, as capital for financing the establishing of the business and the related source of obtaining such funds;

- The needed skills to run the 'show', implement and conduct the specific and required types of business operations;

- The degree of control one wishes to have over the operations;

- The forms and extent of government taxation rules and rates of taxation in the specific type of industry, for business in general, and for business profits, in particular;

- The extent one is willing to be, personally, responsible for debts and claims against the business and also be accountable for the business operational activities and their results;

- The risks one is ready to undertake in carrying out a business for profits;

- Etc.

There are certain advantages and disadvantages associated with the various forms of business organizations enumerated above.

A brief comparison of certain of such characteristics, may be of help.

SOLE PROPRIETORSHIP

Such a form of business organization is characterized by having its owner contributing or investing his own cash and/or other assets in order to set up the business. He may use his savings in this respect, or he may borrow funds from friends and/or different financial institutions.

We can enlist certain advantages and certain disadvantages associated with this kind of business.

ADVANTAGES

- It is easy to establish it;
- It is least subject to the various rules and regulations, comparing with other forms of business;
- The business net profits are taxed as individual or personal income;
- As a smaller and simpler type of business, it is easy to control it and supervise its various activities or operations;
- Flexibility of organization;
- It is an informal kind of organization in its character;
- Small fee for registration with the authorities;
- Less business papers and bookkeeping requirements.

DISADVANTAGES

- The owner must bear the sole responsibility for debts and claims against the business enterprise and he is responsible for controlling it;
- The sole proprietor must procur all the necessary funds to activate and operate the business;
- Sometimes it is difficult to have one person performing all the necessary duties and ensure a smooth performance of the various activities involved;
- The business ceases to exist with the death of the proprietor.

GENERAL PARTNERSHIP

This kind of business organization can come to light when two or more individuals get together and decide to form an enterprise and share profits and sustain eventual losses, in an agreed ratio.

Certain advantages and disadvantages can be mentioned below:

ADVANTAGES

- It is easy to set up;
- No written agreement is necessary, although it is advisable to have one;
- Many management and profit-sharing arrangements are possible to be made;
- It is a more complex form of business organization than the sole proprietorship type of organization, but less complex than the corporate form;
- Each partner can be held liable for the debt or contractual agreement made by the others in the firm.

DISADVANTAGES

- Death or withdrawal of one partner of the firm, or the inclusion of a new one, will, legally, bring the firm to a cessation;

- Liability of the partnership affects the personal assets of the general partners;

- Since it is not a separate legal entity, each partner's shared income is to be reported on an individual basis, for taxation purposes.

LIMITED PARTNERSHIP

It is a more closely regulated type of business than the kind of partnership mentioned above.

One may invest in such a type of business and become a partner in sharing the profits, as agreed. This without having unlimited liability. But he will have control over the business only to a limited extent, and risk only his original contribution or investment into the firm.

It has to be noted that in certain jurisdictions, this form of business, like the general partnership one, is regulated under the so-called Partnership Act.

A limited partnership form of business organization is a more complex form than that of a sole proprietorship one.

Registration of such a form of business organization is required under certain regulations.

THE CORPORATION

This kind of business organization is a separate legal entity, apart from its shareholders (co-owners). In such a capacity it can be entered into contractual legal agreements, held responsible for any eventual liabilities incurred by the entity, receive and deal with claims and pay corporate taxes.

Certain advantages and disadvantages can be associated with such a form of business organization, namely:

ADVANTAGES

- Easy to raise capital funds, by selling shares of the company, to outsiders;

- It can go public;

- Shareholders are limited in their liability(ies) for the firm's debts and/or claims, to the extent of their original investment into the business;

- It has continuity of its existence, namely it is a going concern;

- Shares are transferable, thus the continuity of the business is ensured;

- More capital is available;

− Greater flexibility regarding taxation and certain incentives or taxation advantages may be obtained from time to time and under certain conditions.

DISADVANTAGES

− Complexity of taxation and the need for professional advice in this respect;

− Subject to more elaborate regulations than other forms of business as discussed above;

− Cost of establishing and carrying on such a kind of enterprise can be much higher than expected.

THE LAW, THE RULES AND THE VARIOUS REGULATIONS REGARDING LICENCES AND PERMITS

Under certain jurisdictions there is no need for a licence to set up a business and no formalities are required in this respect. Anyone can provide any goods or services and conduct his business operations.

However, one may need a licence and this because of the nature of the chosen business or because some aspect of the business operations may only be practised under a licence.

The law, the rules and various regulations in use, may apply nationally, provincially or locally, depending on the extent of business operations. The related authorities may be branches of government or agencies, municipalities, professional bodies or the local police.

It has to be stressed that one should know that an undischarged bankrupt may not manage an enterprise or be an executive of one. Also anyone convicted of offence or in breach of certain regulations.

However, any interested person, interested to obtain a permit or licence to carry on a business for profit, should firstly, enquire about the related and specific provisions of the rules and regulations in use in the selected area of his business establishment. It is best to consult a senior officer in charge of the respective department in the government, prior to submitting the application for licencing.

THE NAME SEARCH

Before a business enterprise is established, it is recommended that the given or chosen name of the business be searched with the respective government authority, and a request for name reservation be made.

A related and specific application form should be obtained and the owner or founder of the business should state in it if the entity is already incorporated or registered in another jurisdiction and what type of business is he carrying out, e.g. corporation, sole proprietorship, partnership, etc.

The owner will then indicate a few names as his choice and in their order of preference; this in case one of the selected names is already in use by another business within the jurisdiction.

Usually, the name search and the reservation request, if required by the government authorities, will be obtained for a reasonable fee, in a certain reasonable time. At the same or a higher authoritative level of the government, a declaration for partnership formation and business name is required in order to be entered, legally, in the corporate and central registry. Normally, in such a form, is required that a statment be made regarding the type of business organization the owner is involved in or, as the case may be, if there is a change of business name or change in membership or ownership or change in the nature of business or if a dissolution date is declared.

YOUR BUSINESS RECORDS AND ACCOUNTS

Your business records should be preserved for any future purpose, especially when, at a later date, certain legal authorities will like to examine them and assess your state of business affairs, mainly in respect to taxes.

Records must be maintained in clear writing and kept at the main place of business for a certain period.

It can be stressed that every person carrying on business is required to keep accurate records of all the financial transactions of the fiscal periods.

The law requires taxpayers to keep such records and books of accounts as are needed to determine the taxes payable. The taxation office is authorized to audit such records for any purpose related to the enforcement or administration of the related regulations. In this regard, the taxation office is authorized to request and receive from any person, information, records, documents, etc., within a reasonable time.

The original documents reflecting the business transactions that took place during a given fiscal period, should be, neatly kept in respect to sales, purchases, receipts, disbursements of cash, etc.

The original books of entry like the journals and the ledgers, should also be preserved.

The following represent some noticeable advantages of keeping proper business records:

− Future business plans and future business decisions made by the firm's management, can use past data of information, relevant to many business aspects;

− The financial position of the business, if stated in a sound and fair way can provide better information about the business state of affairs and help forecasting for the future;

− It serves the firm's management for subsequent yearly analysis, on a comparative basis, against prior years results of operations;

− It represents the legal basis of documentation in support of the company's operations, for audit and control purposes;

− Complete and accurate income tax reports can be prepared and other supporting documentation and necessary information for the calculated taxable income;

− Well-kept records will facilitate tax savings, since they constitute also a reminder of eligible deductible expenses, income from sources which are not taxable, etc.

− Also, well-kept records will eliminate certain problems that may arise when taxes are audited;

− It serves other useful purposes like for cash flow projections, budgeting, planning, etc.

Sketchy records, which may represent mere estimates are unacceptable. The records must be keep in the country, at the main place of business.

The type of records a business keeps will normally depend on the following factors:

- the complexity and nature of the business

- the availability of bookkeeping-accounting facilities

- the specific needs of the business

- the legal requirements and those of other authorities and agencies such as banks, etc.

- the firm's own need to keep constantly informed the management about the business state and development.

In this respect, the accounting system should be properly designed to ensure a sound and fair presentation of data and the availability of it for necessary internal information and support daily and periodically the business decision-makers.

It should be emphasized that a poorly designed accounting system and consequently a lack of necessary information by the internal control section of the business under consideration, will most of the time result in business failure.

One may or may not be selected for audit by the government authorities who are conducting audit work from time to time. It is highly advisable that one keep an orderly state of the records and account system which will faciilitate control and assessment whenever the need may arise. In this respect, it is necessary to provide detailed or elaborate information of many facets of the business, for various fiscal periods, as required.

The specific legislation dealing with records and their preservations, provide for a certain number of years, during which the business should have all of its records kept available for examination.

Other records like the minute book, share records, certain contracts and agreements, must be kept indefinitely.

THE STATE OF YOUR BUSINESS RECORDS
Questionnaire
CASH RECEIPTS

What kind of records are in use for cash receipts?
Is a cash register in use? If so, what information is obtained from such a record, for accounting purposes? Is it considered adequate by your accountant?
How is cash verified and reconciled at the end of day?
Are all cash receipts deposited in the bank and separate listings of daily incoming cash kept at the place of business?
How are cash receipts accounted for or recorded by customer or by any eventual other source?

CASH PAYMENTS

How are documents examined, verified and approved for payment? By whom?
Are all bills and invoices paid by cheque? Who is reconciling the bank account? How often?
Is control of a petty cash fund entrusted to someone in your business?
Is such a fund reasonable in size based on the size of your business operations?

What kind of small expenses are paid from petty cash? Who authorizes them?
How is the fund handled and accounted for? Is there an imprest system in place to replenish the fund from time to time?

PURCHASES

What is the purchase cycle in your company?
How are orders for goods (merchandise) prepared?
How are invoices verified and how does your filing system work in this respect?
Where are purchases accounted for or recorded?
Is a separate ledger used for creditors' accounts?
Describe the related account form in use.
What are the sources for recording in such accounts?
How are suppliers' accounts reconciled? By whom? How often?

SALES

What is the procedure for cash sales in your business?
How are credit sales recorded? What are the related records in use?
Who approves them?
Are sales invoices made for all sales?
How are sales invoices verified and how is the filing system in your business set up? Describe it.
Is a separate ledger kept for customer accounts?
What record form is used to handle such accounts?
How often are customers' accounts reconciled? By whom?

STATEMENTS

What is the period of the fiscal year used by your business?
What kind of inventory method is in use and how often is inventory of goods (merchandise) checked?
How often is an inventory taken? Is this done through a physical count or stock recordkeeping information?
What kind of financial statements are prepared?
What is the level of professional or technical knowledge of the accountant who prepares such statements?
Are your books kept on a cash or an accrual basis?
What kind of adjustment entries are made, if any? How often? By whom?
What is the nature of such adjustments? Are they made due to omissions or errors, or for completion of transactions already recorded?
Who is reviewing such entries and/or authorizing them?

It should be emphasized from the start that the need for accurate and sound accounting information, for example, is felt everywhere and by all types of businesses and in various fields of occupation.

It is an already proven fact that poor or incomplete data are in most cases the cause of business failure and may create other problems as well during the normal course of business life in general, and during the early stages of a business development, in particular.

PART TWO

BASIC BOOKKEEPING – ACCOUNTING

A practical study guide

Lack of adequate business records can be the cause of business failure and not an excuse for it.

Good experience teaches us that even the most knowledgeable entrepreneur and best tradesman can get 'lost' in the myriad of business transactions and bring him to the verge of failure.

Trying to correct or redress such a failure can, sometimes, be a costly task for the firm, especially for a small business during its first stage of development.

For multiple purposes, and especially for financing, forecasting, taxation and other matters, well-kept business records should be considered a must.

CONTENTS

Introduction 27

Basic Bookkeeping-Accounting: General Considerations 30

The Bookkeeping-Accounting Cycle: Useful Comments 31

Analysing a Business Transaction: The Rules of the 'Game' 33
- Important Steps..34
- A Useful Illustration 37
- General Journal Entries 39

The Various Books of Entries: The Journal in Use 41
- Relevant Considerations 41

The 'Subsidiary' Ledgers of Accounts: An Inter-relationship............................43

Sales and the Sales Journal 44

Cash Receipts and the Cash Receipts Journal..45
- Practical Illustrations 45
- Cash Management: Certain Relevant Questions...............................49
- Control over Accounts Receivable 50

Purchases: Step-by-Step along its Cycle 51
- Certain Journalising Procedures 52
- Accounts Payable Journal: a Practical Illustration 53

Cheque Payments and Cash Disbursements Journal 54
- The Subsidiary Ledger of Accounts Payable 55

The General Journal of Various Entries 56

Certain Steps in Reconciling the Bank Balance of Account..............................57

The Petty Cash Fund Handling: An Exemplification 58

The General Ledger of Accounts 61

The Worksheet and the Necessary Adjustments to Accounts 62
- The Depreciation; Certain Useful Notes..63
- The Worksheet: A Practical Application 64

General Standards of Financial Statements Presentation 68
- Accounting Principles Explained 70
- Classification of Balance Sheet Items..72
- The Income Statement: The Meaning of Revenue and Expenses.....73

The Closing Entries and the Post-Closing Trial Balance: An Exemplification 75

Analysing Financial Statements: Certain Applications or Ratios in Use 77

LIST OF EXHIBITS
(ANNEXED)

Exhibit
Number

1	The Rules of the Game: A Diagram	33
2	Analysing a Business Transaction - Step I	34
3	Analysing a Business Transaction - Step II A. Re: Balance Sheet	35
4	Analysing a Business Transaction - Step II B. Re: Income Statement	36
5	Opening Balance Sheet: An Illustration	37
6	Illustration of Recording Transactions	38
7	The 'Know-How' to Journalise Transactions	39
8	Compound Journal Entries; An Exemplification	40
9	What Type of Journal to Use	42
10	The General Ledger and its Subsidiary Ledgers: An Interrelation	43
11	Sales Journal	44
12	Cash Receipts Journal: An example for a simple form	46
13	Cash Receipts Journal: An example for a more elaborate form	47
14	Accounts Payable Journal	53
15	Cheques Disbursements Journal	54
16	Petty Cash Journal	59
17	General Journal Entries (Re: Petty Cash)	60
18	Worksheet	64
19	General Journal (Re: Adjustments to Accounts)	67
20	General Journal (Re: Closing Entries)	76
21	The Bookkeeping-Accounting Cycles Explained	82
22	The Bookkeeping-Accounting Cycles - Diagram	83
23	Review of the Sales Procedure	84
24	Credit Memorandum	85
25	Cash Received on Account	86
26	Statement of Account Receivable	87
27	Account Receivable Ageing Analysis	88
28	Aged Listing of Accounts Receivable	89
29	Purchase Order	90
30	Purchase Journal - Trade	91
31	Petty Cash Vouchers illustrated	92
32	Chart of Accounts - Exemplification	93
33	Trial Balance	98
34	Financial Statements	99

Introduction

The Bookkeeping-Accounting work of a business constitutes one of the most important facets of its administrative operations.

The financial transactions of any business should be recorded in an orderly and chronological way, using the machinery of accounting and financial systems.

As stated by an authoritative body, 'Accounting is the art of recording, classifying and centralizing in a systematic way' all the available data expressed in monetary terms, and in order that decisions and predictions will be made on as accurate a basis as possible.

The inflow of important business papers, constituting the so-called primary documentation or the original ones, like invoices, cheques, etc. are analysed, scrutinised or verified, and subsequently recorded in the firm's books of original entry known as books of original entry (the journals and the related general ledger of company's accounts).

The scope is to summarise the figures of the period under consideration, by grouping them according to the nature of the business transactions, under the heading of certain specifically-named accounts in operation for the fiscal period.

The totals of all the business transactions of the period under consideration presented in the form of ending balances of accounts are regrouped, in order to be represented in the form of the financial statements of the firm for a particular selected fiscal period, usually one year. In addition to the financial statements, the accounting process can generate supporting information in the form of various detailed schedules of the accounts included in the respective statements. Thus it will serve the management for analysis of the business operations that took place during the period under treatment.

Nevertheless, the entire accounting work of any fiscal year, together with the schedules of accounts and the various supported documentation and information will serve, at a later date, as a useful basis for analysis and verification, audit or inspection by outside authorities, like taxation offices, banks, etc.

It has to be emphasised that all the accounting work and the related business papers should be preserved by the firm a certain number of years, according to the country's provisions in this respect.

Any business manager should gain familiarity, to a satisfactory extent, with the following:

- what type of journals are in use within the firm;

- the interpretation of the information presented in the ledgers of accounts to include the subsidiary ledgers of accounts receivable and account payable;

- the way of recording the business transactions into the various journals;

- what information can be further obtained through the accounting machinery;

- how to interpret the firm's financial statements of any given period;

- how to communicate with the professionals like the accountants, bankers, and other outsiders, in respect to the end results of business operations;

- how the internal control system should work in order to safeguard the company's assets, minimise the possibility for fraud and errors or omissions, and ensure a smooth line of work in all the company's units.

At the minimum, and in order to grasp the essentials of any basic accounting, the following should be known:

- the bookkeeping-accounting work: its importance;

- the legal requirements regarding the state of business records;

- how the technical and clerical staff of the accounting department should be evaluated for their performances;

- the steps involved in the Bookkeeping-Accounting Cycle;

- the existing rules of the accounting 'game' and how to analyse a business transaction for recording purposes (journalising);

- the various business journals in use, both special and general ones, like the journals for sales, purchases, cash receipts, cash disbursements, etc;

- the various subsidiary journals and other records in use like the ones needed for registering the acquisitions of company's assets;

- the various business forms in use during any given fiscal year of operations;

- the inter-departmental relationship of various incumbents with their related positions and assigned duties, vis-a-vis those involved in the accounting department;

- the flow of various forms and other business papers and memos, within the firm;

- the preservation of records and internal control system, especially in regard to the safeguarding of the company's various assets;

- the payroll information system and the needed specific payroll forms in use;

- familiarity with the company's chart or list of accounts;

- the types of financial statements in use by the company, their usefulness, understanding and interpretation of the end-results of business operations for a given period under consideration;

- the various rules and regulations in force regarding payroll and safety in the particular type of industry;

- the various outside agencies which may make use of the company's business information and related documentation.

- the preservation of records and internal control system, especially in regard to the safeguarding of the company's various assets;

- the payroll information system and the needed specific payroll forms in use;

- familiarity with the company's chart or list of accounts;

- the types of financial statements in use by the company, their usefulness, understanding and interpretation of the end-results of business operations for a given period under consideration;

- the various rules and regulations in force regarding payroll and safety in the particular type of industry;

- the various outside agencies which may make use of the company's business information and related documentation.

BASIC BOOKKEEPING-ACCOUNTING
GENERAL CONSIDERATIONS

The entire machinery of bookkeeping-accounting work together with all its related procedures are of paramount importance in the everyday life of almost any kind of business enterprise and its incumbents.

The best way for anyone on the road to progress and development at the place of work is to try to learn the various elements (the essential ones), step by step, from the simple to the more complex ones, in a clear and concise way. And this, obviously, at one's own pace and ability.

The various illustrations represented by the exhibits of this Part, constitute one of the most selective bodies of technical exemplifications and as such can serve as a useful guide for further adjustments to be made to the already-existing journals and forms, in use, in a certain given firm.

Any effort or endeavour revealed by anyone, at his place of work, should be sustained by assistance sought from a professional in the field, for any problem that may arise during normal course of daily business life within the framework of the bookkeeping-accounting work.

It has been stressed that proper bookkeeping-accounting work supported by adequate documentation of a firm's operations serve a multi-fold purpose, namely:

- They provide the owner(s) and/or management of a given enterprise with the needed information in order to reach fair, sound and timely business decisions of various extents and degrees of importance and usefulness.

- They also represent the legal basis for financial reporting by the firm to its outside authorities, private and governmental ones, including the necessary data for taxation purposes.

- They constitute an important managerial tool for yearly analysis, on a comparative basis and against prior years' performance.

- They may also serve many other useful purposes including those related to planning, projections, etc.

Needless to say, a poorly-designed accounting system and the lack of necessary and timely information associated with this will, more likely, lead to business failure.

While some interested individuals might find the present topic an interesting and easy one to digest, others may as well treat it as a suitable and refreshing chapter that facilitates the grasp of its various elements.

As the needed practical business bookkeeping-accounting skills and knowledge, at any level, cannot be learned from a basic and related technical book only, it is the proper application of the principles, rules and related technical procedures that prevail, if good performances at work are to be attained.

The purpose of the practical descriptions included in this Part is to assist one making progress at taking better steps towards improvement on the job. It is in this way that one can better become familiarised with the specific matters of concern and, perhaps, be on a higher level of knowledge and able to assist others, whenever the need may arise.

THE BOOKKEEPING-ACCOUNTING CYCLE

In performing the bookkeeping-accounting work, the following steps are always taken, namely:

- all the original or source documents, named primary documents, are enlisted or recorded (journalised) into certain special or specific journals, each of them reserved for certain similar types of business transactions, e.g. sales, purchases, receipts, payments, or of a general nature;

- each and every column of each and every month of a given journal is added up and the totals are transferred or posted to the respective and related accounts of the firm's general ledger of accounts.

- at the end of each and every month, the balances of all the accounts of the general ledger are listed in a so-called trial balance of accounts, as a mechanical verification that all the amounts of debit and credit type were posted rightly into the accounts, namely on the related part;

In this way, the bookkeeping work can be accomplished and a higher stage of the accounting performance comprising the following steps, may follow, namely:

- using the already-prepared trial balance of accounts of a given firm, a so-called worksheet is prepared. This will facilitate the needed analysis of the respective accounts in order to make all the eventual needed corrections and adjustments and complete the information leading to the issuance of the company's financial statements for a certain selected period of time;

   In this respect, and prior to the preparation of the financial statements, certain useful schedules of accounts are drawn, based on the analysis made using the worksheet mentioned above;

- the statement of income or earnings comprises, on one hand, the revenue of the firm, like sales, rental income, fees or commissions earned, and on the other, all the related costs or expenses that help generate such a revenue (matching principle). Subsequently, all these accounts are closed, and the end result in the form of a profit or loss is transferred to the capital or equity account, as the case may be depending on the form of business organisation. The profit or loss of each and every period is accumulated into the permanent account of the firm, named Capital account (re: sole proprietorship) or Retained Earnings or Deficit (re: corporation);

- in order to ensure that all the company accounts (revenue and expenses) have been correctly and properly closed, a new so-called post-closing trial balance is prepared;

- finally, all the assets, liabilities and equity accounts are sorted out and the set of required financial statements are issued for a certain selected period of time, usually for one year of operations.

In addition to the above steps, the following work is also performed, namely:

- all the individual amounts comprising the totals of purchases and payments on account, as made, are posted or transferred to the subsidiary ledger of accounts payable, and similarly.

31

-   all the individual amounts comprising the total of sales and receipts journals are posted or transferred to the subsidiary ledger of accounts receivable

It has to be emphasised that the accounting of a firm includes not only the bookkeeping work but also the use of such information, its interpretation and analysis, tax planning, product costing, etc.

ANALYZING A BUSINESS TRANSACTION:

THE RULES OF THE 'GAME'

Each time your assets increase you DEBIT the respective account involved.
Each time your assets decrease you CREDIT the respective account involved.

The opposite rules apply for liabilities and CAPITAL or EQUITY accounts, namely:

Each time your liabilities, for example, increase, you CREDIT the respective account.
Each time your liabilities, for example, decrease, you DEBIT the respective account.

In analyzing a business transaction, one should ask the following questions:

- What accounts are affected?
  The double entry system and the related logic highlight the practical usefulness of the so-called "T" form of accounts, and the equality between the left and right sides, in any given business transaction

- To what group do they belong?

- Sort the accounts which are affected (into assets, liabilities, capital groups of accounts).

- How are these accounts affected? Are they increased or decreased?

Note: The so-called double entry of accounting refers to the fact that for each transaction that takes place, at least two accounts are involved. While one account is debited, another account is credited with the same amount. Subsequent pages deal with practical applications that prove this fact.

For illustration purposes only, the following diagrams are presented below:

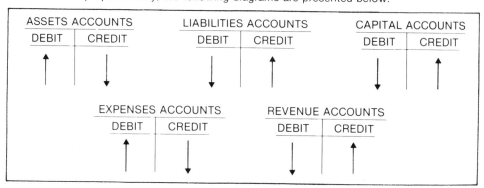

Note: The arrows indicate either increases or decreases in the respective accounts.

To each and every account there are always two sides: debit and credit with, obviously, a certain space designated for the related balance of the respective account.

Debit refers to the left-hand side and it has that meaning only.

Conversely, credit refers to the right hand side, and it has that meaning only.

Exhibit 1

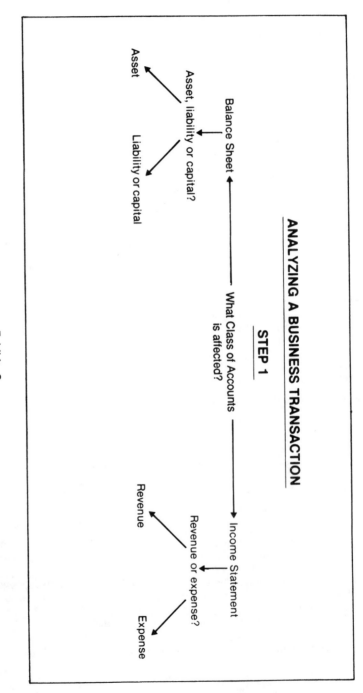

ANALYZING A BUSINESS TRANSACTION

<u>STEP 1</u>

What Class of Accounts is affected?

Balance Sheet

Asset, liability or capital?

Asset

Liability or capital

Income Statement

Revenue or expense?

Revenue

Expense

Exhibit 2

34

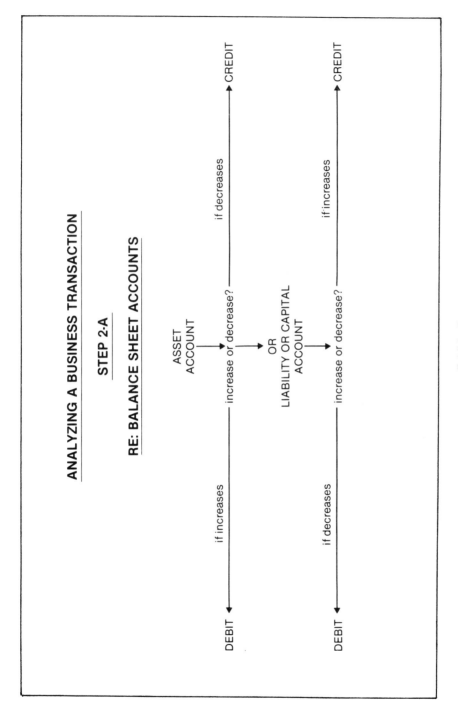

ANALYZING A BUSINESS TRANSACTION

STEP 2-A

RE: BALANCE SHEET ACCOUNTS

ASSET
ACCOUNT

if increases → DEBIT

increase or decrease?

if decreases → CREDIT

OR

LIABILITY OR CAPITAL
ACCOUNT

if decreases → DEBIT

increase or decrease?

if increases → CREDIT

Exhibit 3

ANALYZING A BUSINESS TRANSACTION

STEP 2-B

RE: INCOME STATEMENT ACCOUNTS

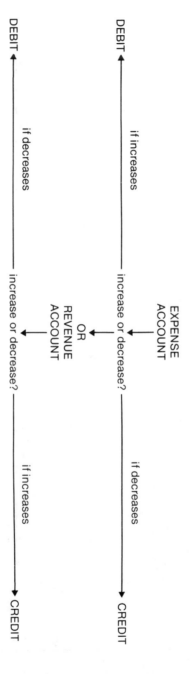

Exhibit 4

Let us examine, for exercise purposes only, a small business's application of the rules as described above:

T. IRELAND CARTAGE SERVICES

BALANCE SHEET

AS AT DECEMBER 31, 1977

1) Opening balance sheet based on owners' contributions at start:

ASSETS		LIABILITIES	
CASH	$ 350.22	BANK LOAN	$ 5000.00
ACCTS. RECEIVABLE	3300.00	ACCTS. PAYABLE	645.36
SUPPLIES	100.00	CAPITAL	
TRUCKS	8020.00	O. KEITH, Capital	6124.86
TOTAL	$11770.22	TOTAL	$11770.22

2) The above information is posted or recorded into the related accounts of the firm's General Ledger of accounts:

(D) **CASH** (C)	
$350.22	

(D) **ACCTS. RECEIVABLE** (C)	
$3300.00	

(D) **SUPPLIES** (C)	
$100.00	

(D) **TRUCKS** (C)	
$8020.00	

(D) **BANK LOAN** (C)	
	$5000.00

(D) **ACCTS. PAYABLE** (C)	
	$ 645.36

(D) **O. KEITH, CAPITAL** (C)	
	$6124.86

Exhibit 5

37

TRANSACTION 1

Jan. 10, 1987. $100.25 cash is received from D. Smith in part payment of his debt.

CASH

DR	CR	BAL.
350.22		
100.25		450.47

ACCOUNTS RECEIVABLE

DR	CR	BAL.
3300.00	100.25	3199.75

TRANSACTION 2

Jan. 15, 1987. A service has been performed for a customer at a price of $50.00 and is paid in cash.

CASH

DR	CR	BAL.
350.22		
100.25		
50.00		500.47

O. KEITH, CAPITAL

DR	CR	BAL.
	6124.86	
	50.00	(6174.86)

TRANSACTION 3

Jan. 25, 1987. $476.00 has been paid to the Bank on loan account.

CASH

DR	CR	BAL.
350.22	476.00	
100.25		
50.00		24.47

BANK LOAN

DR	CR	BAL.
476.00	5,000.00	(4,524.00)

NOTE: If the total debits (left side) are higher than the total credits (right side), then the balance will be called 'BALANCE AT DEBIT' or 'DEBIT BALANCE', and conversely if the total credits (right side) are higher than the total debits (left side) then the balance will be called 'BALANCE AT CREDIT' or 'CREDIT BALANCE'.

Exhibit 6

THE KNOW-HOW TO RECORD TRANSACTIONS

IN THE GENERAL JOURNAL

JOURNAL   Page 1

| 1 | | | | |
DATE	ACCOUNT TITLE AND EXPLANATION	POST. REF.	DEBIT AMOUNT	CREDIT AMOUNT
Oct 05	Equipment ← 2	#24	$ 600.00	
	Cash ←	#10	3	→ $ 600.00
	Purchased typewriter ← 4			

STEP 1 Record the actual date the transaction took place.

STEP 2 Indicate the account to be charged (debited), and the one to be credited.

STEP 3 Indicate the amount to be debited and also credited.

STEP 4 Provide a brief, clear, concise and meaningful explanation for the transaction involved.

Exhibit 7

COMPOUND JOURNAL ENTRIES

In some cases the accounting of a transaction requires more than one debit and credit. For example, let us assume that Ace Plumbing sold a typewriter that they owned, and the typewriter cost them five hundred dollars ($500.00). They sold the typewriter for three hundred dollars ($300.00) cash and two hundred dollars ($200.00) payment due in one month. The entry would be:

1987

Oct 01	Cash	$300.00	
	Accounts Receivable	200.00	
	Office Equipment		$500.00
	To record the sale of a typewriter to Jim Brown, for $300.00 cash and $200.00 payable on October 31, 1987 (unused).		

Exhibit 8

SPECIAL JOURNALS

A journal is referred to as a book of original entry.

This is due to the fact that the primary or source document in support of the transaction is firstly recorded or journalized in such a way.

There are certain positive features presented by a journal:

- it reduces the possibility of error(s)
- it is a 'picture' of recording similar transactions in one place
- it presents a chronological order of all the transactions of a certain period

Special journals have the advantage of possible speed and accuracy in the process of recording transactions, simply by reducing the detailed work and by offering greater separation of personnel involved.

Such journals are periodically (usually, monthly) crossfooted by:

- adding the totals of the credit columns
- adding the totals of the debit columns
- comparing the total DEBITS with the total CREDITS (they must be equal!)

NOTES: 1. When a business has to record a small number of transactions during a fiscal period, it is recommended to use a general journal.
2. When a business has a small number of **similar** transactions, then a combined or synoptic journal may be in use.
3. When a business has a large number of transactions, the special journals will more likely be found in use.

Now, the immediate question for review that may come to one's mind is:

A. WHAT TYPE OF JOURNAL TO USE

The following chart may be used for illustration purposes only:

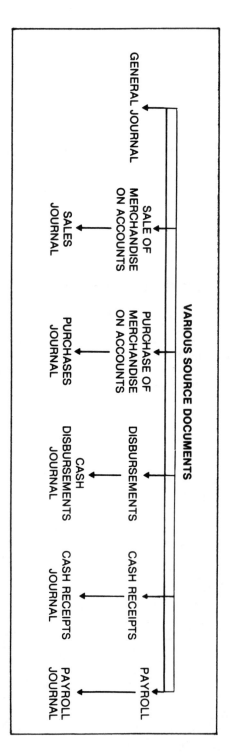

VARIOUS SOURCE DOCUMENTS

GENERAL JOURNAL

SALE OF MERCHANDISE ON ACCOUNTS → SALES JOURNAL

PURCHASE OF MERCHANDISE ON ACCOUNTS → PURCHASES JOURNAL

DISBURSEMENTS → CASH DISBURSEMENTS JOURNAL

CASH RECEIPTS → CASH RECEIPTS JOURNAL

PAYROLL → PAYROLL JOURNAL

Exhibit 9

42

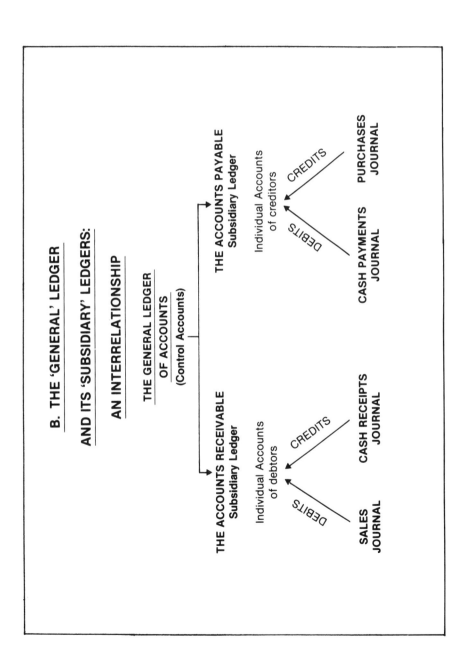

B. THE 'GENERAL' LEDGER

AND ITS 'SUBSIDIARY' LEDGERS:

AN INTERRELATIONSHIP

THE GENERAL LEDGER
OF ACCOUNTS
(Control Accounts)

THE ACCOUNTS RECEIVABLE
Subsidiary Ledger

Individual Accounts
of debtors

CREDITS

DEBITS

SALES JOURNAL

CASH RECEIPTS JOURNAL

THE ACCOUNTS PAYABLE
Subsidiary Ledger

Individual Accounts
of creditors

CREDITS

DEBITS

CASH PAYMENTS JOURNAL

PURCHASES JOURNAL

Exhibit 10

43

C. SALES AND THE SALES JOURNAL

Sales or revenues from sales represent the total amount of goods (e.g. merchandise) sold. Revenue may also include the total amount of services rendered. Goods returned by customers or allowances given from sales must be accounted for and shown as a reduction of total (gross) sales.

Sales are the most important part of one's business and, consequently, the sales records are considered very important.

Various types of business enterprises are using different kinds of patterns for their sales journals. The respective forms or patterns of sales journals should appear to suit particular needs. This has to be seen as the result of many years of owner's or management's experience in the particular field of business.

Prior to any approval of sales on account, certain verification of the customer's credit record should be made and files of such approved credit information and documentation should be kept in the company.

Let's start with a simple example of a sales journal, usually found in certain business enterprises (small ones).

MARVIN'S WHOLESALE TOY STORE

SALES JOURNAL

MAY 1987

DATE	PARTICULARS	INVOICE NUMBER	TERMS	ACCOUNTS RECEIVABLE DR	SALES CR	OTHER INCOME CR
May 04	J. Collins	101	2/10, n/30	600.00	600.00	
07	A. Martens	102	3/10, n/30	1000.00	1000.00	
19	G. Peck	103	4/10, n/30	1500.00	1500.00	
	MONTHLY TOTAL			3100.00	3100.00	
	Account Number			(120)	(340)	

NOTE: The total of the Sales Journal, namely the total of sales, should be posted as a debit to the Accounts Receivable control account and as a credit to the Sales account, in the General Ledger of accounts.

Also, all the individual amounts of the nominal accounts comprising the total of sales charges, will be posted to the individual accounts (debits) in the Subsidiary Ledger of Accounts Receivable.

Exhibit 11

D. CASH RECEIPTS

AND

THE CASH RECEIPTS JOURNAL

NOTE: The total of the cash receipts of the period (usually monthly) will be posted or transferred to the debit of the bank account and the same amount will also be posted to the credit of Accounts Receivable (control) account in the General Ledger of accounts.

On the other hand, all the individual nominal amounts in the cash receipts comprising the respective total of receivables will be posted to the related individual accounts in the Subsidiary Ledger of accounts receivable.

CONTROL OVER CASH RECEIPTS

SOME USEFUL SUGGESTIONS

The following measures should be taken in order to have better control over cash receipts:

- cash receipts should be deposited daily;
- all the incoming cheques should be stamped with the words 'FOR DEPOSIT ONLY';
- bank deposit slips should be stamped by the bank at the time of making the deposits;
- large amounts of money should not be kept on the premises of the business;
- the function of receiving cash should be separated from that of disbursing cash;
- a record of cash received should be made immediately upon receipt;
- the function of cash handling should be separated from that or record keeping;
- each day's receipt should be deposited intact in the bank;
- the deposits shown on the monthly bank statement should be compared with receipts recorded in the Cash Receipts journal, by a responsible or delegated person.

A meaningful type or kind of Cash Receipts Journal is presented below.

In various firms, different patterns or forms of cash receipts journals may be in use, depending on the firm's needs and specific type of operations that may require a particular kind of pattern or form design to be used.

THE GREAT VARIETY STORE

CASH RECEIPTS JOURNAL

FOR THE MONTH OF NOVEMBER 1987

DATE 1987	CLIENT	INV. NO.	ACCTS. REC.	CASH	SALES	SALES DISC.	FROM OWNER	BANK LOAN	OTHER ACCTS. AMOUNT ACCTS.
NOV	1 J. Collins	150		300	300				
	4 J. Owen	201		800	800				
	5 G. Perk	72	200	196		4			
	7 A. Queen	24	400	375					DR 25 Sales Return (402)
	9 L. Smith	5	450	441		9			
	14 R. Roger	103		900	900				
	18 D. Williams	204	700	686		14			
	22 N. McGreggor			1000			1000		
	25 D. Smith			1000					CR 1000 INV. (305)
	30 Royal Bank			5000				5000	
	TOTALS		1750	10698	2000	27	1000	5000	975
	Account Number		(109)	(101)	(400)	(401)	(120)	(300)	
	Debits/Credits		CR	DR	CR	DR	CR	CR	

Exhibit 12

NOTES: The amounts not credited to sales but to accounts receivable, represent amounts received on account of prior sales made. Then, the sales account was credited and the accounts receivable was debited. Now, the accounts receivable are discharged (credited) with the amounts received (on account of prior sales).

The numbers in brackets represent the account numbers to which the amounts are posted or transferred into the General Ledger of accounts.

The same amounts of accounts receivable are posted also to the individual accounts in the subsidiary ledger of accounts receivable (credit) and the total is posted also to the controlling account in the General Ledger of accounts (credit).

A more elaborate form of cash receipts journal is presented below. A closer examination of the respective entries will make possible to gain insight into the related way of accounting for the transactions involved.

THE GREAT CO. LTD.

CASH RECEIPTS JOURNAL

FOR THE MONTH OF APRIL 1987

DATE 1987	ACCOUNT	CASH BANK	SALES DISC.	NOTES REC.	LOSS ON SALE OF STOCK	OTHER	ACCOUNT	ACCTS. REC.	SALES	SHARE-HOLD.	EQUIP.	GAIN ON EQUIP.	STOCK	OTHER
APRIL 2	Investment	14000					J. Collins Advance			14000				
3	Cash Sale	2000					Sales		2000					
9	Don's Co. Invoice	400		2600			Don's Co.	3000						
12	Sale of Equipment	4000					Equipment				3500			
							Gain on sale of equip.					500		
14	Gino's Co. Invoice (2%)	2940	60				Gino's Co.	3000						
18	Sold Stock	1950			50		Stock						2000	
25	Cash Sale	5000					Sales		5000					
30	Brown Co. Invoice (2%)	3920			80		Brown Co.	4000						
TOTAL		34210	60	2600	130		TOTAL	10000	7000	14000	3500	500	2000	
Account		(101)	(402)	(102)	(140)		Account	(103)	(400)	(305)	(120)	(405)	(110)	

DEBITS — CASH BANK, SALES DISC., NOTES REC., LOSS ON SALE OF STOCK, OTHER

CREDITS — ACCTS. REC., SALES, SHARE-HOLD., EQUIP., GAIN ON EQUIP., STOCK, OTHER

Exhibit 13

Explanatory Notes:

APRIL 2   1) shareholders advance to the business.

3   2) to record total cash sales of the day

9   3) received partly cash, partly on account (a note received) and to discharge the existing account receivable

12   4) sale of equipment at a gain

14   5) to discharge an existing account receivable, paid in full

18   6) sale of stock at a loss

25   7) to record total cash sales of the day

30   8) to discharge an existing account receivable, paid in full

CASH MANAGEMENT AND CERTAIN RELEVANT QUESTIONS

Learning to manage the cash is a matter of necessity.... In the process of running a business, this constitutes a must.

In this line of thought, one's involvement in the daily or periodical banking operations, cash receipts, collection of the amounts receivable and making various payments on their due dates will, undoubtedly, bring him on the road of improved practical knowledge.

As there is no one best way of handling the financial matters, due to the complexity of various factors involved in the business operations, it is advisable that one will seek the guidance of a professional accountant, especially during the first stage of business development.

Constant efforts, self-discipline and good management, good experience and knowledge are needed on the path to success.

Tentatively, we can outline a certain number of useful and interesting questions regarding cash management, like the following:

- to what extent are you vulnerable to rising costs, fluctuating sales figures and shortages of supplies and materials?

- in what way(s) do you succeed to preserve the needed cash?

- are you making daily deposits of receipts?

- are you paying your bills and invoices when due and taking advantage, as the case may be, of discounts allowed?

- are you making use of cash term-deposits (interest bearing)?

- are you involved in any form of tax planning?

- does your accountant consultant advise you about possible tax deferrals, whenever the opportunity arises?

- what useful accounting practices are in place in your business, and how sound is your internal control system?

- are you reviewing regularly your accounts or amounts receivable and concentrating your attention on the doubtful collectable amounts?

- do you have outlined any sales and organisational or distribution plans in force?

- what is your purchasing policy and the main duties of the people involved in this department?

- do you inspect, regularly, your accounts or amounts payable?

- do you keep your inventory of goods for re-sale to the minimum while ensuring the right amount and the right diversity of items in stock?

- what measures are in operation in order to ensure the safeguarding of your assets, like machinery, equipment, etc.

E. CONTROL OVER

ACCOUNTS RECEIVABLE

Good control over the accounts receivable in any business has to do with sound credit and sales policies, like the following:

RE: CONTROL

- a Subsidiary Ledger of accounts receivable should be in place;
- pre-numbered sales invoices and the control of receipts for credit sales should take place;

RE: COLLECTION

- Aging of accounts receivable proves very useful and important for analysis purposes and business decision-making;

It has to be emphasized that the better the control over the accounts receivable, the less losses will be incurred.

The handling of the Accounts Receivable ledger should be completely separated from the function of cash handling.

All accounts receivable should be reviewed regularly, at least once a month, with special consideration to past due accounts.

The person who handles the Accounts Receivable subsidiary ledger should not have access to cash.

Certain Considerations Regarding Uncollectible Amounts (accounts)

The provision for uncollectible amounts of accounts receivable is an estimate of expense to be sustained by the business. This method is known as the Balance Sheet approach: It is applied by aging the accounts receivable at a certain date, usually, at the year end (for financial statement purposes) and estimating the uncollectible portion of these receivables.

A separate account known as Provision or Allowance for Uncollectible Amounts (accounts) is kept and adjusted to equal the estimated uncollectible amount included in the Accounts Receivable account. In analysing the aged list of accounts receivable, the management or owner's best judgement based on past experience in dealing with clients, will result in a best estimated figure of uncollectibles to be recorded.

The Income Statement Approach of estimating uncollectible amounts is an alternative approach to the one mentioned above and it consists of computing the charge to uncollectible accounts expense as a percentage of the net sales for the year under consideration. It simply means determining the average percentage relationship of uncollectible expense to the year's net sales.

The Direct Charge-Off Method: Under this particular method, when individual accounts receivable are determined to be uncollectible, they are charged off by debiting the Uncollectible Accounts Expense also known as the Bad Debts Expense account.

F. PURCHASES

THE PURCHASE CYCLE EXPLAINED:

STEP-BY-STEP

1. Daily, the stock record cards should be inspected in order to determine the need to re-order items close to minimum quantity in stock.

2. The clerk in charge will decide how much more of a particular item should be ordered.

3. A purchase requisition form is completed and transferred to the purchases department or to the purchases clerk, as the case may be.

4. The purchases order as made, is sent to the firm's established supplier. Here, detailed specification should be indicated regarding quantity, price, standards, etc..

5. The invoice received from the supplier is checked or verified against both the firm's order and the actual goods received as confirmed by the receiving clerk.
   Note: Corrections will eventually be made for any discrepancies. A debit memo will be sent to the supplier for any overcharges due to shortages, errors in computation, etc..

6. The goods received will be recorded on the stock card to agree with the quantity in stock in the firm's warehouse.

7. The purchases invoice and the supporting documentation will serve as the basis to journalize the information in the purchases journal for accounts payable-trade.

8. All the pertinent information will be kept safely in the respective supplier's file for future access to needed information and for later reconciliation of accounts.

NOTE: The purchase order, the invoice, and the receiving report are the necessary documents to assess that a purchase transaction took place and that the related amount involved should be paid or credited to the supplier's account.

The total of the purchases from the Purchases Journal should be posted as a debit to the Purchases account or Inventories, as the accounting system requires, and as a credit to the Accounts Payable account, in the General Ledger of accounts.

Also, the individual amounts comprising such a total, will be posted to the respective related individual and nominal accounts in the Subsidiary Ledger of Accounts Payable.

When a business has in use an Accounts Payable journal, the following procedures should be known:

A voucher payable is issued which is a serially numbered document. It includes all the needed information (recorded) regarding a liability and requires approval or confirmation for each step in the inspection and also approval of the liability created..All vouchers of a certain period are recorded or listed in a so-called Voucher Register which is considered a book of original entry. A related Cheque Register will be in use as a simplified pattern of Cash Payments journal.

One of the noticeable advantages of such a system is that it provides assurance that every cost is systematically verified before payment is made.

What we have in fact is a replacement of the Purchase journal with a Voucher Register where all kinds of assets and all kinds of expenses incurred are recorded.

A debit memorandum may be issued by the company receiving a shipment of goods (merchandise) in any of the following possibilities:

- the quantity of merchandise received is less than the quantity specified in the sale invoice.

- some of the goods are damaged or defective, and

- the seller's invoice specifies an excessive price or has an arithmetical error that is revealed by the wrong or overstated amount of the invoice.

It has to be mentioned in this respect that the use of a Purchase Returns and Allowance account is to show the amount of returns in relation to total purchases. The Purchase Returns and Allowance account, usually, has a credit balance, in contrast with the Purchase account and has to be treated as a reduction of the total purchases as the sales discounts is treated similarly as a reduction of the total (gross) sales to obtain the net figure of sales.

WIDE VARIETY STORE

ACCOUNTS PAYABLE JOURNAL

FOR THE MONTH OF FEBRUARY 1987

DATE	SUPPLIER/ CREDITOR	TERMS	INV. NO.	ACCTS. PAYABLE DR	ACCTS. PAYABLE CR	PURCHASE DISC.	INVENT.	FREIGHT	TEL.	OTHER ACCOUNTS	OTHER DR	OTHER CR
FEB 1	ABC CO.	n/30	52		180		180					
4	Great West Rail	n/30	103		10			10				
5	Adone Off. Supplies	n/30	95		25					off. exp. (508)	25	
7	Chevrolet Co.	n/10	70		80					auto exp. (510)	80	
14	Dino's Co.	n/30	23		320		320					
17	Specialty Ltd.	n/30	180									
21	Variety Co.	n/30	209	35			(35)					
26	Amero Serv.	n/30	106		40				40			
28	Bon Appetite	n/30	32		32		32					
	TOTALS			35	687		497	10	40		105	
	Account Number			(300)	(300)	(501)	(110)	(502)	(503)			
	DEBITS/CREDITS			DR	CR	DR	DR	DR	DR		DR	

Exhibit 14

G. CASH PAYMENTS AND THE DISBURSEMENTS JOURNAL

A well-structured cash payments (disbursements) journal is presented below. A closer examination of the respective entries will give you insight into the related way of accounting for the transactions involved.

CHEQUES DISBURSEMENTS JOURNAL   C/D1
FOR THE MONTH OF APRIL 1987

DATE 1987	PARTICULARS (Account)	CASH IN BANK	PURCH. DISC.	OTHER ACCOUNTS ACCT.	AMT.	PARTICULARS (Account)	ACCTS. PAYABLE	PURCH.	OTHER ACCTS. ACCT.	AMT.
APR 01	Purchased gov't. bonds	1000				Gov't. bonds-asset			(108)	1000
02	April rent	500				Rent expense			(502)	500
04	Bought office equipment	200		note pble.	1600	Office equipment			(109)	1800
09	Repairs, automobile	100				D. Smith towing			(200)	100
11	Dunn Co. invoice 2%	588	12			Dunn Co.	600			
18	Cash purchases	3000						3000		
21	Two-year insurance	350				Unexpired Ins.			(110)	350
24	Cash purchase	2000						2000		
25	Monthly commission	1000				Comm. exp.			(150)	1000
28	Cash purchases	5000						5000		
30	Monthly salaries	4000				Salaries exp.			(162)	4000
TOTALS		17738	12		1600		600	10000		8750
Account number		(100)	(501)		(306)		(307)	(500)		
Credits/Debits		CR	CR		CR		DR	DR		DR

Exhibit 15

The following measures should be considered important and must be taken in order to have control over disbursements:

- cheques should be prenumbered

- invoices should be stamped with the word 'PAID'

- no expense should be made directly from the receipts before depositing them to the bank.

In certain firms where purchases discount is taken, a more elaborate type of cash disbursements journal is kept to record both the cash discounts taken and the cash and/or cheques paid for other types of accounts representing services received for which payments are due.

H. THE SUBSIDIARY LEDGER

OF

ACCOUNTS PAYABLE

NOTE: It has been mentioned that the Subsidiary Ledger of Accounts Payable functions like the Subsidiary Ledger of Accounts Receivable while the rules of accounting in respect to debit and credit apply here in the opposite way.

What in a certain company is considered an account receivable, in another company, based on the same transaction, is considered an account payable. Thus, depending on whether the company is in a seller position or buyer position, the seller will open a receivable account when he sells on credit, and the buyer will open for the corresponding transaction, an account payable record.

I. THE GENERAL JOURNAL

OF

VARIOUS ENTRIES

The General Journal is reserved for certain entries that are not related to any special or specialized journal described above, for example: calculations of depreciation and amortization of assets, segregation of prepaid or unexpired costs from the expired (consumed) ones, etc. Also any correction or 'adjustment' for error(s) or omission(s) are included here. Such entries are posted regularly to the General Ledger of accounts, along with other postings from the various and already existing journals.

It must be stressed that it is highly recommended that all such entries, as made into the General Journal of accounts, be reviewed regularly by the owner or the authorized or delegated person by the owner, before the postings take place. This will make possible any eventual investigation(s) if needed.

Adjusting and closing entries are made in the General Journal.

NOTE: It is recommended that the number of entries recorded in such a journal be kept at the minimum, whenever possible, in order to facilitate audit and control, at a later date.

CASH CONTROL

Many owners and managers in any small business do seem to have a practical way of controlling the cash. This due to the fact that such people are usually very down-to-earth as revealed in their daily business practice.

The bank account reconciliation can only be useful for the business if the business has a sound machinery of bookkeeping-accounting in place that gives all the needed information in order to be able to reconcile the bank account.

It is highly recommended that the bank account reconciliation be prepared by an employee other than one who may have access to cash or to accounting records.

CERTAIN STEPS

IN

RECONCILING THE BANK BALANCE OF ACCOUNT

A bank statement usually indicates:

1) the amount on deposit at the beginning of the month

2) Cheques and any other amounts deducted from the account (debits)

3) Deposits and any other amount added to the account (credits)

4) Ending balance (as at end of a certain day, usually the last day of the month)

Items which cause the bank statement to differ from the book balance:

1) Outstanding cheques (not cleared yet - end of same date)

2) Unrecorded deposits (in transit or omitted)

3) Charges for services and uncollectable items (debit memos, NSF, returned cheques)

4) Collections - collected by the bank not recorded by the company (from accounts receivable)

5) Errors of various kinds (contemplate!)

Steps in reconciling the bank statement (ledger vs bank statement):

1) Compare deposits and note discrepancies.

2) Compare cheques with bank statement listings (for errors).

3) Arrange cheques in numerical order and check with own records; note discrepancies.

4) Note debit memorandums and credit memorandums.

5) Check for errors in recording and make the necessary adjustments.

6) Journalize (record) adjustments.

7) Post adjustments as journalized to the various ledger accounts.

8) Ensure review and confirmation of ending balance as reconciled.

NOTE: It is desirable to have this reviewed and approved by a senior officer of the Company.

THE PETTY CASH FUND

A small petty cash fund is almost always needed for small expenditures.

In this respect, a certain maximum amount is established, to be on hand in the firm and entrusted with someone to handle all kinds of small disbursements. Such an amount may vary, depending on the size of the enterprise.

For any incurred small expenditure, a petty cash voucher will be issued to show the kind of expense, the amount involved, the date of payment, and to whom it was paid. Such vouchers should always bear the approval or confirmation of the manager or the person delegated by him. The vouchers should be prenumbered in order to ensure the complete accountability of them.

From time-to-time, the total amount spent from the petty cash fund will be replenished, at request. This procedure is known as the 'imprest' system of accounting for petty cash.

It has to be emphasized that the petty cash fund should be of a modest amount and kept at a reasonable minimum size. Theft will then become impossible without unreasonably frequent replenishment of the fund.

DORY'S BEAUTY SALON

PETTY CASH REGISTER

FOR THE MONTH OF SEPTEMBER 1986

DATE	PARTICULARS	VOCH. NO.	PETTY CASH FUND AD. VANCED	PETTY CASH FUND PAID EXPENSE	AUTO EXPENSE	OFFICE EXPENSE	MAINT. EXPENSE	OTHER ACCTS.	AMOUNT
SEPT 04	Neil Kam		100						
15	B. Smith	1		5	8			travel (515)	$ 5
16	T. Owen	2		8	12				
18	N. Cole	3		12	15				
19	R. Roberts	4		15					
22	C. Neils	5		10		10			
23	O. Donell	6		20			20		
26	Neil Kam		70						5
30	**TOTALS**		170	70	35	10	20		
	Balance on hand		100						
	Account number		(105)	(105)	(501)	(502)	(510)		
	Debits/Credits		DR	CR	DR	DR	DR		

Exhibit 16

DORY'S BEAUTY SALON

GENERAL JOURNAL

FOR THE MONTH OF SEPTEMBER 1987

DATE	PARTICULARS	ACCT. NO.	DEBIT	CREDIT
SEPT 04	Petty Cash Fund	110	$100 00	
	Cash	105		$100 00
	To establish a petty cash fund			
	with M. Neilsen			
26	Travel Expenses	515	5 00	
	Automobile Expenses	501	35 00	
	Office Expenses	502	10 00	
	Maintenance Expenses	510	20 00	
	Cash			70 00
	To replenish the petty cash fund			
	based on attached vouchers.			

Exhibit 17

THE GENERAL LEDGER OF ACCOUNTS AND THE TRIAL BALANCE

The General Ledger of accounts, in any given form, is comprised of all the total accounts of the firm, known also as the firm's Chart of Accounts.

Each account in the General Ledger of accounts has a similar pattern or form design which is almost universally valid, as the attached exhibit shows.

A trial balance shows whether or not the Ledger of accounts is in balance; that is whether an equality of debits and credits has been preserved throughout the recording or journalizing process of transactions, postings to the ledger, and computation of account balances.

A trial balance is merely a listing of all the firm's accounts kept in the General Ledger of accounts and it serves a two-fold purpose, namely:

- To verify the mathematical correctness of the work performed in the General Ledger of accounts, and

- To facilitate the preparation of the firm's Financial Statements over a certain period (e.g. month, quarter, year).

However, it has to be emphasized that there are a number of noticeable limitations that are characteristic of any trial balance. If a trial balance reveals that total debits (of balances) are equal to the total of the credits (of balances), it represents a mathematical correctness only.

Even if the trial balance will balance, certain transaction(s) could have been omitted through incorrect posting from the journals into the General Ledger of accounts, entries could have been debited and/or credited to the wrong accounts, or entries could have been posted more than once to certain accounts in the General Ledger of accounts.

NOTE: Total assets and expense accounts with debit balances will equal total liabilities and revenue and capital accounts with credit balances. This must be the case in order for a trial balance to 'balance'.

THE WORKSHEET:

The worksheet is prepared before adjusting entries are journalized and transferred to the General Ledger of accounts.

The existence of such a worksheet offers some assurances that the necessary adjustments and corrections and other end-of-year (or other selected period) procedures were correctly made.

The adjusted trial balance columns in the worksheet should be totalled before the individually adjusted figures are extended to the Income Statement or Balance Sheet columns. If this is not done, difficulties may arise later in locating eventual errors.

The process of extending amounts horizontally across the worksheet should start from the top down, a line at a time. This will further assist in speeding up the process of work while eliminating the possibility of omission(s) of certain amounts to be extended, or errors of duplication (extending an amount in two or more columns).

Segregation of expired from unexpired costs will also be made on such a worksheet. Unexpired costs which will provide benefits to future periods appear in the balance sheet as assets. Examples include unexpired portions of rent, unexpired insurance, supplies on hand, and undepreciated costs of certain fixed assets like building, machinery, equipment, automotive and the like.

DEPRECIATION: CERTAIN USEFUL NOTES

Unlike other operating expenses, depreciation does not require regular periodic outlays of cash. Depreciation is recorded simply by an entry in the accounts based on a certain method of calculation which estimates the cost of the depreciable asset which has expired during the current period under consideration.

For example: After the first year of using an automobile for business purposes, an annual depreciation expense (let's say 30% of the original cost) is calculated as follows:

$$30\% \text{ on } \$10,000.00 = \$3,000.00$$

$$\text{Monthly depreciation expense will be } \frac{\$3,000.00}{12} = \$250.00$$

The adjusting entry to be made at the end of each and every month is journalized in the General Ledger of entries as follows:

Depreciation expense: Automobile	$250.00	
Accumulated Depreciation: Automobile		$250.00

To record depreciation for one month on automobile

Such a kind of expense will be found among the other expenses in the Income Statement.

The accumulated depreciation will be shown on the balance sheet as a reduction of the respective fixed asset. It is a reserve which does not consist of cash. It is an account with a credit balance showing how much the original cost of the assets have been reduced as a result of the related depreciation expenses since the acquisition of the assets.

There are various methods for calculation of depreciation and in various firms different methods can be found in use.

The selection of one method over another depends on the company's policy and this has to do, in most cases, with the desire of the owners to minimize their income tax liability in the current year, thus claiming the maximum capital cost allowance permitted (e.g. acceleration depreciation method).

Other firms adopt a depreciation method which more closely measures the expiration of the potential service of the assets (straight line method) and this is for financial reporting purposes

GOOD SERVICES COMPANY

WORKSHEET

FOR THE MONTH ENDED DECEMBER 31, 1986

ACCT NO.	ACCOUNT	TRIAL BALANCE DR	CR	ADJUSTMENTS DR	CR	ADJUSTED TRIAL BAL. DR	CR	INCOME STATEMENT DR	CR	BALANCE SHEET DR	CR
100	Cash	$ 67000.00				$ 67000.00				$ 67000.00	
101	Prepaid tax cost	2000.00			a) 1000.00	1000.00				1000.00	
102	Unexpired insurance	1000.00			b) 500.00	500.00				500.00	
103	Prepaid repairs cost	800.00			c) 200.00	600.00				600.00	
104	Materials	30000.00			d) 1000.00	29000.00				29000.00	
105	Equipment	10000.00				10000.00				10000.00	
106	Accumulated deprec. equip.		$ 2000.00		e) 1600.00		$ 3600.00				$ 3600.00
200	Jim Brown, capital		40000.00				40000.00				40000.00
201	Jim Brown, drawing	15000.00				15000.00				15000.00	
300	Revenues		100000.00				100000.00		$ 100000.00		
400	Automobile expense	3000.00				3000.00		3000.00			
401	Wages expense	12000.00		f) 2500.00		14500.00		14500.00			
402	Promotions expense	1200.00				1200.00		1200.00			
		$ 142000.00	$ 142000.00								
403	Tax expense			a) 1000.00		1000.00		1000.00			
404	Insurance expense			b) 500.00		500.00		500.00			
405	Repairs expense			c) 200.00 d) 1000.00		1200.00		1200.00			
406	Depreciation expense			e) 1600.00		1600.00		1600.00			
350	Wages payable				f) 2500.00		2500.00				2500.00
	Net Income										
				6800.00	6800.00	146100.00	146100.00	23000.00	100000.00	123100.00	46100.00
								77000.00			77000.00
								100000.00	100000.00	123100.00	123100.00

a) business tax expense for December
b) insurance expense for December
c) repairs expense for December
d) materials expense for December
e) depreciation expense for December 20% on (10000.00-2000.00)
f) wages earned but not paid during December

Exhibit 18

ADJUSTING THE ACCOUNTS AND PREPARING THE STATEMENTS

For the purpose of calculating reports and determining taxes, the life of a business is divided into periods. These accounting periods are usually one year in length.

There is a need for adjustments before statements are prepared. At the end of an accounting period there will be costs incurred that will not have been properly assigned as costs. In order to present a true picture of the amounts of assets, liabilities, owners' equity and income, these accounts must be adjusted.

This conforms to the matching principle which says that costs must be matched with revenues in the period in which they occur.

I. **Adjusting the accounts**

1. **Pre-paid expenses**

A pre-paid expense is an asset which turns into an expense as it is consumed. If a portion of the pre-paid expense has been consumed, but not recorded as such at the end of an accounting period, this must be adjusted to record the amount consumed as an expense.

2. **Depreciation**

The expiry of a plant asset in its "quantity of usefulness" is known as depreciation. Depreciation is an expense and is recorded as an adjusting entry at the end of the accounting period.

3. **Accrued expenses**

Most expenses are recorded during the accounting period when they occur. However, when a period ends there may be a few expenses that have been incurred but have not been recorded because payment is not yet due. Examples of expenses that can accrue include salaries and interest.

4. **Unearned revenues**

An unearned revenue results when payment is received for goods or services in advance of their delivery. This results in a liability. At the end of the accounting period, some of the revenue may have actually been earned and this must be transferred from the liability to the revenue account.

5. **Accrued revenues**

An accrued revenue is a revenue that has been earned but has not been collected because payment is not due. When revenue is earned, it should be recorded in the period in which it is earned.

NOTE: All the accrued amounts will be subsequently reversed at the start of the next period.

II. **The adjusted trial balance**

The purpose of an adjusted trial balance is to ensure accounts are in balance after the accounts have been adjusted, and to provide a working basis for the balance sheet and the income statement.

III. The adjustment process

The adjustment process is based on two accounting principles:

1. **Recognition principle:**

   Requires that revenue and expenses be recorded when they are earned or consumed, not necessarily when cash is received for revenues or paid for expenses.

2. **Matching principle:**

   Requires that revenues and expenses be matched so that a fair representation of income can occur.

GOOD SERVICES COMPANY

GENERAL JOURNAL   Page 1

FOR THE MONTH OF DECEMBER 1986

ADJ. NO.	ADJUSTING ENTRIES	ACCT. NO.	DR	CR
a)	Business Tax expense Prepaid tax expense - cost Business tax expense for December 1986	403 101	$1000.00	$1000.00
b)	Insurances expense Unexpired insurance Insurance expense for December 1986	404 102	500.00	500.00
c)	Repairs expense Prepaid repairs cost Repair expense for December 1986	405 103	200.00	200.00
d)	Repairs expense Materials Materials used for repairs during month	405 104	1000.00	1000.00
e)	Depreciation expense - Equipment Accumulated depreciation - Equipment Depreciation expense for 12 months - (20% on 10000.00-8000.00)	406 106	1600.00	1600.00

Exhibit 19

67

FINANCIAL STATEMENTS:

GENERAL STANDARDS OF FINANCIAL STATEMENTS PRESENTATION

The process of communication of business information is highlighted through financial reporting. In this respect it has to be stressed that full disclosure of the essential and material facts are a must in order to meet the requirements of investors, creditors, government authorities, etc.

Financial statements usually include the Balance Sheet Statement, the Income Statement or Statement of Earnings (or simply stated Profit or Loss Statement), the Retained Earnings Statement and the Statement of Sources and Applications of Funds.

General and minimum standards of financial statements presentation are as follows:

- information included in such statements should facilitate their interpretation and understanding;

- preparation of financial statements on a comparative basis is desirable, if this makes them more meaningful;

- if the accounting system includes changes, they must be disclosed in particular, as notes to the respective statements (regarding changes in practice, methods, principles, etc.);

- explicit statements should be made regarding the basis of valuation of assets;

- if assets were pledged as security against liabilities, this fact must be disclosed, in detail;

- explicit statements should also be made regarding the basis of monetary translations from foreign currency(ies).

In analyzing a business entity, one of the prime concerns is the ability of that business to earn a profit on its sales of goods or services it provides.

THE BALANCE SHEET indicates what the business owns and what it owes on a certain particular date, and the difference as the net worth or the owner(s)' or shareholder(s)' interest or equity on that date.

THE INCOME STATEMENT indicates how much money the business has earned, during a certain (selected) period, from the sale of goods or services rendered and how much it has spent for purchases and operating expenses and how much was left as profit, if any (or incurred as a loss). An income statement indicates a reasonably accurate estimate of net income, not an exact measurement of earnings. It shows the amount by which a firm's revenues are higher or lower than its expenses for the period under review or consideration.

THE STATEMENT OF RETAINED EARNINGS OR DEFICIT shows how much of the profit for the period was paid out and how much was retained to accumulate for future use or distribution.

THE STATEMENT OF SOURCES AND APPLICATION OF FUNDS indicates the inflow and outflow of funds over the period under consideration.

Usually, a small business issues, in most cases, only the first two financial statements mentioned above. Such a statement of changes in financial position shows the sources and application of funds (working capital), thus offering the possibility to assess the way in which the company handled its financial resources during the period and the source(s) of fluctuations in working capital.

Financial statements reflect the end results of the business operations, following, usually, one year. They may be prepared monthly, quarterly or semi-annually. Financial statements are brief reports which summarize the accounting information of a certain period under consideration. The two principal financial statements are the balance sheet, which shows the financial conditions at a certain selected point in time, and the income statement, which shows the profitability of the business during a certain period.

FINANCIAL STATEMENT PRESENTATION

AND

THE ACCOUNTING PRINCIPLES

The following are the five most known accounting principles to be observed:

1. **Accounting for Current Operations:**

   Current operations are recorded in the accounting system at the time when the contractual agreements are fulfilled, namely when the seller ships the goods and when the purchaser receives the goods. The amounts accounted for are taken from the respective invoices, and the related discounts will reduce these amounts.

2. **Accounting for Revenues:**

   Revenue is considered earned under the following conditions:

   - the selling invoice serves as an indication for the seller to record the revenue;

   - certain costs related to the sale will be recorded based on the indication in the contract as to the party who sustains such costs (seller or purchaser);

   - revenue must be recognized only if supported by documentation that goods have been actually sold or services have been actually provided.

3. **Matching Revenues and Expenses:**

   Under this principle, the requirement is that all the expenses of a certain period under consideration will be matched only against the revenue of the same period since such expenses help generate the revenue of the related period.

4. **Evaluating Balance Sheet Items:**

   Useful references can be made regarding some of the most common balance sheet items and the related standards that apply to each:

   - accounts receivable are shown at par value less a provision for doubtful collectible amounts (accounts);

   - inventory includes all the costs incurred for acquisition and warehousing of the goods;

   - fixed assets are presented at their original costs at acquisition less their related accumulated depreciation;

   - accounts payable are shown at par value less cash discounts taken or allowed, based on the respective contractual agreements;

   - long-term debts are shown at the present value of the future commitment for payment;

   - issued authorized capital stock is shown at the value agreed upon at the time it was actually issued and was legally recorded as such;

- Retained Earnings or Deficit are presented cumulatively, namely as the aggregate of all the earnings, less all losses and declared dividends, since the start of the company's operations.

5. **Presentation of the Financial Statements:**

The main requirement under this principle is that all the figures presented in the financial statements must reveal soundly and fairly the company's state of affairs and in such a way that they do not lead to misinterpretation by any user(s) of such statements like creditors, investors, etc.

CLASSIFICATION OF BALANCE SHEET ITEMS

Accounts are normally grouped on the balance sheet by similar characteristics.

Assets may be categorized as:

A. **Current Assets**

These include cash on hand and in the bank(s), stocks, bonds, receivables, inventory, prepaid costs, and any other assets which can be converted into cash during the normal operation of the business, usually within one year or within the current operating cycle, whichever is longer.

B. **Long-Term Investments**

These include stocks, bonds and promissory notes which will be kept for more than one year, and land that is not presently being used by the business, but is held for future expansion.

C. **Plant and Equipment**

Plant assets are relatively long term tangible assets that are used in the production or sale of other assets or services (for example, equipment, buildings and land).

D. **Intangible Assets**

These are assets having no physical nature. Their value is derived from the owner's rights of possession (for example, goodwill, patents and trademarks).

Liabilities may be categorized as:

A. **Current Liabilities**

These are debts or other obligations which are required to be paid or liquidated within one year or within the normal operation cycle. Current assets are required in the payment or liquidation of these liabilities.

B. **Long-Term Liabilities**

These include debts and liabilities which are not due and payable within one year or within the current operation cycle.

Retained Earnings

These constitute the accumulated earnings (including prior period adjustments less dividends declared) since incorporation. If this account shows a debit balance, then it will be placed in the equity section of the balance sheet as a deduction, known as Deficit.

NOTE: Working Capital is the difference between current assets and current liabilities. It is seen as a 'fund of liquid resources'.

THE INCOME STATEMENT:

THE MEANING OF REVENUES AND EXPENSES

REVENUES

The revenues that are reported in the income statement of a firm represent the total prices of all goods (merchandise) sold and services provided to customers during a certain period.

The revenue recorded in the accounting books of a business increases its assets and consequently its owner's equity. Commissions earned (like in real estate), fees earned (like in legal, accounting fields), rents earned (like in rental of property), and sales of goods constitute various types of revenues we come across during our daily business life.

It has to be emphasized that incoming cash in a business does not necessarily mean revenue. It can simply be received on account of future or past performance(s). Revenues are considered earned if, and only if, goods have been actually sold (shipped or delivered) or services actually rendered or provided to customers.

In this line of thought, certain selective and suggestive statements can be made:

- the total prices of goods sold and services provided to clients are revenues when such sales are made for cash or credit or other valuable trade-in considerations;

- the revenue of a firm generates income from clients;

- the following transactions or events stand as relevant examples that indicate the earning or revenues:

  - rendering of plumbing repair services to customers on account;
  - sale of parts by an automotive supplier;
  - earning of interest by a business, from a financial institution.

EXPENSES

The expenses that are reported in the income statement represent the costs of goods and services consumed (expired) and help generate revenues. The expenses transactions of a business decrease its assets and consequently its owner's equity. It has to be emphasized that when goods are purchased, their related cost price at that point in time is an asset, but once the respective goods enter the production line or are consumed, the cost becomes an expense (or expired cost). Examples of various kinds of expenses are supplies used, depreciation expense, insurance cost that expired, promotion expense, wages of employees, cost of goods sold, etc. It has to be emphasized that expenses are not incurred by simply paying cash, but by using the goods or services in the process of generating revenues. Along this line of thought, the following should be stressed, for better illustration or exemplification:

- costs of goods or services provided always become expenses when such goods or services are used up or consumed in the process of creating revenues;

- the source of costs of goods or services that can become expenses may come from purchases either by cash or credit (on account);

- expenses may include cost of goods sold, if incurred;

- simply repaying a loan to a financial institution does not mean that an expense is incurred. This is merely a reduction of the cash and also of the debt;

- thus not all cash payments are expenses since only costs of goods or services used up in the process of creating revenues are expenses;

- the cash purchase of assets like automobiles, equipment, furniture, fixtures or machinery, for example, means a decrease in cash only (one type of asset decreases, while another one increases).

A business is considered to have incurred an expense in situations like the following ones:

- use of telephone answering service for a period of time;

- use of promotional service that has not yet been paid for;

- the estimated cost of an automobile used up for business purposes during a period of time (known as depreciated value);

- heat, water, light, natural gas and other utilities consumed during a period.

THE CLOSING ENTRIES

Revenue and expense accounts are closed at the end of each accounting period by transferring their balances to a so-called Income Summary account. A debit balance stands for a net loss for the period while a credit balance in this summary account stands for net income for the period.

Finally, after the issuance and approval of the Financial Statements for the period under consideration by the Owner(s) or Management (directors), the Statement of Income accounts are closed to bring them to 'NIL' or '0' balance and the resulting difference between revenue and expenses of the same period (namely the profit or loss) is transferred to the Capital Account known as Retained Earnings or Deficit Account (in a corporate type or form of business organization).

NOTE: It has to be mentioned that there is not a rigid demarcation between the so-called bookkeeping work and accounting work. One may rightly assume that a bookkeeper presents a trial balance to an accountant who is on a higher level of knowledge and can further analyze the accounts and prepare financial statements that are recognized and accepted, officially and legally, by outside authorities including a country's fiscal authorities. (see attached Exhibits)

GOOD SERVICES COMPANY

GENERAL JOURNAL

FOR THE MONTH OF DECEMBER 1986

DATE 1986	CLOSING ENTRIES	ACCT. NO.	DR	CR
Dec 31	Revenues	300	100000.00	
	Income Summary	380		100000.00
	To close revenue account			
31	Income Summary	380	23000.00	
	Automobile expense	400		3000.00
	Wages expense	401		14500.00
	Promotions expense	402		1200.00
	Tax expense	403		1000.00
	Insurance expense	404		500.00
	Repairs expense	405		1200.00
	Depreciation expense	406		1600.00
	To close expense accounts			
Dec 31	Income Summary	380	77000.00	
	Jim Brown, Capital	200		77000.00
	To close Income Summary account			
31	Jim Brown, Capital	200	15000.00	
	Jim Brown, Drawing	201		15000.00
	To close owner's drawing account			

Exhibit 20

ANALYZING FINANCIAL STATEMENTS

One should be familiar firstly with certain definitions of terms used in computing ratios, like the following:

- capital funds
- common equity
- current liabilities
- long-term debt
- inventory
- net worth
- operating profit
- profit margin
- sales
- senior charges
- total debt
- working capital
- adjusted current assets
- cash and equivalent
- adjusted fixed assets

A dictionary of accounting terms can be very useful in this respect.

The following constitute a suggested list of ratios to be used in any analysis of financial statements:

- sales capital funds
- sales common equity
- profit margin/sales
- sales/working capital
- profit margin/capital funds
- profit margin/net worth
- operating profit/capital funds
- sales/inventory
- inventory/working capital
- fixed assets/net worth
- sales/fixed assets
- current assets/current liabilities
- acid test ratio
- total debt/net worth
- funded debt/working capital
- current liabilities/net worth
- common equity/capital funds
- times senior charges earned
- average collection period

NOTE: As more advanced knowledge is required in order to apply such ratios, it is advisable that, for a certain period of time, a professional accountant be asked to assist at this level.

CERTAIN ILLUSTRATIONS

IN ANALYZING FINANCIAL STATEMENTS

A. **Comparative Statements**

Facilitates the noting of the changes in the financial position of the company while comparing subsequent years of operations.

B. **Analyzing and Interpreting Comparative Statements**

When working with comparative statements, evaluate the reasons for changes and the advantages and disadvantages of the changes.

C. **Calculating Percentage Increases and Decreases**

The increase or decrease of the item is divided by the amount shown in the base year.

D. **Trend Percentages**

1) Choose a base year and assign a value of 100%.
2) Percentages for subsequent years are determined by the dollar amounts of the base year.

E. **Common Size Comparative Statements**

These statements reveal the percentage change in one item on a statement as compared to other items on the statement.

'Net Sales' is assigned a value of 100% for an income statement.

The items of costs, expenses, and profit will balance this. Thus the amount of every sales 'dollar' attributed to costs, expenses, and profit is indicated.

The business efficiencies and inefficiencies are revealed by common size percentages.

F. **Analysis of Working Capital**

Working capital equals the excess of a company's current assets over its current liabilities.

To remain competitive, a company needs adequate working capital so that it can maintain adequate inventories, meet current debts, capitalize on cash discounts, and provide favorable terms to its customers.

	COMPANY I	COMPANY II
CURRENT ASSETS	$200,000.00	$40,000.00
CURRENT LIABILITIES	190,000.00	20,000.00
WORKING CAPITAL	$ 10,000.00	$20,000.00

In this particular example, note that Company I needs to convert its current assets to cash more quickly than Company II. If a great part of Company I's current assets were in inventory, it would have to be sold very quickly to keep the company in a favorable cash position.

G. Current ratio $= \dfrac{\text{current assets}}{\text{current liabilities}}$

Company II – current ratio $= \$\ 40,000.00/\$\ 20,000.00\ =\ 2{:}1$
Company I – current ratio $= \$200,000.00/\$190,000.00\ =\ 1.05{:}1$

Although 2:1 current ratio is considered to indicate an adequate working capital situation, other factors have to be taken into consideration, like the following ones:

1) The nature of the business – how does it compare with industry?

2) The rate of turnover of assets.
   For example, in Company II, if there was a quick inventory turnover and the current assets are monthly in inventory then a lower current ratio is acceptable.

3) The nature of current assets.
   Let us suppose that a large portion of current assets is accounts receivable. These accounts must be collected in enough time to create cash to pay current debts.

While the current ratio is a useful indicator, the accounts comprising current assets and current liabilities must be considered as well.

H. Acid Test Ratio

This ratio is a ratio of assets (that can quickly be converted to cash) to current liabilities. The so-called quick assets are represented by cash, notes receivable, accounts receivable and marketable securities. An acid test ratio 1:1 is considered acceptable.

I. Day's Sales Charges Uncollected

It indicates how fast the money is received from sales.

$$\dfrac{\text{ACCOUNTS RECEIVABLE}}{\text{CHARGE SALES}}\ \text{X}\ 365$$

J. Turnover of Merchandise Inventory

The number of times a company sells its average inventory during an accounting period is called merchandise turnover. By industry standards, good merchandising is indicated by a high turnover of inventory. In considering working capital, the faster the inventory is turned over, the less capital is required assuming the same sales and the same span for collection of accounts receivable.

$$\dfrac{\text{COST OF GOODS SOLD}}{\text{AVERAGE INVENTORY ON HAND}}\ =\ \text{MERCHANDISE TURNOVER}$$

$$\text{Average inventory on hand}\ =\dfrac{\text{Beginning inventory}\ +\ \text{Ending inventory}}{2}$$

K. Comparison Standards

When turnovers and ratios are used to analyze financial statements, it is best to use similar sized companies in the same industry. This information can be found in certain business publications (e.g. Dunn & Bradstreet).

It takes great will and determination from any business education student in order to confront and cope with any problem one may encounter at the place of work and in any area of business.

It is only through trial-and-error that one may reach a fruitful result while working on available alternatives toward a tentative solution.

ADDITIONAL EXHIBITS

OF

THE BOOKKEEPING RECORDS

THE BOOKKEEPING CYCLE

THE ORIGINAL OR SOURCE DOCUMENTS (PRIMARY)
(analyzed, verified and approved)

↓

ARE LISTED OR RECORDED (JOURNALIZED) INTO SPECIFIC JOURNALS AND
(re: sales, receipts, purchases, payments)

↓

ALL THE TOTALS OF THE JOURNALS' COLUMNS ARE POSTED TO THE GENERAL
LEDGER.
(see firm's list of accounts, named chart of accounts)

↓

THEN ALL THE INDIVIDUAL AMOUNTS COMPRISING THE TOTAL OF SALES AND
RECEIPTS JOURNALS ARE POSTED TO THE SUBSIDIARY LEDGER OF ACCOUNTS
RECEIVABLE

↓

AND SIMILARLY, ALL THE INDIVIDUAL AMOUNTS COMPRISING THE TOTALS OF
PURCHASES AND PAYMENTS ON ACCOUNT ARE POSTED TO THE SUBSIDIARY LEDGER
OF ACCOUNTS PAYABLE.

↓

A TRIAL BALANCE IS TAKEN OR PROVIDED USING THE INFORMATION FROM THE
GENERAL LEDGER.
(listing the individual accounts with their related balances)

NOTE: Bookkeeping is, usually, referred as the recording of transactions, the record-'build-up'
stage of accounting. However, there is not a clear or rigid demarcation between the
bookkeeping and accounting cycles.

THE ACCOUNTING CYCLE

↓

A WORKSHEET IS PREPARED USING THE TRIAL BALANCE AS A STARTING POINT.
THIS IS FOR FURTHER ANALYSIS AND CORRECTION(S) AND COMPLETION OF
INFORMATION.

↓

THEN FINANCIAL STATEMENTS AND THE RELATED SCHEDULES OF CERTAIN
IMPORTANT ACCOUNTS ARE PREPARED.

↓

FINALLY, THE STATEMENT OF INCOME IS CLOSED AND THE PROFIT OR LOSS IS
RECORDED IN OR TRANSFERRED TO THE EQUITY ACCOUNT
(RETAINED EARNINGS/DEFICIT).

↓

A POST-CLOSING TRIAL BALANCE IS PROVIDED TO AGREE WITH THE BALANCE SHEET
STATEMENT.

↓

END

NOTES: In some firms, a senior accountant or controller, as the case may be, is performing
these steps, which are later reviewed or confirmed by an outside accounting firm
engaged to issue the firm's financial statements.

Accounting includes not only the stage of bookkeeping but also the use of this information, its
interpretation and analysis, tax planning, product-costing and auditing, etc.

Exhibit 21

For some learners, the following diagram may prove to be more useful in following the bookkeeping-accounting steps of the cycle:

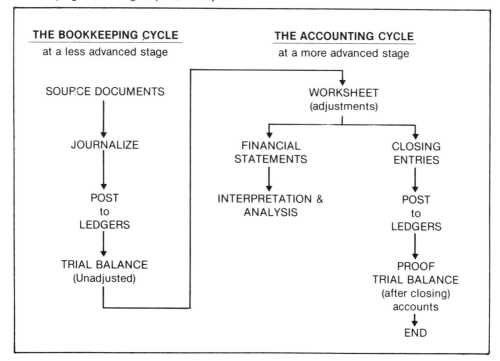

Exhibit 22

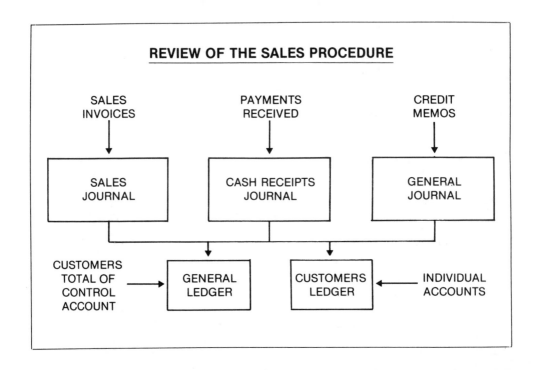

REVIEW OF THE SALES PROCEDURE

SALES INVOICES → SALES JOURNAL

PAYMENTS RECEIVED → CASH RECEIPTS JOURNAL

CREDIT MEMOS → GENERAL JOURNAL

CUSTOMERS TOTAL OF CONTROL ACCOUNT → GENERAL LEDGER

CUSTOMERS LEDGER ← INDIVIDUAL ACCOUNTS

Exhibit 23

CREDIT MEMORANDUM

FROM: _____

_____

_____   NO. _____

_____   DATE: _____

CLIENT'S NAME: _____

ADDRESS: _____   DELIVERED OR
SHIPPED TO:_____

_____

_____   _____

DATE	YOUR ORDER No.	OUR INVOICE No.	TERMS	SALESPERSON

UNITS	PARTICULARS	PRICE PER UNIT	TOTAL VALUE

EXPLANATORY NOTE(S) FOR CREDIT GIVEN:

TOTAL

APPROVED BY

Exhibit 24

85

The diagram below is self-explanatory to understand the recording of payment received on account on a sales invoice (goods already shipped in the past).

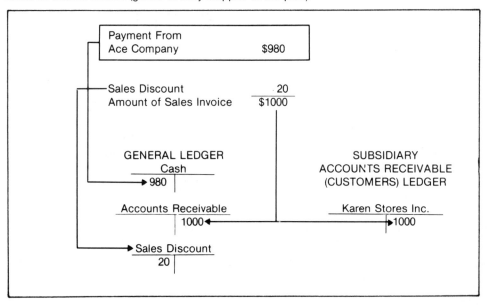

Exhibit 25

Usually, monthly, a statement of account receivable is sent out to all the firm's customers. This serves a two-fold purpose, namely:

1) To ask for payment of the balance of the account, as shown on the statement, and
2) To depict any eventual discrepancy(ies) between the respective firm and the customer.

STATEMENT

CUSTOMER NUMBER _____

NAME_____

ADDRESS _____

Please detach top portion and return with your remittance.

DATE	INV. NO.	INV. DATE	TERMS.	AMOUNT			BALANCE
				DEBIT (CHARGES)	CREDIT (PAYMENTS)		
				PREVIOUS BALANCE ⟶			

CURRENT	OVER 30 DAYS	OVER 60 DAYS	OVER 90 DAYS	OVER 120 DAYS		

BALANCE OUTSTANDING TO PAY ⟶

THANK-YOU

Exhibit 26

An illustrative information listing of accounts receivable is presented below for analysis:

COMPANY _____

ACCOUNTS RECEIVABLE AGING ANALYSIS

AS AT NOVEMBER 30, 1987

NAME	TOTAL	1 - 30 DAYS	31 - 60 DAYS	61 - 90 DAYS	OVER 90 DAYS
M. Blair	$ 400	$ 200	$ 80	$	$ 120
J. Clark	600	600			
N. Collins	72	72			
T. Dunn	190	100	80	10	
L. Gerry	60	60			
B. Hall	200		200		
K. Hogan	73				73
P. Holt	260	60	200		
A. Jones	160		100		60
D. Kaiser	140		140		
H. Knight	800		400	200	200
F. MacRae	1,300				1,300
G. Mann	1,000	1,000			
E. McLean	290	100	120	70	
C. Monroe	250	150	100		
K. Miller	170			100	70
L. Moore	58				58
N. Smith	30	30			
I. Smith	300	100			200
D. Thompson	120	100			20
M. Townsend	300	100		200	
J. Travis	300		100		200
TOTALS	7,073	2,672	1,520	580	2,301

Date submitted _____   Done By _____

Management approval _____

Exhibit 27

NOTE: Preparation of an aging analysis of accounts receivable periodically, will keep the owner or management timely informed of the progress of collections and state of the receivables. It's useful to show not only the dollar amount of receivables in each column but also the percentage relationship of each group to the whole.

AGED LISTING OF ACCOUNTS RECEIVABLE

COMPANY _____

as at _____ 19 _____ .

NAMES OF DEBTORS (Show Address)	TOTAL	CURRENT	31 - 60 DAYS	61 - 90 DAYS	OVER 90 DAYS	HOLD-BACKS	OFFSETTING ACCOUNTS PAYABLE	DOUBTFUL AMOUNTS (ACCTS.)	EXPECTED DATE OF PAYMENTS	OBSERVATIONS
			OMIT CENTS							
— SUB TOTALS										
— AGGREGATE OF ACCOUNTS UNDER...										
— NUMBER OF ACCTS.										
TOTALS										
PERCENTAGES CORRESPONDING TOTALS _____ 19 (PREVIOUS MONTH OR QUARTER)	100%	%	%	%	%	%				
PERCENTAGES	100%	%	%	%	%	%				
CORRESPONDING TOTALS _____ 19 (PREVIOUS YEAR)										
PERCENTAGES	100%	%	%	%	%	%				

Exhibit 28

PURCHASE ORDER

FROM

NO. _____

DATE _____

SUPPLIER'S NAME AND ADDRESS _____   SHIP TO _____

_____   OR DELIVER TO_____

_____   _____

REQUISITION NO.	TERMS	SHIP VIA	DELIVERY DATE	F.O.B.
UNITS	DESCRIPTION		PRICE PER UNIT	TOTAL VALUE
TAX EXEMPT NO. (IF APPLICABLE)	APPROVED BY			

Exhibit 29

90

In respect to the purchases of goods (trade accounts only) the following simple pattern for listing or journalizing is suggested:

PURCHASES JOURNAL · TRADE ONLY

DATE	SUPPLIER'S NAME (For goods purchased only)	DATE of INV.	TERMS	FOLIO	AMOUNT

Exhibit 30

VOUCHER NO. 3

PAID OUT

DATE Sept. 18, 1986

NAME: N. Cole

EXPLANATION: Automobile 12 00

RECEIVED AMOUNT SHOWN ABOVE

SIGNATURE

VOUCHER NO. 4

PAID OUT

DATE Sept. 19, 1986

NAME: R. Roberts

EXPLANATION: Automobile 15 00

RECEIVED AMOUNT SHOWN ABOVE

SIGNATURE

Exhibit 31

RON'S AUTO REPAIR SERVICES LTD.

A SUGGESTED

CHART OF ACCOUNTS

Exhibit 32

ASSETS

CURRENT

CASH & EQUIVALENTS

100 - Petty Cash Fund
101 - Undeposited Cash
102 - Cash in Bank (general business account)
103 - Term Deposit(s); (% interest earned)

RECEIVABLES

110 - Customers' Accounts Receivable
110A - Allowance (Provision) for Doubtful Collectible Accounts
111 - Other Receivables
112 - Advances to Employees
113 - Advances to Shareholder(s)

INVENTORIES

120 - Parts and Accessories
121 - Paint and Shop Materials
122 - Work in Progress - Labor
123 - Supplies and Non-Automotive Merchandise

PREPAID COSTS

130 - Taxes
131 - Insurance
132 - Rent
133 - Interest
134 - Other

FIXED

140 - Automobile(s)
141A - Accumulated Depreciation - Automobile(s)
142 - Shop Equipment and Machinery
142A - Accumulated Depreciation - Shop Equipment and Machinery
143 - Office Furniture, Fixtures & Equipment
143A - Accumulated Depreciation - Office Furniture, Fixtures & Equipment
144 - Land
145 - Building
145A - Accumulated Depreciation - Building
146 - Leasehold Improvements
146A - Accumulated Amortization - Leasehold Improvements
147 - Goodwill
147A - Accumulated Amortization - Goodwill

LIABILITIES

CURRENT

ACCOUNTS PAYABLE

200 | - Trade Creditors
201 | - Dividends Payable
202 | - Customers' Deposits
203 | - Sales Tax Payable
204 | - Provision for Income Taxes
205 | - Advances from Shareholder(s)
206 | - Net Payroll Due (clearing)
207 | - Payroll Deductions & Benefits (payable to Taxation Office)

ACCRUED LIABILITIES

210 | - Interest
211 | - Payroll
212 | - Insurance
213 | - Taxes - Other than Income
214 | - Income Taxes - Previous Year
215 | - Income Taxes - Current Year
216 | - Utilities
217 | - Telephone

NOTES PAYABLE

220 | - Bank - Current
221 | - Other - Current

LONG-TERM LIABILITIES

230 | - Notes Payable - Bank
231 | - Notes Payable - Other
232 | - Lease & Rental Units Financed

NET WORTH

300 | - Capital Stock Outstanding
301 | - Retained Earnings or Deficit
302 | - Profit or Loss - Current Year

EXPENSES

A - SHOP

400	- Advertising
401	- Warehousing
402	- Automobile(s)
403	- Depreciation/Amortization
404	- Maintenance and Repairs - Buildings
405	- Maintenance and Repairs - Equipment & Machinery
406	- Equipment Rental
407	- Rental of Space
408	- Deliveries
409	- Wages
410	- Employees' Benefits
411	- Foremen's (Supervisor) Salaries
412	- Subcontracting Work
413	- Occasional Labor
414	- Insurance
415	- Utilities
416	- Purchases of Parts and Accessories
417	- Purchases of Paint and Shop Materials
418	- Purchases of Supplies and Non-Automotive Merchandise
419	- Freight-In
420	- Taxes - Other than Income

B - OTHER THAN SHOP: (Administrative, General, Financial, Selling)

450	- Management Salaries
451	- Office Salaries
452	- Employees' Benefits
453	- Stationery and Office Supplies
454	- Memberships, Dues & Publications
455	- Charitable Donations
456	- Legal Fees
457	- Consulting Fees
458	- Accounting Fees
459	- Advertising
460	- Sales Promotion
461	- Travelling
462	- Entertainment (Other than for sales promotion)
463	- Collection Fees
464	- Postage
465	- Training & Educational Seminars, Lectures, etc.
466	- Other Miscellaneous Expenses
467	- Interest
468	- Rental of Space - Office
469	- Bad Debts (uncollectible accounts)
470	- Depreciation/Amortization
471	- Maintenance & Repairs - Building & Grounds
472	- Taxes - Land and Building
473	- Taxes - Other than Land, Building & Income

474	- Maintenance & Repairs - Office Furniture, Fixtures & Equipment
475	- Insurance
476	- Business Identity Signs
477	- Penalties
478	- Interest and Service Charges - Bank
479	- Loan Interest
480	- Discounts Allowed
481	- Utilities
482	- Telephone

REVENUE

SALES

500	- Sales of Service - Labor
501	- Sales of Parts and Accessories
502	- Sales of Shop Materials and Paint
503	- Sales of Supplies and Non-Automotive Merchandise

OTHER INCOME

510	- Cash Discount Earned
511	- Interest Earned
512	- Commissions Earned
513	- Other Income

RON'S AUTO REPAIR SERVICES LTD.

GENERAL

TRIAL BALANCE

Page 1

(Prior to Adjustments)

As at Jan. 31, 1987

ACCT. NO.	ACCOUNT	DEBIT	CREDIT
100	Petty Cash Fund	$ 200.00	
102	Cash in Bank	13,563.00	
110	Customers' Accounts Receivable (Control)	12,576.00	
113	Advances to Shareholders	100.00	
131	Prepaid Insurance	300.00	
132	Prepaid Rent	1,000.00	
140	Automobile(s)	8,000.00	
142	Shop Equipment & Machinery	26,400.00	
143	Office Furniture, Fixtures & Equipment	1,200.00	
200	Trade Creditors (Control)		$ 4,000.00
202	Customers' Deposits		200.00
203	Sales Tax Payable		119.00
205	Advances from Shareholder(s)		50,200.00
207	Payroll Deductions & Benefits due to the Taxation Office		1,586.00
220	Bank Note Payable		10,000.00
300	Capital Stock Outstanding		100.00
400	Advertising	500.00	
402	Automobile Expense	40.00	
404	Repairs & Maintenance - Shop	200.00	
407	Rental of Space	1,000.00	
409	Wages - Shop	2,900.00	
410	Employees' Benefits - Shop	144.00	
412	Subcontracting Work	1,900.00	
416	Purchases of Parts and Accessories	4,500.00	
417	Purchases of Paint and Materials	2,500.00	
418	Purchases of Shop Supplies	700.00	
419	Freight-In	220.00	
450	Management Salaries	2,000.00	
451	Office Salaries	1,200.00	
452	Employees' Benefits - Office	142.00	
453	Stationery & Office	25.00	
456	Legal Fees	300.00	
464	Postage	20.00	
478	Interest and Service Charges	10.00	
500	Sales of Services - Labor		14,250.00
501	Sales of Parts & Accessories		765.00
502	Sales of Paint and Materials		420.00
	Totals (for control only)	$81,640.00	$81,640.00

Exhibit 33

ACE DRAPERIES LTD.

FINANCIAL STATEMENTS

YEAR ENDED AUGUST 31, 1986

(PREPARED WITHOUT AUDIT)

Exhibit 34

Public Accountants

_____
_____
_____

ACCOUNTANTS' COMMENTS

We have prepared the accompanying balance sheet as at August 31, 1986 and the statements of income and retained earnings and changes in financial position for the year then ended from the records of Ace Draperies Ltd. and from other information supplied to us by the company. In order to prepare these financial statements, we made a review consisting primarily of enquiry, comparison and discussion, of such information. However, in accordance with the terms of our engagement, we have not performed an audit and consequently do not express an opinion on these financial statements.

Place: _____
May 20, 1987   Public Accountants

ACE DRAPERIES LTD.
(Incorporated as a private company under the laws of the Province)

BALANCE SHEET

AUGUST 31, 1986
(with comparative figures at August 31, 1985)

ASSETS

	1986	1985
CURRENT		
Cash	$ 419.00	$ 3,500.00
Accounts receivable	7,847.00	915.00
Inventory	4,200.00	3,813.00
Due from shareholders (Schedule 1)	19,594.00	541.00
	32,060.00	8,769.00
FIXED		
Vehicles	850.00	850.00
Furniture and equipment	800.00	800.00
	1,650.00	1,650.00
Less accumulated depreciation	778.00	492.00
	872.00	1,158.00
Due from affiliate	1,301.00	302.00
Incorporation costs	531.00	531.00
	$34,764.00	$10,760.00

On behalf of the Board:

_____ Director

_____ Director

LIABILITIES AND SHAREHOLDERS' EQUITY

	1986	1985
CURRENT		
Accounts payable	$ 284.00	$ 439.00
Income taxes payable	7,561.00	2,084.00
	7,845.00	2,523.00
SHAREHOLDERS' EQUITY		
Share capital –		
Authorized:		
20,000 common shares,		
no par value		
Issued:		
100 common shares	100.00	100.00
Retained earnings (deficit)	26,819.00	8,137.00
	$26,919.00	$ 8,237.00
	$34,764.00	10,760.00

See accompanying notes

ACE DRAPERIES LTD.

STATEMENT OF INCOME AND RETAINED EARNINGS

YEAR ENDED AUGUST 31, 1986
(with comparative figures at August 31, 1985)

	1986	1985
REVENUE:		
Sales	$71,493.00	$39,585.00
Cost of Sales	32,409.00	13,657.00
Gross Profit	39,084.00	25,928.00
EXPENSES:		
Advertising	785.00	1,540.00
Bank charges and interest	161.00	127.00
Depreciation	287.00	388.00
Office	50.00	111.00
Professional fees	172.00	2,610.00
Rent	6,000.00	6,000.00
Subcontractors	920.00	50.00
Telephone	1,714.00	1,752.00
Travel	913.00	89.00
Vehicle	3,923.00	1,907.00
	14,925.00	14,574.00
Income before income taxes	24,159.00	11,354.00
Income taxes	5,477.00	2,084.00
Net income for the year	18,682.00	9,270.00
Retained earnings (deficit), beginning of the year	8,137,00	(1,133.00)
Retained earnings, end of year	$26,819.00	$ 8,137.00

See accompanying notes

PREPARED WITHOUT AUDIT

ACE DRAPERIES LTD.

STATEMENT OF CHANGES IN FINANCIAL POSITION

YEAR ENDED AUGUST 31, 1986
(with comparative figures at August 31, 1985)

	1986	1985
Sources of working capital		
Operations –		
Net income for the year	$18,682.00	$9,270.00
Add (deduct) items not involving funds:		
Depreciation	287.00	388.00
Total funds from operations	18,969.00	9,658.00
Application of working capital		
Advance to affiliate	1,000.00	1,152.00
Increase (decrease) in working capital	17,969.00	8,506.00
Working capital, beginning of year	6,246.00	-2,260.00
Working capital, end of year	$24,215.00	$6,246.00

See accompanying notes

PREPARED WITHOUT AUDIT

ACE DRAPERIES LTD.

DUE FROM SHAREHOLDERS

YEAR ENDED AUGUST 31, 1986
(with comparative figures at August 31, 1985)

	1986	1985
Due from (to) shareholders, beginning of year	$ 541.00	$(3,725.00)
Add advances to shareholders	30,972.00	13,751.00
	31,513.00	10,026.00
Deduct:		
Repayments by shareholders	5,919.00	3,485.00
Rent payable to shareholders	6,000.00	6,000.00
	11,919.00	9,485.00
Due from shareholders, end of year	$19,594.00	$ 541.00

See accompany notes

PREPARED WITHOUT AUDIT

ACE DRAPERIES LTD.

NOTES TO FINANCIAL STATEMENTS

YEAR ENDED AUGUST 31, 1986

1. Significant accounting policies.

The financial statements of the company have been prepared in accordance with generally accepted accounting principles consistently applied. Because a precise determination of many assets and liabilities is dependent upon future events, the preparation of financial statements for a period necessarily involves the use of estimates and approximations which have been made using careful judgement. The financial statements have, in management's opinion, been properly prepared within reasonable limits of materiality and within the framework of the accounting policies summarized below:

Inventory:

Inventory is valued at the lower of cost or replacement value.

Fixed Assets:

Fixed assets are carried at cost. Depreciation is provided on a declining balance basis at rates of 20% and 30% which are designed to amortize the cost of the assets over their estimated useful lives.

PART THREE

SELECTIVE EXERCISES AND SELF-TESTING QUESTIONS

IN THE FIELD

OF

BASIC BOOKKEEPING-ACCOUNTING STUDY

CONTENTS

Introduction 109

Accounting Procedures 111

Accounting: its meaning and usefulness...112

General Relevant Matters 114

Bookkeeping-Accounting Terminology..115

Selective Questions on Various Matters 117

Analysing a Business Transaction 119

The Journals 122

The General Ledger...124

Journalising Transactions 126

Banking Matters 129

Payroll-Related Issues 133

Petty Cash Fund Handling 134

Financial Statements...138

Multiple Useful Questions on Selective Matters 146

Chart of Accounts..149

INTRODUCTION

The present collection of a limited number of exercises and self-testing questions in the field of basic bookkeeping-accounting study has its primary scope to serve individuals from everywhere who are interested in the subject matter and strive to apply and test themselves, to a certain degree and extent, in some particular areas.

This part is also designed to assist those who are searching for a more direct, easy to read and practical approach in this specific and technical line of study.

As there is sometimes a tendency by writers on this subject to address readers in a rather more sophisticated language, one may sense the need to approach bookkeeping-accounting study from a more direct, simple and practical angle. Thus my endeavour to satisfy a larger group of people rather than write for a particular segment of interested learners.

The purpose of the diagrams included in this chapter is to make available to the interested individuals some basic knowledge in the application of the accounting 'game' and its interesting rules in respect to the various categories of accounting grouping of business transactions (assets, liabilities, equity, revenue and expenses) whenever the need may arise and in order to analyse the business transactions taking place in a firm.

The practical knowledge of specific or concrete steps in recording business transactions in a given firm's journal of accounting, for example, should be considered paramount and as such it can be found at the very core in any study of basic bookkeeping-accounting study.

Yet another type of suitable exercise to be used is that regarding the recording of the various source documents in their related journals.

The diagram used for understanding the application of the rules of 'Debit-Credit' sides is also considered an important one. In this way, one will be able to grasp the functional operations in respect to purchases, payments, sales, receipts and other transactions.

Another good exercise is represented by the bank account reconciliation for the verification of the bank balance of account, as a crucial step in the cash control over the bank, on one hand, and over the business accounting in respect to cash, on the other. By applying such an exercise, one may gain, when used often, the needed versatility in mastering this precious tool of cash control.

The practice of working and exercising with the financial statements, for example, can be of much help to anyone interested in reaching the stage of familiarity with such statements on hand, and also be able to construe, whenever the need may arise, similar statements while confronted with such related tasks, in the real business of life. The knowledge of distributing or listing the specific company's accounts, in a certain order, by their degree of convertibility into cash, should be considered a very useful one that facilitates the handling of the various accounts of a given firm in respect of its assets as presented on the example sheet.

The relevant schedules to be found at the end of this Part constitute a good guide for analysis of a manufacturing kind of business firm, for example, when trying to follow up the results during the subsequent periods of operation. The figures can be taken from a public firm's financial statements in order to exercise them. Further to this, a useful judgement of the different costs incurred by a given firm under consideration can take place when such costs are compared against the revenue that was generated based on the respective and related costs, for the stated periods of time.

Similarly, a fruitful analysis, in certain respects, of a given firm can be made by using the included illustrative models that should be completed and the figures compared for various periods of time. It is in this way of exercising that one may gain insight into a company's business operations and their interpretation and at the same time reaching the ability of structuring similar schedules, in the future, whenever necessary.

Lastly, by completing the missing figures in the illustrative Condensed Profit and Loss Statement of a manufacturing enterprise, one can become familiar with the type of accounts in use, on one hand, and with certain useful calculations of the company's various results of its operations, on the other.

Explain the following steps of the accounting procedures characteristic of any business enterprise:

1 - Journalizing or listing transactions;

2 - Posting or transferring amounts to ledger accounts;

3 - Preparation of a trial balance;

4 - Making the end-of-period necessary adjustments;

5 - Preparation of an adjusted trial balance;

6 - Preparation of financial statements;

7 - Journalizing and posting closing entries;

8 - Preparation of an after-closing trial balance.

QUESTIONS

Complete, in your own words, the following:

1) Accounting is concerned with _____

_____

_____

and it aims to _____

2) Accounting tries to meet the following objectives (name three):

a) _____

b) _____

c) _____

3) Accounting, as a system, attempts to accomplish the following things:

a) _____

_____

b) _____

_____

4) The relationship between the assets, liabilities and capital, as revealed on a simple balance sheet, indicates the fundamental accounting equation. Try to illustrate and explain it below.

_____

_____

_____

_____

_____

_____

5) What kind of management decisions are made, based on accounting information? List three of them.

a) _____

b) _____

c) _____

6) What types of services are most commonly provided by an accountant?

a) _____

b) _____

c) _____

7) Describe briefly the business 'going on concern' concept.

_____

_____

_____

8) How can one figure out the worth of a business entity? Describe briefly.

_____

_____

_____

9) What accounts comprise the OWNER'S EQUITY part of a general ledger of accounts in a given business enterprise?

a) _____

b) _____

c) _____

d) _____

10) Explain in your own words the meaning of the accounting term of accrual.

_____

_____

_____

_____

Answer, briefly, the following questions.

1) Why familiarity with accounting terminology and concepts is useful to people of other occupations than that of accounting?

2) What is the meaning of a business transaction? Give four examples of different categories of accounting classifications.

3) Is there any difference between bookkeeping and accounting? Explain.

4) What is your understanding of financial statements? What purpose(s) are they serving?

5) What does an account or ledger account represent? Give three examples.

6) What are the basic elements of account?

7) How does the double-entry method of accounting work? Illustrate.

8) What is the difference between a journal and a ledger? What is their common feature?

9) Why is a trial balance always needed? What are the advantages and the limitations of such a technique?

10) What are the real meanings of revenue and expenses?

11) We are told that an income statement does not present an exact measurement of earnings. Explain this.

12) Explain in your own words, why the revenue and expenses accounts are closed at the end of each accounting period. How is this accomplished?

13) How are unexpired costs reflected in a balance sheet? Base your explanation on a few examples.

14) At what stage in the bookkeeping-accounting cycle is there a need to prepare a work sheet? What is its usefulness?

15) What kind of accounts are included in current assets and current liabilities? Give five examples of each category.

16) Why is it advisable to use a Purchase Returns and Allowances account?

17) What are the different methods of accounting for inventory? Explain the characteristics of each and their field of application(s).

18) What measures may you suggest in order to have control over a company's cash funds? List and explain five of them.

19) What are the different kinds of journals in use? Explain the nature of each and the field of applicability, with their advantages and disadvantages for such use.

20) What is the difference between a capital expenditure and an extraordinary repair?

Define or explain, in your own words, the meaning of the following bookkeeping and accounting terms:

1) Balance Sheet

2) Capital

3) Asset(s)

4) Liability(ies)

5) Credit

6) Debit

7) Business transaction

8) Double-entry

9) Account

10) Trial Balance

11) Revenue

12) Expenses

13) Depreciation

14) Work Sheet

15) Amortization

16) Income Statement

17) Long-Term Liabilities

18) Order of Liquidity

19) Debit Memorandum

20) Credit Memorandum

21) Closing Entry(ies)

22) Prepaid Costs

23) Compound Entry

24) Adjusting Entry(ies)

Answer briefly, the following questions:

1) What are the advantages and disadvantages of the following types of business organization: (Name three of each).

   Sole proprietorship or sole ownership;
   Partnership and
   Corporation

2) What are the differences amongst these types?

3) What is meant by limited partnership?

4) What information is contained in an individual earning record of an employee in comparison with the information needed in the payroll journal. Comment briefly on this point.

5) What useful things are accomplished through a WORKSHEET?

6) The performance of adjusting and closing entries, help us to attain the following:

7) The following constitute the steps in the bookkeeping-accounting cycle:

8) The meaining of current liabilities can be described as follows:

9) The kind of financial statements that can be prepared are the following:

10) The financial results of a business state of affairs can be used by certain outside parties like the ones listed below (name five):

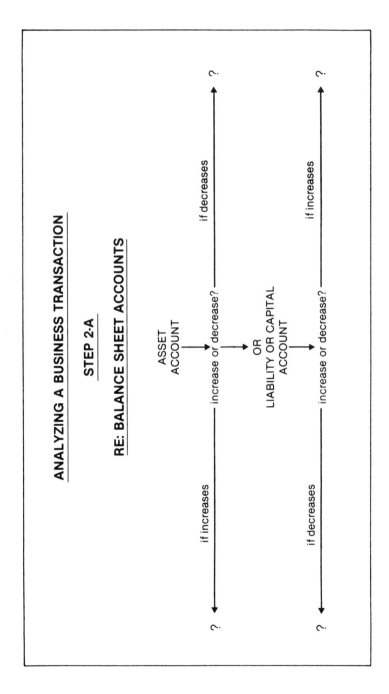

ANALYZING A BUSINESS TRANSACTION

STEP 2-A

RE: BALANCE SHEET ACCOUNTS

ASSET ACCOUNT

if increases → ?

increase or decrease?

if decreases → ?

OR

LIABILITY OR CAPITAL ACCOUNT

if decreases → ?

increase or decrease?

if increases → ?

Exhibit 35

Please replace the question marks by correct and brief answers.

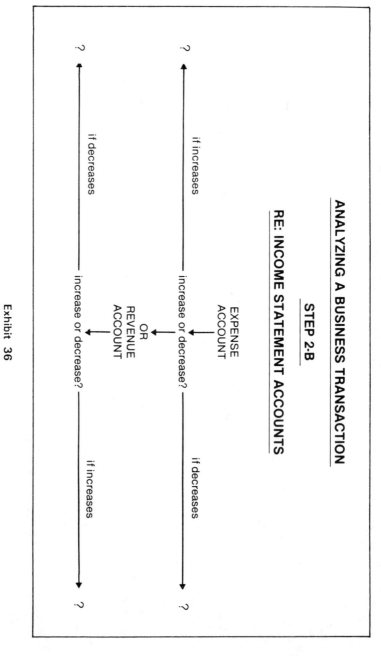

ANALYZING A BUSINESS TRANSACTION

STEP 2-B

RE: INCOME STATEMENT ACCOUNTS

EXPENSE
ACCOUNT

OR
REVENUE
ACCOUNT

if increases — increase or decrease? — if decreases

if decreases — increase or decrease? — if increases

?

?

?

?

Exhibit 36

Please replace the question marks by correct and brief answers.

THE KNOW-HOW TO RECORD TRANSACTIONS

IN THE GENERAL JOURNAL

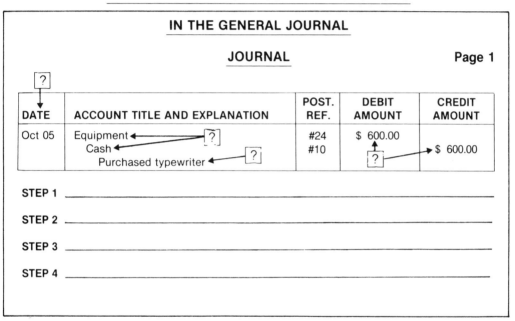

JOURNAL — Page 1

DATE	ACCOUNT TITLE AND EXPLANATION	POST. REF.	DEBIT AMOUNT	CREDIT AMOUNT
Oct 05	Equipment ◄── [?]	#24	$ 600.00	
	Cash ◄──	#10	[?]	► $ 600.00
	Purchased typewriter ◄── [?]			

STEP 1 _____

STEP 2 _____

STEP 3 _____

STEP 4 _____

Exhibit 37

Please explain briefly the required steps to be followed
in analysing a business transaction.

THE JOURNALS

Now, the immediate question for review that may come to one's mind is:

A. WHAT TYPE OF JOURNAL TO USE

The following chart may be used for illustration purposes only:

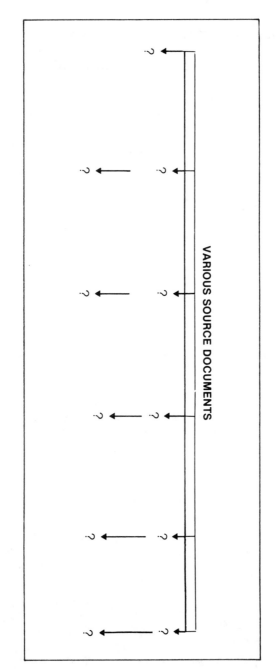

VARIOUS SOURCE DOCUMENTS

Exhibit 38

Please replace the question marks by correct and brief answers.

Answer, briefly, the following questions:

1) What are the main and necessary elements of information to be included in the following accounting journals:

   - Cash Reciepts Journal;
   - Cash or and Cheques Payments;
   - Sales Journal;
   - Purchases Journal;
   - General Journal;
   - Payroll Journal;
   - Petty Cash Journal.

2) What measures of control should be instituted in most of the existing firms in order to safeguard their assets. Explain.

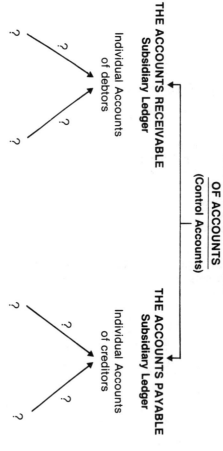

THE 'GENERAL' LEDGER

AND ITS 'SUBSIDIARY' LEDGERS:

AN INTERRELATIONSHIP

THE GENERAL LEDGER
OF ACCOUNTS
(Control Accounts)

THE ACCOUNTS RECEIVABLE
Subsidiary Ledger

Individual Accounts
of debtors

?   ?

?   ?

THE ACCOUNTS PAYABLE
Subsidiary Ledger

Individual Accounts
of creditors

?   ?

?   ?

Exhibit 39

Please replace the question marks by correct and brief answers.

JOURNALIZING TRANSACTIONS

A. Journalize the following transactions, in the General Ledger of a company, using the enclosed format:

March 2   Jim Smith commenced business with 6,000.00 cash, deposited into his new business account;

March 2   Paid in advance, last month shop rental space, in the amount of 1,000.00, as a security deposit;

March 3   Bought goods for re-sale, from Mr. E. Taylor, for 650.000, on account;

March 4   Bought Office furniture for 1,400.00 cash;

March 6   Paid Utility security deposit for 500.00;

March 12   Cash Sales of 300.00 is recorded end of day, from the cash register information;

March 15   Paid semi-monthly net payroll, in the amount of 1,500.00

March 17   Paid 3300.00 to E. Taylor, on account.

March 26   Mr. Jim Smith withdrew 200.00 from the bank account for his personal use.

B. 1) Using the pattern of the General Journal provided in the subsequent pages, perform the following accounting entries:

January 5 Mr. T. Hall, owner of the cartage company, opened a new bank account for current business purposes, contributing with 1,000.00 from his personal savings;

January 6 Mr. T. Hall performed services, on account, for Mr. B. Smith, valued at 200.00;

January 7 The owner transferred certain of his assets, as listed below, into the business, for its use:

Truck	8,000.00 at net book value
Automobile	3,000.00 at net book value
Furniture	600.00 at net book value
Office Equipment	400.00 at net book value

January 8 Mr. Hall obtained from his bank branch a current business loan of 5,000.00 in order to stimulate his business activities through promotions and advertisements;

January 9 Mr. Bill Smith forwarded to Mr. T. Hall a cheque of 100.00, on account;

January 10 A new typewriter is purchased for cash from D.J. Office Equipment Supply Co.

January 11 300.00 value of office stationery supplies are purchased from Grand Company Ltd. but were not paid for.

January 12 A new truck is purchased from XYZ Motors Ltd., at a cost of 9,000.00, with a 3,000.00 down payment;

January 14 The owner of the business withdrew 600.00 cash from the business bank account, for his personal use;

January 21 Paid 10,000.00 cash to Grand Company Ltd. in part payment of the debt owed to them;

January 24 An amount of 60.00 is prepaid to the telephone company in lieu of a security deposit, for opening a new line of communication;

January 28 The bank branch charged the account with 300.00 as a part payment of the loan balance.

2) Using the suggested pattern or format presented below, indicate schematically, how the entries of above should be 'judged';

3) Finally, produce a Balance Sheet for the enterprise, to find out Mr. T. Hall's net worth of the business.

Trans. No.	What accounts are affected?	What group of account is affected?	Are accounts increased or decreased?	Are accounts debited or credited?	Amount debited	Amount credited

Company _____

A Simplified 'Pattern'
of
General Journal (Entries)
For the Month of _____   Page 1

Date		Description	p.r.	Debit	Credit

Exhibit 40

BANK STATEMENT

ACE OMEGA LTD.　　　　　　　　　**ACCOUNT NO.**
620 · 8 AVE. S.W.

PERIOD ENDING DEC. 31/87

CHEQUES	CHEQUES	DEPOSITS	DATE	BALANCE
		2,000.00	DEC 01	2,000.00
40.00			02	1,960.00
20.00			07	?
		100.00	09	2,040.00
			12	1,580.00
70.00	50.00		14	1,460.00
		200.00	16	1,660.00
300.00	600.00		19	?
			23	1,160.00
40.00			26	1,120.00
	100.00		29	1,010.00
2.50			29	?
BEGINNING BALANCE	TOTAL DEPOSITS	TOTAL CHEQUES	TOTAL CHARGES	ENDING BALANCE
-0-	2,700.00	1,690.00	2.50	1,007.50

NUMBER DEPOSITS MADE	NUMBER OF CHEQUES PAID	NUMBER OF OTHER CHARGES
4	10	1

NOTE: See attached list of possible codes

Exhibit 41

Please replace the question marks with correct figures of ending balances.

BANK RECONCILIATION STATEMENT

As at May 31, 1986

Balance Shown on Bank Statement $10000.00   Balance Shown in the Ledger Acct. $13250.00

Plus Deposits in Transit

Date	Amount
May 29	$200 00
May 30	500 00
May 31	100 00
Total Deposits in Transit	$
SUBTOTAL	$10800 00

Less Cheques Outstanding

Number	Amount	
121	$50 00	
133	80 00	
146		
160	30 00	
161	20 00	
Total Cheques Outstanding	$ 200 00	
ADJUSTED BANK BALANCE	$	

According to the bank
statement of account

Less Charges and Fees

Description	Amount	
Service Charge	$ 25 00	
Ins. Authoriz.	75 00	
NSF Cheques	500 00	
Bank Loan Pmts.		
Bank Loan Int.	50 00	
Total Charges and Fees	$ 2650 00	
ADJUSTED LEDGER ACCT. BAL.	$	

Accounting Clerk _____   Reviewed by _____

Date _____

Exhibit 42

Please fill in the blanks with correct figures.

EXERCISES

A. You are presented below with certain information in order to prepare a bank reconciliation for the Diversified Company, at December 31st, 1987.

1 - Cash per company s General Ledger of account at December 31st, amounted to 19,420; the bank statement at this date indicates a balance of 15,882.

2 - The cash receipts of 4,822 on December 31st were sent out to the bank but not recorded by the bank during December;

3 - The paid cheques cleared by the bank included a cheque for 500 which had been paid in error by the bank since it belongs to a different company.

4 - The following slips of information for charges accompanied the bank statement:

a) A debit memo for 11 for service charges for December.

b) A debit memo attached to a 600.00 cheque of a customer, Mr. B. Smith, marked signature required.

5 - The following cheques had been issued by Diversified Company but were not included among the cleared cheques sent by the bank: no. 320 for 856, no 324 for 734, and no. 401 for 805.

B. You are presented below with the summary of cash transactions of the Western Company for the month of November 1987.

1) As of November 30, cash balance of the account per General Ledger was 3232.45; the bank statement balance as at same date was 3,232.45.

2) Cash receipts of 1,211.44 on November 30 were not deposited until December 1.

3) Certain information was attached to the bank statement, namely:

   a) A debit slip of inforamtion for various charges for the month of November, 10.12

   b) A debit slip of information together with a cheque of J. Collins marked post-dated for 98.99.

   c) A credit slip of information for 355 indicating the correction made by the bank for the previous bank charge in error of a cheque that did not belong to the Western Company.

4) Certain cheques issued and mailed out by the company were not cleared by the bank and did not appear in the bank statement of the respective month sent by the bank with cleared cheques: no. 222 for 253, no. 241 for 62.80, and no 301 for 36.42.

Instructions:
- Prepare a bank reconcilation of the account as of November 30.

- Make the general journal entries in order to reflect in the company books the necessary adjustments to the accounts.

- Indicate the balance of the cash account which should be shown in the balance sheet of November 30, 1987.

QUESTIONS

1) Indicated the kind of taxes that most firms are required by Law to withhold from their personnel payroll. Name the accounts which would be credited to reflect the amounts withheld.

2) What are the characteristics that assist us to discriminate between the status as an employee and that of an employer, according to the rules or/and regulations of the country?

3) Indicate which of the taxes listed below in respect to an employee's remunerations are sustained by the employee, and which by both the employee and the employer:

   a) Pension Plan;

   b) National Insurance;

   c) Federal or national taxes on income.

4) Give 3 examples of types of information representing output of the payroll work in any firm, and 5 examples constituting input to such work.

EXERCISES

Mr. Bill Smith is the owner of a coffee shop in the downtown area of the city. He entrusted Mr. James Collins, his manager, with the handling of the petty cash fund, limited to 400.00 at all times.

The fund is required to be replenished monthly, based on the imprest system in place.

During the month of January, the following transactions took place:

1. On January 5th, a cheque of 400.00 is make payable to Mr. James Collins, in order to establish the fund;
2. On January 6th, a voucher of automobile expense for 25.00 is submitted by the delivery clerk, Mr. Noel Poole.
3. On January 8th, another voucher for 20.00 for postage is submitted by the owner;
4. On January 15th, the last voucher of the month is issued for 45.00, as reimbursement for travelling expenses incurred by the delivery clerk, for business purposes.

The company policy requires that the petty cash fund be replenished at the end of each month. In this way all vouchers in the fund will be charged to expense accounts, before closing the month of operations.

Based on the above information, perform the following:

1. Issue the individual nominal vouchers of petty cash amounts, based on the attached illustrations;
2. Record the transactions into the petty cash register, using the attached format as a guide;
3. Journalize the transactions and indicate the amount to replenish the Petty Cash fund at the end of the month.

PAID OUT — VOUCHER NO. 1

DATE: JAN. 06, 1987

NAME: Rebecca Heart

EXPLANATION

NOTE: See attached receipt

RECEIVED AMOUNT SHOWN ABOVE

SIGNATURE

PAID OUT — VOUCHER NO. 2

DATE: JAN. 08, 1987

NAME: Rebecca Heart

EXPLANATION

NOTE: See attached receipt

RECEIVED AMOUNT SHOWN ABOVE

SIGNATURE

PAID OUT — VOUCHER NO. 3

DATE: JAN. 15, 1987

NAME: Ron Smith

EXPLANATION

NOTE: See attached receipts

RECEIVED AMOUNT SHOWN ABOVE

SIGNATURE

Exhibit 43

PETTY CASH REGISTER

DATE 1987	PARTICULARS	VOUCHER NO.	PETTY CASH FUND			ALLOCATIONS OF PAID-OUTS				
			ON ACCT.	PAID OUT	POST. EXP.	STAT. EXP.	AUTO EXP.	NAME OF OTHER EXP.	AMT.
Jan 05									
06		1							
08		2							
15		3							
31	TOTAL								
	Balance on Hand								
	TOTAL (for control only)								

Exhibit 44

A. Mr. J. Collins is the owner of a Cartage Company. As of October 30th, 1988, the company's books included the assets and liabilities as listed below.

From this information provided to you, you are asked to prepare the October 30th, 1988 Balance Sheet for this company, and complete the format provided below.

List of Assets and Liabilities

Petty Cash Fund	100.00
Cash in Bank account	2,000.00
Mr. G. Peck (a debtor)	400.00
Mr. H. Nickson do	300.00
Supplies-shop	250.00
Office equipment	1,000.00
Automobile (net book value)	9,000.00
Truck (net book value)	12,000.00
Jim's Supply Co. (a creditor)	350.00
O'Neil Co. (a creditor)	600.00

J. COLLINS COMPANY

(Sole Proprietorship)
BALANCE SHEET
As at October 30, 1988

ASSETS		LIABILITIES	
	......		......
	......		......
	......		......
	......		......
	......		......
	......		......
	......	CAPITAL	
	......		......
	......		
	......		
TOTAL		TOTAL	

Exhibit 45

B. The Balance Sheet of Great Company, at the close of business on November 30, 1988 is as follows:

GREAT COMPANY

Balance Sheet
As at November 30, 1988

ASSETS		Liabilities	
Cash	2,000.00	Bank loan payable	5,000.00
J. Noris	400.00	Mortgage payable	14,000.00
S. Vello	300.00	Dixon Company	900.00
Supplies	200.00	Total	19,900.00
Land	20,000.00		
Building	40,000.00	Owner's Equity	
Equipment (net)	10,000.00	J. Donn	53,000.00
Total	72,900.00		72,900.00

Exhibit 46

Instructions:

1) Analyze and journalize the transactions presented below and record the changes in an Account format of Debit/Credit/Balance. in a separate sheet;

- J. Noris paid cash of 400.00 on account in order to liquidate in full his balance;

- The proprietor withdrew 200.00 cash from his bank account for his own use;

- A payment of 250.0C was made off the mortgage payable account;

- Acquisitions of supplies of 175.00 was made from Dixon Company, on account.

2) Prepare a Balance Sheet as at December 1st. 1988, the date of close of business. after including the above listed transactions.

C. 1) Set up, in the accounting form, the schedule of cost of good sold of Great Toys Company Ltd., as for the year ended December 31st, 1987, based on the information provided below:

Merchandise Inventory, January 1, 1987	4,227.00
Purchases of good during the year	11,220.00
Delivered cost of purchases	?
Freight-In	200.00
Merchandise Inventory, December 31st, 1987	4,379.00

2) Complete the following information that is part of the Income Statement for the year ended December 31st, 1987 of G & G Stores Ltd.:

Total operating expenses	60,000.00
Net Income	?
Gross Profit on sale	128,000.00
Net Sales	228,000.00
Cost of goods sold	?

BALANCE SHEET

AS AT JANUARY 31st, 1987

ASSETS

CURRENT

Petty Cash Fund	$ 200.00	
Cash in Bank	13563.00	
Accounts Receivable - Trade (less allowance for doubtful collectible accounts)	?	
Prepaid Costs	1250.00	
Inventories at cost	3700.00	$31189.00

FIXED

Automobile	$ 8000.00	
Shop Equipment & Machinery	?	
Office Furniture, Fixtures & Equipment	1200.00	
Subtotal	$35600.00	
Less: Accumulated Depreciation	?	?
TOTAL		$66129.00

LIABILITIES AND EQUITY

Liabilities

CURRENT

Bank Loan payable	$10000.00	
Trade Creditors	4000.00	
Customers' advances	200.00	
Other payables	?	
Accrued liabilities	1100.00	
Advances from Shareholder	50100.00	$67105.00

CAPITAL STOCK

Issued and Fully Paid:

100 common shares	$ 100.00	
DEFICIT	?	?
TOTAL		$66129.00

APPROVED BY MANAGEMENT

Please replace the question marks with correct figures.

Exhibit 47

AUTO REPAIR SERVICES

STATEMENT OF INCOME

FOR THE MONTH OF JANUARY 1987

REVENUE:

SALES		$15435.00
Less: **Cost of Goods Sold**		
Purchases of merchandise	$ 7700.00	
Freight-In	220.00	
Wages & Benefits	?	
Subcontracting work	1900.00	
Subtotal	$13364.00	
Less: Inventory-end	?	?

GROSS PROFIT — $ 5771.00

OVERHEAD

Management Salaries	$ 2000.00	
Office Salaries	?	
Rental of Space	1000.00	
Depreciation	660.00	
Advertising	500.00	
Legal Fees	300.00	
Utilities	250.00	
Repairs & Maintenance	200.00	
Taxes	200.00	
Employees benefits	142.00	
Loan Interest	100.00	
Bad Debts	100.00	
Telephone	50.00	
Insurance	50.00	
Automobile	40.00	
Stationery & Office	25.00	
Postage	20.00	
Interest & Service Charges	10.00	?
NET LOSS		$ 1076.00

APPROVED BY MANAGEMENT

Please replace the question marks with correct figures.

Exhibit 48

ALBERT'S MANUFACTURING COMPANY

CONDENSED PROFIT AND LOSS STATEMENT

FOR THE FISCAL YEAR ENDED DECEMBER 31, 1986

REVENUE:
(Gross) Sales of goods ....$ 500,000.00
  Less: Discounts allowed............................ ?
    Refunds.. 2,000.00...........$?

(Net) Sale ....$ 488,000.00

LESS: Cost of Goods Sold
  – Inventories, at start ....$?
  Add: Purchases of goods 200,000.00
    Freight-In 2,000.00
    Direct Labour 30,000.00
    Benefits costs..................................$ 4,000.00
    Subtotal...$ 276,000.00
  Less: Inventories, at end....................... ?

GROSS MARGIN (PROFIT) ....$ 246,000.00

EXPENSES:
    Factory overhead...$?
    Selling 20,000.00
    General and administrative 25,000.00
    Financial 15,000.00
    Total ....$ 110,000.00

NET OPERATING PROFIT (LOSS)..$?

Add: Other income... 5,000.00

NET PROFIT – PRE-TAXES...$ 141,000.00
PROVISION FOR INCOME TAXES (deduct)............................... ?

NET PROFIT (LOSS) FOR THE FISCAL PERIOD.........................$ 113,000.00

Please replace the question marks with correct figures.

Exhibit 49

142

Complete the needed information in the statement presented below:

Great Manufacturing Co. Inc.

Statement of Cost of Good Manufactured
For the Year of 1987

Stock in process of work, at start of period			85,500
Raw materials use:			
In stock, at start of period:	45,000		
Acquisitions made	150,000		
Deduct: Allowances and returns	?	?	
Freight-in		3,000	
Cost of raw materials ready for use		190,000	
Deduct: stock at end of period		?	
Cost of raw materials consumed		161,000	
Direct wages and benefits		325,000	
Overhead costs (total)		360,000	
Total manufacturing cost			?
Total cost of items in process during period			931,500
Less: Stock in process at end of period			?
Cost of goods manufactured			891,500

Please replace the question marks with correct figures of ending balances.

Exhibit 50

143

GREAT WESTERN COMPANY INC.

Income Statement
For the Year Ended November 30, 1987

Net sales (after discounts and allowances)		550,000
Less: Cost of goods sold:		
Finished goods inventory, at start		
Cost of good manufactured	400,000	
Total value of finished goods ready for sale, at cost	?	
Less: Finished goods inventory, at end	70,000	
Cost of goods sold		?
Gross margin (profit) on sale		160,000
Operating expenses:		
Sales expenses:		
Promotions	20,000	
Commissions on sales	?	
Other costs	6,000	
Total selling expenses		
Administrative and General expenses:		
Salaries of administration	?	
Bad debts (uncollectables)	4,000	
Other costs	12,000	
Total general and administrative expenses	76,000	
Total operating expenses		147,000
Net income from operations (margin)		?
Deduct: Interest expense		1,000
Income before taxes		12,000
Income taxes		?
Net income after taxes		9,500

Please replace the question marks with correct figures.

Exhibit 51

From the following information, you are required to prepare two financial statements: a Balance Sheet and an Income Statement.

Great Western Company

Sole Proprietorship

Adjusted Trial Balance as at December 31, 1988

ACCOUNT	DEBIT	CREDIT
Petty Cash Fund	100.00	
Current Bank Account	1,000.00	
Accounts Receivable-Trade	5,555.00	
Allowances for doubtful collectible amounts		666.00
Prepaid costs	2,345.00	
Inventory of Office Supplies	450.00	
Office furniture & equipment	3,000.00	
Accumulated Depreciation of office equipment		1,000.00
Land	10,000.00	
Building	60,000.00	
Accumulated Depreciation-Building		20,000.00
Automobiles	15,000.00	
Accumulated Depreciation-Automobile		4,000.00
Accounts Payable-Trade		2,000.00
Bank Loan Payable		25,000.00
Net Payroll Clearning		7,500.00
Jim Brown, Capital		8,284.00
Jim Brown, Drawings	10,000.00	
Revenue: Sales of Goods		100,000.00
Expenses (Total	61,000.00	
GENERAL TOTAL (For control only)	168,450.00	168,450.00

Exhibit 52

For the multiple choice questions presented below, please, circle the letter of the right answer:

1) An account indicating what is owned by a business is
   a) an account payable
   b) a current asset
   c) an account receivable
   d) all of the above
   e) none of the above

2) Which of the following transactions will not be recorded in the cash payments journal?
   a) received a refund for goods returned
   b) received payment on account from a client
   c) owner made a contribution of cash to the business
   d) all of the above
   e) none of the above

3) Special journals are created mainly
   a) as internal control devices
   b) for reporting information
   c) as accounting tool for recording transactions
   d) all of the above
   e) none of the above

4) The total of the Accounts Receivable Ledger Trial Balance must agree with the balance in the
   a) Accounts Receivable control account
   b) Accounts payable ledger
   c) Sales account
   d) all of the above
   e) none of the above

5) The entries in the Sales account are posted daily to the
   a) Accounts Payable journal
   b) Accounts Receivable journal
   c) Cash Receipts journal
   d) all of the above
   e) none of the above

6) Each individual amount in the Accounts Receivable debit column of the cash Receipts Journal is
   a) posted to the credit side of the respective customer's account
   b) posted to the debit side of the respective customer's account
   c) posted to the credit side of a client account
   d) all of the above
   e) none of the above

Exhibit 53

146

7) Special journals have the advantage of

    a) increasing recording of transactions
    b) increasing the number of postings
    c) increasing the delegation of responsibility
    d) all of the above
    e) none of the above

8) Some people decided to take courses in accounting because

    a) accounting appears to be an interesting course
    b) to them it is a useful course
    c) it enlarges ones field of knowledge
    d) all of the above
    e) none of the above

9) Accounts in a subsidiary ledger for debitors are classified

    a) alphabetically
    b) chronologically
    c) numerically
    d) all of the above
    e) none of the above

10) Which kind of business form will serve as a basis to debit a supplier's account?

    a) cash receipt slip
    b) cheque voucher
    c) sales invoice
    d) all of the above
    e) none of the above

11) A purchase invoice is a business form issued

    a) by a seller of goods when there is a credit sale
    b) by a purchaser when there is a cash purchase
    c) by a purchaser when there is either a cash or credit purchase
    d) all of the above
    e) none of the above

12) The inventory balance of account constitutes

    a) goods purchased during the period of a year
    b) goods sold during the period of one year
    c) goods in stock at the start of a fiscal period
    d) all of the above
    e) none of the above

Classify the following accounts of a given company in the automotive field. The classification should be made by categories and in the order of the degree of convertibility into cash, whenever applicable.

Also, number the accounts, as for their better identification.

CHART OF ACCOUNTS

Petty Cash

Lease & Rental Unit Expense

Undeposited Cash

Other Deductions

Customer's Accounts Receivable

Cash Discount Allowed

Allowance for Doubtful Accounts

Lease & Rental Unit Income

Cash Sales

Other Income

Other Receivables

Sale of Scrap

Parts and Accessories

Interest & Commissions Earned

Paint & Body Shop Materials

Cash Discount Earned

Work in Process - Labor

Sales of Materials and Supplies

Supplies and Non-Automotive Merchandise

Sales of Parts

Taxes

Sales of Services - Labor

Insurance

Provision for Income Taxes

Rent

Bonuses

Interest

Corporate Identity Signs

Other

Employee Benefits

Parts & Accessories Equipment

Depreciation - Other than Buildings

Depreciation - Parts & Accessories
Equipment

Maintenance of Equipment

Service Equipment

Taxes - Other than Land, Buildings & Income

Depreciation - Service Equipment

Taxes - Land & Buildings

Furniture & Fixtures

Maintenance - Building & Grounds

Depreciation - Furniture & Fixtures

Amortization of Leasehold Improvements

Service Vehicle

Rent

Depreciation - Service Vehicles

Provision for Doubtful Accounts

Leaseholds Improvements

Interest

Amortization - Leaseholds Improvements

Other Miscellaneous Expense

Advances to Employees

Training

Trade Creditors

Postage

Dividends Payable

Telephone & Telegraph

Customer Deposits

Legal, Auditing & Collection Expense

Interest

Travel & Entertainment

Payroll

Institutional Advertising & Sales Promotion

Insurance

Contributions

Taxes - Other than Income

Memberships, Dues & Publications

Income Taxes - Previous Year

Stationery & Office Supplies

Income Taxes - Current Year

Payroll Taxes

Bank - Current

Other Salaries and Wages

Other - Current

Salaries - Office

Notes Payable - Bank

Salaries - Office Supervision

Notes Payable - Other

Salaries - General Manager

Lease & Rental Units Financed

Salaries - Owners or Officers

Capital Stock Outstanding

Proprietor's Investment

Subcontracting Work

Partners' Investment

Salaries

Retained Earnings

Inventory Control

Dividends

Freight and Express

Drawing Account(s)

Depreciation - Maintenance, Repair & Rental-Equipment

Profit or Loss - Current Year

Absentee Wages - Production Personnel

Delivery Expense

Vehicle Expense

Advertising

Warehousing

At the termination of working with the present self-testing exercises, it is advisable that one will review the answers and/or solutions to the questions, with an experienced person in the respective field of work.

While this will reinforce one's positive or desirable good knowledge, it will also increase one's confidence in the acquired abilities in the related area of study.

PART FOUR

THE PAYROLL WORK: ITS IMPORTANCE

A PRACTICAL STUDY GUIDE

The entire Payroll work with all its intricacies and the related Country's legislation must be known by anyone involved with such a type of work. This, especially nowadays, when the employer-employee relationship is a paramount factor in the working environment, everywhere and all the time, and the labour movement reveals, increasingly, the sensible nature of the work relationships.

CONTENTS

Introduction 157

General Considerations 158

Employment-Rental Status 163

The Company's Policies and Regulations with respect to Payroll
-     Aims and Objectives 167
-     Records under Examination...168
-     Certain Considerations regarding the required procedures 169
-     Elements involved in any Control and Verification 169

Illustration of a Payroll Procedure in a certain firm during a given month 170

The Required and/or Necessary Payroll forms - their Pattern or Design 171

Private Business Forms
-     Employee's Individual Earning Records..172
-     Payroll Accounting Journal or Register 174
-     Weekly Time Card..176
-     Bi-Weekly Time Record of Work 176
-     Monthly Time Working Record 177
-     Time-Off in lieu of Overtime 177
-     Shift Schedule 178
-     Pay Statement..178
-     Overtime Record 179

Suggested Payroll Tables in Use 181

The Accounting for Payroll - General Considerations 193

The Payroll Expenses and Liabilities Accounts...194

The Payroll Journal 196

General Ledger of Accounts 197

The Payroll Function in a Computerised Environment...199

Procedures involved in the Data Processing Cycle 201

Selective and Suggestive Payroll Audit Schedules...203
-     Key Points for consideration 205

A Suggestive Questionnaire for a Payroll Procedures Manual 217

List of Exhibits

LIST OF EXHIBITS

Exhibit Number	Description	Page Number
54	- Monthly Payroll Journal	183
55	- Weekly Time Card	184
56	- Employee's Clock Card	185
57	- Bi - Weekly Record Card	186
58	- Bi - Weekly Time Card	187
59	- Shift Schedule	188
60	- Statement of Earnings	189
61	- Pay Statement	190
62	- Schedule of Overtime	191
63	- Vacation Schedule	192
64	- The Payroll Work: An Inter - Relationship	193
65	- The Payroll Journal: An Illustration	196
66	- The Payroll Accounts: An Exemplification	197
67	- A Suggested Audit Programme	207
68	- A Summary of factory Payroll Distribution Entries	208
69	- Accrued Payroll Taxes (Schedule)	209
70	- Accrued Liabilities - Summary Schedule	210
71	- Accrued Expenses - Audit Schedule	211
72	- Auditor's Notes Regarding Payroll	212
73	- Payroll Tests: An Audit	213
74	- Auditor's Notes to the Schedules	214
75	- Auditor's Report Regarding Tests of Factory Payroll	215

Introduction

One may agree that in any type of business enterprise and in any area of occupation, it should be instituted one best accounting system to ensure a streamlined clerical procedures in all it's units, sections and departments. This will also facilitate to generate prompt and reliable data obtained through the operational system of the respective firm. All the necessary forms and records in use should be made simple, clear and meaningful, to avoid unnecessary copying of original data. Thus, an adequate or proper reporting system can be in place. In many areas of various enterprises, the payroll costs represent a higher percentage than other costs, as part of the total operational costs. A sizable portion of such totals can be identified with respect to specific accounts. In the operation of a business, like an airport, for example, one of the characteristics that should be a part of the system of accounts is that timekeeping must be a constitutive element of such system, for payroll purposes and for cost control. In the accounting machinery for firms like architects and engineers, it's main element is the recording of time. Here, the labour hour becomes the primary component.

Needless to say, the recording of time in any enterprise should be accurately stated and promptly submitted. In most of the firms using a cost accounting system, the overhead costs are allocated by using the method of labour costs. In this line of thought, it can be emphasised that the simplest cost system is based mainly on hourly work performance.

Another important factor in reaching a successful level of accomplishment in dealing with payroll work and related matters, is to attain a satisfactorily result in selecting the best possible clerical and technical personnel. Both the designed system of payroll accounting and the personnel force should make possible to reach a noticeable progress at taking better steps towards consistent improvement of the system and of the skills of the personnel involved.

The payroll accounting work and it's related matters are of paramount importance in the everyday life of almost any business enterprise and it's employees.

The accounting information and its related documentation of a firm's operation serve a multi-fold purpose, namely the following:

- It provides the owner(s) and/or management of the firm with the required information much needed to make fair, sound and timely decisions of various degree and extent of importance and usefulness;

- it constitutes the legal basis of financial reporting to the country's established authorities represented by various agencies, and mainly for tax considerations.

- It serves the company's management for subsequent yearly analysis and on a comparative basis against prior years of performance;

- It constitutes the legal basis of documentation in support of the company's operations for audit and control purposes, and

- Finally, it can serve many other useful purposes like planning, projections, etc.

General Considerations

The payroll work executed in any business enterprise, anywhere around the world, and in any type of occupational area, constitutes a very important and useful segment of the record-keeping-accounting system in use. Such an attested importance requires that streamlined clerical procedures be in place, approved or confirmed by the firm's professional accountant and based on the best company's needs and stated interests. This will further facilitate to generate prompt and reliable data needed by management and outside authorities, on a periodical basis, like weekly, semi-weekly or semi-monthly, monthly, quarterly, semi-annually or annually, at the least.

It has to be emphasized that all the specific and related payroll forms in use in a particular firm under consideration, together with the related records, should be made simple, meaningful, clear and understandable to any user of such information and documentation. This in order to eliminate duplication of original data. It is well-known by many that the payroll costs constitute, in many cases, larger amounts than other of company's costs, as part of either direct costs or indirect or operational costs (overhead costs).

In this line of thought, it is also important to note that the records of time be accurately stated and reach the payroll clerk or the accounting department, its related unit, as soon as possible. This, especially when the cost system is based, mainly, on hourly work performance.

Any managerial skill, anywhere and at anytime, has to do also with the satisfactorily selection of best possible or available clerical and technical and reliable personnel, to include those to be occupied in the payroll unit of the accounting machinery of a given firm.

It is desirable that constant supervision and training on the job take place, regarding, especially, those involved at lower echelons in the payroll unit, and their up-to-date briefing about the various eventual changes of the particular legislation in force, in the country, and the province, as the case may be.

The payroll accounting work and its related matters, of any firm in operation, serves useful purposes for many, both internally and externally, along the other financial and accounting matters used by the management of a firm under consideration.

Any future audit work in respect to payroll, will verify and examine the supporting documentation and other related information and records, in order to obtain the proof that all the payroll charges are, in fact, for actual services or performances as claimed as being provided to the respective firm under scrutiny.

Another useful purpose of accurate payroll records is to facilitate an adequate and consistent allocation or distribution of payroll costs, to the various categories of accounts.

Certain examples of useful records one may find in a firm, can be enumerated below, as following:

– Company's manuals, policies, rules, procedures and instructions;

– Employees time information sheets, tables, records or cards;

– Individual earning records of the firm's employees;

- Documentation regarding rates of pay and eventual changes in such rates, etc.

- Personnel records;

- Overtime agreements, if required;

- Payroll accounting journal or register;

- Shift schedules;

- Statement of earnings;

- Payroll bank account reconciliations, if a separate payroll bank account is in use;

- Timely payroll reports made, as required from time to time.

- Etc.

Any supervision, inspection, verification, examination or audit that take place anywhere, on the payroll data and the supporting documentation, will present certain advantages for the firm invovled, namely the following:

- Depicting eventual fraud, errors and omissions and reducing the frequency of their occurrences;

- Improved measures for control purposes;

- Increased confidence and satisfaction;

- Reduce operational costs;

- Increase efficiency and productivity at work by recommending eventual changes and improvements at work;

- Improved equipment use;

- Reduced time and costs involved in payroll work and related matters;

- Etc.

Good management in respect to payroll work and related matters, has to do with the following:

- Right allocation of duties amongst the existing personnel;

- Safe preservation of the respective records and supporting documentation;

- Written or clear instructions for the assigned payroll duties, jobs, etc

- Proper supervision of the existing personnel;

- Adequate distribution of duties or separation of tasks in order to safeguard the payroll funds;

- Periodical inspection of the payroll work and recommendations for improvement;

- Constant communication with the professional accountant and follow-up on important payroll matters, etc.

It is quite possible to present a certain general illustration of a payroll procedure in a firm, during a given month, as a relevant illustration in respect to payroll work performance:

- Payroll information is firstly obtained, in respect to the following:

  - hours worked;

  - piece work performed;

  - days, weeks, etc., worked;

  - rates of pay for the period, etc.

- Calculation process of gross earnings in respect to the following:

  - regular earnings;

  - overtime earnings

  - vacation pay.

- Transfers of the due payments, as calculated, into the individual earning records of the particular employees and, at the same time, in the payroll journal or register for the specific period under consideration (weekly, bi-weekly, monthly, semi-monthly, etc.)

- Preparation of the individual pay statements of the individual earnings for each and every employee of the firm, as journalized by the accounting process.

- Monthly payroll bank account reconciliation, if a separate account is kept with the bank; some bank accounts are used for all purposes, in respect to all kinds of payments made by the firm.

- Monthly remittances are made to the taxation office, for all kinds of legal deductions made from the employees' payments of gross earnings.

- All the above information, as journalized, is posted or transferred into the general ledger of accounts, in respect to payroll calculations.

It has to be stressed, that from an accounting and audit point of view, it is highly desirable that all the payroll calculations, as revealed by the payroll records, be reviewed by a senior official of the firm, each and every time, and confirmed regarding inspection and eventual verification of details involved.

Every manager should become familiar with certain provisions in respect to payroll matters, like the following:

- What payroll records are legally required to be in use and what information must be kept or preserved and for how long;

– What is the minimum wage (guaranteed hourly wage, guaranteed daily wage or salary) and its relationship to age, as the law of the country or the province stipulate;

– What the restrictions on hours of work are and for what type of occupations, and what is the treatment of benefits under the law (included and excluded);

– How overtime should be calculated;

– The legal requirement for notification of hours of work by the firm;

– Compulsory and optional deductions;

– Treatment under the Law regarding different kinds of employees, like adolescents, maternity cases, etc.

A computerized payroll program gives reports in the form of a printout of the payroll, pay slips, bank credit slips, and if needed, a list of cheque payments. At the end of each taxation year, the payroll program can print the necessary data for employees and for the Taxation Office.

Some of the reasons for having a computerized payroll system, either within the company or outside it (at a specialized agency), are as follows:

1. It can increase substantially the productivity and efficiency in generating the required information.

2. The availability of capable or trained personnel who can reconcile the manual payroll system against the computerized one obtained from the payroll unit.

3. The computer's capability to store and retrieve large amounts of data, thus increasing information.

4. The promptness of information released by the computer unit.

5. The relative reduced costs for using the computer unit vis-a-vis the prompt availability of useful and needed information for various business purposes like the reporting and record-keeping ones.

6. In the light of growing need for more detailed information required by the management for decision-making and the development of the company's operations, there is also a greater desirability to develop its system of internal documentation by using the computer generated data.

Along this line of thought, some benefits resulting from using a computerized payroll system should be stressed:

– The computer constitutes a basis for comparisons of calculations in order to eliminate erros or to notice errors and subsequently making possible, promptly, the eventual corrections or adjustments.

– It represents a counter-control of the correctness of the accounting clerk in charge of operations and helps to eliminate eventual fraud and negligence.

- It makes it possible for management to obtain timely information for decision-making and various analysis and reports, upon request.

- It offers accurate cumulative records for later use by other parts of the company and for various purposes like budgets, costing, forecasting, reports, etc.

- It facilitates control and serves as a stronger or more powerful measure of any internal control. Also it safeguards the company's information, especially within the competitive world.

In spite of the noticeable and useful advantages the computerized payroll system presents, there are also certain possible negative implications to individuals and society, such as the following:

- It causes a reduced level of employment in certain industries, and in certain areas, due to increased productivity, production and efficiency of operations.

- Computer-based systems are considered by some as impersonal systems, dehumanizing and depersonalizing human activities.

- The right of privacy can be seriously affected due to the enormous capability of the computer to store and retrieve information. The very existence of widely integrated systems of information makes possible and increases the chances for misuse of computer-stored information. It is only through severe legislation that this danger can be greatly reduced.

- Computerized crime fraud or errors may result from computer usage.

- The higher dependency upon computers may have drastic consequences following any malfunctioning of a computer-based system.

- The tendency towards mechanization compels people to conform to the system.

- Since the computer cannot reason, the ability of people is the key factor for directing and operating the information process.

Note: Only to a certain degree and extent, do these disadvantages apply to various firms.

EMPLOYMENT RELATED STATUS

There are certain criteria or factors for analysis that can assist one in establishing the employment related status. These factors or criteria should be seen as important elements of the concept of employment. In this respect, a tentative enumeration of them is presented below:

-   The existence of a contract of service or agreement
    Such an agreement can be oral or written;

-   Direction, supervision and control;

-   Method of remuneration or compensation for service;

-   Ownership of Tools, Furniture, Equipment, Machinery, etc.;

-   Schedule of hours of work;

-   Facilities made available for work performances;

-   Regulations, rules and policies to obey or comply with certain instructions, orders, etc..;

-   Training provided either in-house or outside the firm;

-   Personally recognized performances of work;

-   Time working schedules and routines;

-   Regular required reports of work performances;

-   Payor's premises;

-   Right to dismiss someone at work;

It has to be emphasized in respect to the above noted criteria or factors used in any analysis to study the concept of employment, that there are certain specific rules and regulations characteristic to various countries around the world, dealing with clarification of different cases, notions and aspects of labour relations in this field.

As for immediate need, one should not hesitate to contact the nearest district office, should any eventual need for clarification(s) arise.

The existence of a contract of service or agreement
The Employer-Employee or Master Servant relationship constitutes one of the most important and major element for consideration in any analysis of an employment related status. Should a legal dispute arise in this respect, one should, firstly, look into whether or not a contract of service was in existence in the given context of work relationship.

In this line of thought, a contract of service is said to be in effect, when a party called the servant or employee expresses his agreement to work for the other party called master or employer. This can be in regard to full time or part time employment, indefinitely or for a certain specified period of time.

Direction, Supervision and Control
Another criterion of testing the concept of employment is the factor of directing, supervising and controlling. In this respect, it can be mentioned that it is enough to admit the existence of such a factor if, at least, the authority to exercise control over someone at work exist, namely, as to when the work will be performed and the modality or ways to perform. This even the actual control was not exercise, yet.

Method of remuneration or compensation for service(s)
This aspect represents a useful and important indicator as to what kind of relationship is in existence at a given place of work. Undoubtedly, if one is paid by hourly rate or by a work-piece performance rate or by month, this constitute an immediate and obvious clue of an employer-employee relationship. There are many cases , dealt by the Courts in various countries around the world in which the status of a salary or wage earner was in debate, and the Court found that the existence of a salary or wage is a stronger or a better indicator in testing the concept of employment for ana-lyzing an employee-employer relationship.

Ownership of Tools, Furniture, Equipment, Machinery and the like
Ownership of such assets can serve as an instrument of testing the concept of employment in a given case. Whenever the procurement of certain necessary materials, tools, furniture, fixtures, equipment, machinery and the likes takes place, we have a good indication of the existence of the factor of control by the payor over the employee. However, in certain areas or types of occupations it is customarily or normally accepted that workers can provide and use their own hand tools. Again, in such instances, one should look into the nature of agreement and the specific type of work relationship.

Schedule of hours of work
The scheduling of the hours of work by the payor and the implied requirement to observe such a schedule, constitute an indication of the status of employee within a framework of an employee-employer relationship. In this respect it can be mentioned that the freedom given to someone to select his or her own hours of work does not represent a decisive evidence of control.

Facilities made available for work performances

An employer is said to exercise control over an employee if he is providing or making available the necessary facilities on his premises in order that work performances take place, as expected and required in normal conditions. Whenever a material or substantial amount of money is spent in creating or providing such facilities for use is a good indication of an independent status in testing the concept of employment. Regulations, rules and policies to obey or comply with certain instructions, orders, etc..

Quite often one can find cases when regular reports, either oral or written are required for submission to the payor by the earner, and this constitute an indication of the existence of a control factor since an account of work performances is required through such a submission. Also, any stipulation that a person should comply with instructions or orders as to when, where and the mode of performance(s), constitutes an indication of an employee-employer relationship.

Training provided either in-house or outside the firm

The offer and the actual assistance given by the payor through training of an earner using an experienced person at the place of work or outside the firm's premises, at the discretion of the payor, represents a factor of control since it means that the payor intended to have the work done or performed in a certain way. The training may take various forms, like meetings in certain places, at different times, general or technical courses relevant to the job performances or required duties, etc.. This indicator becomes especially relevant if the execution of training takes place periodically or with some noticeable degree of frequency.

In this line of thought, it can be emphasized that one who enjoys the status of an independent contractor, normally makes use of his or her chosen methods or techniques for work performances and is given no training by the payor who is expecting to benefit from his services.

Personally recognized performances of work

This is an indication that the person requiring the services and ready to pay for them is interested not only in the methods and techniques of work performances but also in the results of the operations and also who is the actual performer of the given job under consideration.

Time working schedules and routines

As the payor may know his own needs and interests at his place of business, he may also indicate to the worker the order or sequence for him to perform, and this in accordance with certain specified instructions thus depriving the worker from the freedom of his choice to follow his or her own mode or way of work performance. In many firms around the world there are in existence certain established schedules and routines required to be observed permanently.

Regularly required reports of work performances

An obvious and strong indication of control by the payor over the earner is said to exist, when regular reports, either written or oral, are required to be submitted, namely when the performer is asked to comply and account for his expected and actual performed duties at the place of work, as assigned to him.

Payor's premises

The requirement that the work is to be performed on the payor's premises is an indication that the person (the earner) will be within the payor's sphere of direction and supervision or control. In this respect, and as a further recognition of the element of control, it is often found that the earner, during the performances of his or her duties, is using also certain facilities needed and made available by the payor, like a desk, telephone, office, equipment like calculators, etc..
However, the worker may, sometime, have the option of using or not such facilities.

Right to dismiss someone at the place of work

This right constitutes an important element of judgement in establishing the status of an employer-employee relationship. It is in fact the existence of the right of dismissal which makes the worker to comply with the payor's instructions. In the case of an independent contractor, if he measures his or her performances up to his contract stipulations or clauses and related details, he cannot have his services interrupted without liability incurred to the payor.

THE COMPANY'S POLICIES AND REGULATIONS
WITH RESPECT TO PAYROLL

Each firm may have special policies and regulations regarding the time worked and the payment procedures. You may find that some of these regulations are negotiated and are already included in a union-contract. In any event, each firm may have its own regulations suitable for the particular type of business. For example:

−   A firm may have decided that its salaried employees do not receive overtime pay but receive time off for extra time worked.

−   The overtime is calculated to the nearest quarter hour.

−   Employees are allowed a certain number of minutes for lateness above which they may lose 15 minutes pay.

−   Regular hours for work are 9.00 a.m. - 1.00 p.m. and 2.00 p.m. - 6.00 p.m.

−   Any time worked above the regular hours (over 15 minutes) and on Saturday is considered overtime.
    (It is assumed that the firm is on a 40 hour weekly working timetable).

After gaining familiarity with the existing state of the company's affairs and after gathering all the various existing payroll forms, you should try to understand their specific pattern or design and compare them against our suggested forms that are presented in a separate section of this text. This will help you make improvements and the necessary or eventual adjustments to the already existing forms in use by the company.

Aims and Objectives

One of the paramount objectives in respect to payroll control and verification is to verify that all payroll charges constitute bonafide actual services or performances supplied for the firm under consideration.

Another important and useful objective to be mentioned is that all the stated services or work performances provided for the firm by its various incumbents or personnel, have been adequately and consistently allocated or distributed to the various categories and properly accounted for and classified.

Finally, there is a need to verify that all the stated services either claimed, recorded or performed for the firm have been in their entirety received and also recorded in the company's accounting books and supported records (subsidiary ledgers, registers, etc.).

Records Under Examination

- Company's manuals, general and specific ones in respect to payroll;

- Company's policies, rules and written procedures and instructions to be followed up in respect to payroll;

- Employees time information sheets, tables, records or cards;

- Individual earnings records of employees;

- Documentation regarding rates of pay, changes in rates of pay, etc..

- The required or necessary government forms to be used;

- Personnel records required as permanent business records;

- Overtime agreements and related rates, as approved;

- The payroll accounting journal or register in use;

- Documentation regarding time-off approved, in lieu of overtime;

- Notifications of hours of work;

- Shift schedules, as approved;

- Statement of earnings;

- Pay statements;

- Overtime records and related calculations;

- Classification made for accounting purposes;

- Proper accounting for payroll, in the ledgers of accounting;

- Payroll bank account reconciliation by month, if in use;

- Any other related documentation and written information in use in the respective firm, in support of various payments made during the period under consideration.

- Timely payroll reports made to the various authorities, including the governmental agencies;

- Periodic remittances of various taxes deducted at source from the employees earnings and company's contributions of various costs for different established funds;

- Transfers of payments or any other amounts or funds in respect to payroll.

- Personnel files.

Certain Considerations
Regarding The Required Procedures

A tentative outline of important procedures as part of a eventual wider plan of audit and verification, can be enlisted below :

- All the existing payroll records should be reviewed for the firm in question.

- The individual earning cards or records sheets should be examined thoroughly;

- All the necessary and relevant information and related details should be obtained, especially regarding the technical and clerical personnel involved in working with payroll and payroll related matters.

- Examination of the periodic payroll summary;

- Examination of the time cards, time information records sheets or tables, authorized earnings records, piece work or tickets for work performances by various employees of the firm under audit, etc..

- Verification of the various related payroll calculations, recalculations of various payroll figures like gross earnings based on authorized rates, various related deductions from the gross amounts as recorded and due, and the finding out of the ending net payroll amounts due to the various employees.

- A proper test cut-off performance should be made, suitable under the circumstances faced by the auditor in question, and of reasonable sampling size in order to facilitate a fair and sound conclusion based on the available evidence.

Elements involved in any control and verification:

- wages, salaries and other forms of earnings or retributions;

- authorized hourly rates;

- piece work performances, reports, various assignments accomplished;

- departments and sections involved;

- various positions, offices, included in the audit plan;

- weekly payments for instance.

ILLUSTRATION OF A PAYROLL PROCEDURE

IN A CERTAIN FIRM DURING A GIVEN MONTH

STEP I: OBTAIN INFORMATION REGARDING:
- WORK AS PERFORMED
  - e.g. – hours
    - piece work
    - days, weeks, etc.
- RATE OF PAY (hourly, weekly, etc.).

STEP II: CALCULATE GROSS EARNINGS:
- REGULAR
- OVERTIME
- VACATION PAY (when applied)

STEP III: COMPLETE ALL THE NECESSARY/REQUIRED INFORMATION IN THE PAYROLL JOURNAL OF ACCOUNTING:
- WEEKLY, BI-WEEKLY, SEMI-MONTHLY, MONTHLY based on the company's practice of accounting work.

STEP IV: ALL THE ACCOUNTING FOR PAYROLL, AS JOURNALIZED, MUST BE REFLECTED OR RECORDED IN THE RESPECTIVE EMPLOYEE'S INDIVIDUAL EARNINGS RECORDS TO AGREE WITH THE TOTAL OF THE PAYROLL JOURNAL OF THE GIVEN PERIOD.

STEP V: PREPARE THE INDIVIDUAL PAY STATEMENTS AND RELATED PAY CHEQUES.

STEP VI: MONTHLY RECONCILIATIONS:
- RE: bank account for payroll, employees' deductions payable, net (balance) payroll due, and outstanding cheques.

STEP VII: PREPARE MONTHLY DEDUCTIONS REMITTANCE TO THE INLAND REVENUE.

STEP VIII: POST/TRANSFER THE TOTALS OF ALL THE COLUMNS FROM THE PAYROLL JOURNAL INTO THE RELATED ACCOUNTS OF THE GENERAL LEDGER AND PRIOR TO THE RECONCILIATION OF CERTAIN RELATED ACCOUNTS OF PAYROLL.

NOTES: It is recommended that all the payroll entries and totals, etc., be approved or certified by a senior supervisor in line, or a person in authority delegated by the head of the firm. And this should be done at least on a monthly basis, if not each and every time work is performed.

Make sure that you update your individual payroll records, especially when changes in the rate(s) of pay occur, and/or when other important information changes, such as tax coding number, addresses of the employee, etc., take place.

THE REQUIRED AND/OR NECESSARY
PAYROLL FORMS EXPLAINED:

First of all, and in support of the self-learning process under this section, certain legal provisions should be known since they constitute important requirements for correct payroll calculations.

Here, the following points should be considered; for example:

- what payroll records are legally required to be in use and what information must be kept or preserved and for how long

- what the minimum wage (guaranteed hourly wage, guaranteed daily wage) is and its relationship to age

- what the restrictions on hours of work are and for what type of occupations, and what the treatment of benefits under the law (included or excluded) is

- how overtime should be calculated (for salaried, piece-workers, etc.); here, a step-by-step approach regarding the way(s) of calculations will facilitate the process of learning

- how to treat **time off in lieu of overtime** as an available option

- the need for an overtime agreement to be in place and its useful elements

- the legal requirement for notification of hours of work by the company

- pay periods on a regular basis [and company's related policy(ies)]

- compulsory and optional deductions

- hours of work with regard to industrial variations and occupational exceptions, if any

- special considerations that relate to general holiday and vacation pay and how it should be calculated and especially at the time of termination of employment

- treatment under the Act of the following:

    - adolescents, young persons

    - subcontractors

    - maternity cases

    - termination (dismissal)

All of the above should be considered based on the law and related legislation.

Each employer must maintain certain necessary records concerning his employees, at each place of business, for a certain length of time.

The following are some of the necessary and useful payroll records forms in use, privately:

- Individual Earning Records for each calendar year

- Payroll Accounting Journals, usually summarized by month (records the weekly, bi-weekly, semi-monthly or monthly pay)

- Weekly time cards/bi-weekly time records, as the case may be

- Monthly time working records

- Overtime records - all hours in excess of 8 in a day or 40 in a week, for example

- Overtime agreement

- Statement of Earnings or Pay Statements

- Statement of Earnings (Where the Employee is paid for overtime, certain information must be given to him)

- Statement of Earnings (If the employer has agreed to provide take time in lieu of overtime pay, some additional information must be given to the employee).
- Shift Schedule
- Vacation Schedule/Plan of Employees' Vacation time

EMPLOYEE'S INDIVIDUAL EARNING RECORDS - FIRST PART

It should contain the following information:

Name of employee completely stated (including middle name, if any)

Address of residence

Mailing Address

Place of work (unit); Department, Section

Type of work or Position

Marital Status

National Insurance Number

Date of Birth

Number of Dependants

Tax code number and changes of code numbers, if any

Employee number/clock number assigned by the firm

Date of commencement of the present term of employment or date started

Date left or terminated

Reason for termination

Basic salary or rate and effective date to apply it; Approved by . . .

Overtime rate and effective date to apply it; Approved by . . .

Commission rate and effective date to apply it; Approved by . . .

Time off in place of overtime provided and taken;

Changes in Rate(s) of pay and Authorization for Change;

- first change—effective date—new rate—approved by . . .
- second change—effective date—new rate—approved by . . .
- third change—effective date—new rate—approved by . . .

Vacation Pay Recap:

Each annual vacation granted should contain:

- the dates of commencement and of completion
- vacation (calculation period) taken from . . . to . . .
- the period of employment covered by the annual vacation
- amount of vacation pay paid

SECOND PART - MAINLY THE CALCULATIONS SECTION

- Number of Regular Hours Worked

- Rate of Regular Pay

- Total of Regular Pay

- Number of Overtime Hours Worked

- Rate of Overtime Pay

- Total of Overtime Pay

- Vacation Pay

- Gross Earnings

- Paid Taxable Benefits

- Gross Income (Gross Earnings plus Paid Taxable Benefits)

Deductions (Compulsory):

- Income Tax

- National Insurance contribution

Other Deductions (Voluntary):

- Insurance premiums such as group life plans

- Payments for loans to a credit union

- Acquisition of Firm's shares

- Pension Plans premiums (re: company or private plans)

- Contributions to various social clubs, saving funds accounts, charitable organizations, etc..

Also, whenever the case may be, advances to employees and garnishees by order of Court can be deducted.

Total of all deductions

Net Earnings (Total Gross Income less Total Deductions)

Add: Non-Taxable Allowances

Total Payable

Pay Period ending (weekly, bi-weekly, semi-monthly, monthly).
If paid by cash it has to be noted as such.
If paid by cheque, indicate cheque number issued and date of cheque.

It is important to emphasize that at the close of each pay period, it is necessary to know the cumulative earnings of the employee for the year-to-date in order to determine whether his earnings for the current period are still subject wholly, or in part, to certain taxes.

Another use of the employee's earnings record is in preparing the annual report required from the employer by the Taxation Office.

These earnings records may serve a variety of other incidental purposes such as the calculation of bonuses or the proof of compliance with the Minimum Wages and Maximum Hours of Work Laws.

Periodically, the earnings records should be pencil-added and cross-balanced. This procedure acts as an error check and also reduces the end-of-the-year work load.

PAYROLL ACCOUNTING JOURNAL OR REGISTER
(Summarized by month, usually)

Certain calculations are necessary in order to determine the due amounts to the Company's employees.

The gross earnings, the deductions subtracted from gross earnings, and the net pay due to the employees, must be listed or recorded for each employee and for each and every pay period. This is needed in order to centralize and group all the information for a certain period - usually a month -for accounting purposes. The related accounting form on which these calculations are made is called a Payroll Register or Payroll Journal.

Certain proofs are necessary to be performed in order to avoid errors. They are:

1. Regular Earnings plus Overtime equals Gross Earnings

2. Gross Earnings - Total Deductions equals Net Earnings

3. Sum of all the Individual Deductions equals Total Deductions

In fact, the payroll journal is a summary of all the individual earnings record sheets for a certain given period, in order to account for the respective related totals of the period under consideration.

Prior to performance on the payroll journal, all the existing individual earning record sheets in operation will be grouped by the department and by alphabetical order; for example: management salaries, sales personnel salaries and commissions, purchasing department, shop or plant direct wages, indirect or auxiliary personnel (e.g. for repairs and maintenance of machinery).

The payroll journal should indicate who performed the calculations, who approved the calculations as made, and the related dates. Obviously, this will be treated and preserved with the utmost confidentiality (payroll information).

The title of the payroll journal will indicate the period of payroll covered, such as weekly, semi-monthly, bi-weekly, monthly.

Regardless of whether payment is made by cheque or deposit to a bank account, the Payroll Record/Register should be treated as a book of original entry and the column totals posted directly from the Record of Payroll Journal or Register to the General Ledger.

The Payroll Journal or Register will contain the following information, for example:

TITLES:

- Company's name
- Kind of Pay (weekly, bi-weekly, semi-monthly, monthly)
- Done By . . . Approved By . . . Date . . .
- Page Number
- Category of Expense (Management Salaries, Office Salaries, Sales Salaries, Commission, Shop Wages, etc. . . .)
- Employee Number/Clock Number
- Employee's Name

Regular Earnings:

- Number of hours
- Rate of hourly pay
- Regular earnings (total)

Overtime Earnings:

- Number of hours
- Rate of hourly pay
- Overtime earnings (total)

Vacation Time Pay (If it applies or if it is calculated in the pay period)

Gross earnings (total)

(ADD) Paid Benefits (Specify)

GROSS INCOME (Gross Earnings plus Paid Benefits)

Less: DEDUCTIONS OF ALL KINDS

- Compulsory (specified)
- Voluntary (specified)
- Other deductions like employee's advances, garnishees by order of a Court

TOTAL OF ALL DEDUCTIONS

NET EARNINGS (Gross Income Minus Total of All Deductions)

(Add: Non-taxable Allowances)

Total Payable

Cheque number issued, pay period ending, and employee's name (obtain the signature to confirm payment if paid by cash)

PLEASE NOTE: All the columns must be added and cross-added before payments are made or cheques issued. This is done in order to avoid errors.

It has to be emphasized that, for the most part, the payroll journal contains the same information and the pattern as the individual employee's earning records. This is due to the fact that the payroll journal is nothing more that a recap or a centralization of all the information of payments and deductions contained in the individual earning records.

The very purpose of the payroll journal is to make possible the accounting for payroll.

NOTE: 1) The related exhibit is purposely presented in the form of a "basic" or "simplified" framework or pattern, since it is left up to you, having in mind your firm's needs, to add information to these specific patterns or business forms, in order eventually to produce the newly needed specific business forms or records.

WEEKLY TIME CARD - FOR EXEMPLIFICATION ONLY

It contains:

Employee's Complete Name

Employee Number/Clock Number

Job Name or Number

Kind of Work Done (Job identification number or brief job description)

Week Ending

Number of Hours Worked Each Day of the Week

Total Number of Hours per Job or Kind of Work Done

Total Number of Hours per Each Day of the Week

Rate per Hour for Each Job or Kind of Work Done

Total Amount for Each Job Number or Kind of Work Done

General Total for the Respective Week

Approved By

Deductions Related to Above

Total Deductions

Net Pay

Date Paid

Paid by Cheque No. . . . (if paid by cheque)

BI-WEEKLY TIME RECORD OF WORK

It contains:

Employee's Complete Name

Employee Number/Clock Number

DATE AND DAY WORKED

TIME IN

TIME OUT

TOTAL NUMBER OF HOURS ACTUALLY WORKED EACH DAY (Specify time of lunch allowed)

MONTHLY TIME WORKING RECORD

It contains:

The Month Under Consideration

Daily Hours Worked Each Day and for Each Week Ending

Total Hours Worked for Each Week Ending

Total Regular Hours for Each Week Ending

Total Overtime Hours for Each Week Ending

Regular Rate for Each Week ending

Overtime Rate for Each Week Ending

TIME-OFF IN LIEU OF OVERTIME

Both the employer and the employee have an option available to them, namely for time-off in lieu of overtime.

For example, certain provisions may be in force:

1. The agreement must be in writing

2. At the minimum, at least for one hour overtime worked, one hour time-off must be given.

3. The time-off should be taken only during normal working hours.

4. Regular wages should be paid at the time the time-off is taken, and based on a rate of pay in force on the day the time-off is taken.

5. Time-off should be used within the three months of the end of the pay period in which it was worked. (An extension may be obtained from the Director).

6. If the employee decides not to take the time-off in lieu of overtime, he must be paid out at time-and-a-half, at the rate of pay in force on the day the three months came to an end.

7. It is necessary to have two weeks notice by either party in case of cancellation. In this case the parties must agree to a cash basis at time-and-a-half.

NOTIFICATION OF HOURS OF WORK

Overtime should exist only if it is both authorized and needed by the company. It should be emphasized that a shift notice should be posted to the attention of the employees. Every employer should notify the employees of the period of time when work begins and ends, whenever shift work applies and time at which a shift begins and ends. This acknowledgement can be carried out by any other suitable means the Director decides. In case of a change of shift, advanced written notice shall be given to employees and a certain time of rest between shifts should exist.

NOTE: No Overtime Without Permission should take place. This is in order to avoid eventual disputes.

SHIFT SCHEDULE

It contains:

Week Ending . . .

Shift: First, Second, Third, etc. . . .

- For each day of the week an indication of the name of the employee should be in place.

STATEMENT OF EARNINGS - Where the employee is paid for overtime, the following information should be given to him:

Name of Employee

Pay Period

Wage Rate

Regular Hours and Wages

Overtime Hours and Wages

Total Wages Regular for Each Week Ending

Total Wages Overtime for Each Week Ending

GENERAL TOTAL OF EARNINGS for each Week Ending

MONTHLY TOTALS FOR HOURS, RATE, WAGES, TOTAL OF EARNINGS

Deductions Calculated:

- Compulsory (specified)
- Voluntary (specified)
- Other eventual deductions (specified)

Total Deductions

Net Pay

STATEMENT OF EARNINGS: For example, if the employer has agreed to give the "take time-off" in lieu of overtime pay, some additional information must be given to the employee.

PAY STATEMENT - At the end of each pay period, an employer must provide certain information in writing to the employee.

NOTE: The employee should retain this record of earnings and deductions. This will facilitate control at a later date, whenever necessary.

The pay statement contains the following information:

Employee number
Regular hours worked
Regular rate of pay
Regular earnings
Overtime hours worked
Overtime rate of pay
Time-Off in place of overtime pay provided and taken
Vacation pay paid
General holiday pay
Other Earnings: Hours and Wages
Gross Pay: Hours and Wages

DEDUCTIONS

- Compulsory (specified)
- Voluntary (specified)
- Other eventual deductions (specified)

NET EARNINGS

OVERTIME RECORD

SPECIAL CONSIDERATION IN RESPECT TO CALCULATIONS

ALL HOURS IN EXCESS OF 8 IN A DAY OR 40 IN A WEEK - for example

The record contains for calculation purposes the following:

- total number of all hours for each week

- separately, the total number of all hours for each week - regular and overtime

As an example, assume that an employee is paid a monthly salary of 2,000:

	$2,000	(Monthly Salary)
Divide By:	4.33	(Number of Weeks Per Month)
Equals:	$461.89	(Weekly Salary)

If the company is on a 38 hour week, then an hourly wage rate and an overtime rate would be figured out as follows:

$12.15 (Hourly Wage Rate)
38/461.89 (Weekly Salary)
then $12.15 × 1.5 = $18.22 (Overtime rate)

In case of payment made on a piece-work basis, or by commissions or by any way that brings the employee's wages to vary from one pay period to another, it is necessary to calculate an overtime rate every pay period where overtime occurs.

In order to complete this kind of calculation, it is necessary to figure out an hourly rate of pay. This can be obtained by dividing all the amount earned in a given pay period by all the hours the employee actually worked in that particular pay period.

This will constitute the regular hourly wage for the respective employee for the related pay period.

For example, if a piece worker during December earned total wages of $1,644.00 by working 164 regular hours and 14 overtime hours (total 178), the calculation of wages would be as follows:

STEP 1:   Calculate December Wage Rate :

Divide Total Wages by all Hours Worked $1,644/178 = $9.24

$9.24 (December Wage Rate)

1,644/178 (Overtime Rate should be $13.86 or 1 1/2 hour)

STEP 2:   Regular 164 Hours × \$9.24 = \$1,515.36
14 Hours × \$13.86 =   194.04

Gross Wage   \$1,709.40

SUGGESTIVE
PAYROLL TABLES IN USE

A closer analysis of the useful diagrams and the interesting tables that can be found in the subsequent pages may have a tremendous impact on the road of gaining familiarity with a diversity of business operations one may be confronted during the business life. This, on a national and/or international level.

It has to be acknowledged that the payroll work of any kind of business enterprise around the world constitutes one of the most important and useful segments of the machinery of accounting.

MONTHLY PAYROLL JOURNAL

Category of Expense	Emp. No.	Regular Hr.	Rate	Pay	Overtime Hr.	Rate	Pay	Total Earnings	Nat. Ins.	Pen-sion	Tax	Hosp Care	Gr. Ins	Advances CD	Amt	Total Deductions	Earnings	Total Pen-sion to date	Ck. No.	Pay Period Ending	Employee Name	Code
Management	1			2000.00				2000.00	32.51	46.84	378.45	14		2	100.00	571.80	1428.20	150.20	51	06/30	Jim Brown	1
Office	2			1600.00				1600.00	25.35	37.60	269.05	14		2	100.00	446.00	1154.00	120.40	52	06/30	Bill Smith	1
Sales	3			1400.00				1400.00	21.75	32.90	213.60	14		2	100.00	382.25	1017.75	100.10	53	06/30	Greg O'Neil	1
Purchasing	4			1300.00				1300.00	19.95	30.55	191.80	14		2	100.00	356.30	943.70	90.40	54	06/30	Harold Sharlow	1
Shop	5	160	.16	2560.00				2560.00	42.59	46.84	563.50	14		2	200.00	866.93	1693.07	240.50	55	06/30	Ken Smith	1
	6	160	.12	1920.00				1920.00	31.11	45.12	355.75	14		2	100.00	545.98	1374.02	140.05	56	06/30	Roy Love	1
Sub-total								4480.00														
Aux. Personnel	7	160	.10	1600.00				1600.00	25.35	37.60	269.05	14		2	100.00	446.00	1154.00	120.40	57	06/30	Brian Hogan	1
Totals								12380.00	198.61	277.45	2240.20	98			800.00	3615.26	8764.74					
								Salaries -DR	Pay -CR	Pay -CR	Pay -CR	Hosp Pay -CR	Gr. Ins Pay -CR	Misc. Deductions		Total Deductions	Salaries Pay -CR	Total Pension to date				
								(1)	(2)	(3)	(4)	(5)	(6)	(7)		(8)	(9)					

Proof Columns 1 - 8 $8764.74

Column 9 $8764.74

Total Columns: 2, 3, 4, 5, 6 + 7 $3615.26

Column 8 $3615.26

Exhibit 54

WEEKLY TIME CARD

Employee Name _____ No. _____

Week Ending August 17 1985

Job Name or No.	Kind of Work Done	S	M	T	W	T	F	S	Hours	Rate	Amount
3426			2	1	2	3	2		10	8.00	$ 80.00
4972			4	3	1	1	1		10	6.00	60.00
6851			1	1	2	1	3		8	7.00	56.00
1293			1	1	1	1	1		5	6.00	30.00
2452			1	1	1	1	1		5	9.00	45.00
TOTALS									38		$271.00

		Deductions:	$6.37	$4.01	$41.05		Total	$ 51.43
Approved			Nat. Ins.	Pen- sion	Tax		Net Pay	$219.57
Date Paid: Aug. 19, 1985	Check No. 342							

Calculations done by _____   Reviewed and Approved by _____

Exhibit 55

EMPLOYEE'S CLOCK CARD

No.: 102

Name of Employee: Mr. Bill Smith

Week Ending: March 27th, 19 _____

Day	In	Out	In	Out	Total Hours
Monday	0802	1200	1301	1804	9
Tuesday	0759	1201	1258	1740	9
Wednesday	0806	1203	1300	1800	9
Thursday	0809	1159	1259	1706	8
Friday	0803	1158	1304	1600	7
TOTAL:					42

Ordinary time: 40 hours @ $3.00 $ 120

Overtime: 2 hrs @ $4.50 $ 9

Total Gross Wages $ 129

Exhibit 56

		IN	OUT	HOURS

NAME Jim Brown

CLOCK NO. 21

Employee No. 5.

1985

		IN	OUT	HOURS
SUNDAY	AUGUST 18			
MONDAY	AUGUST 19	9:00	6:00	8.
TUESDAY	AUGUST 20	8:59	6:31	8½
WEDNESDAY	AUGUST 21	9:01	6:01	8.
THURSDAY	AUGUST 22	9:02	7:04	9.
FRIDAY	AUGUST 23	8:57	6:03	8.
SATURDAY	AUGUST 24	9:00	7:30	9½
SUNDAY	AUGUST 25			
MONDAY	AUGUST 26	8:57	6:00	8.
TUESDAY	AUGUST 27	9:01	6:00	8.
WEDNESDAY	AUGUST 28	9:02	8:30	10½
THURSDAY	AUGUST 29			
FRIDAY	AUGUST 30	9:01	6:30	8½
SATURDAY	AUGUST 31	8:57	8:00	10

LUNCH: 1:00 p.m. - 2:00 p.m.

NOTE: Foreman's or supervisor's confirmation should be obtained.

Calculations done by

Reviewed and Approved by

Exhibit 57

MONTH OF JULY, 1986

WEEK ENDING	DAILY HOURS WORKED							HOURS			RATE		WAGES		TOTAL
	S	M	T	W	T	F	S	TOTAL	REG.	OVER TIME	REG.	OVER TIME	REG.	OVER TIME	
July 5		9	7	9	8½	7½	6	47	44	3	6	9	264	27	291
July 12		9	4	7	10	9	3	42	38	4	6	9	228	36	264
MONTHLY TOTAL															

Calculations

Done by _____

Reviewed and Approved by _____

Exhibit 58

SHIFT SCHEDULE   WEEK ENDING _____

	S	M	T	W	T	F	S
FIRST SHIFT 7AM - 4PM (Lunch 11 - 12)		MIKE	MIKE	MIKE	MIKE	MIKE	
SECOND SHIFT 9AM - 6PM (Lunch 1 - 2)		GREG	GREG	GREG	GREG	GREG	
THIRD SHIFT 8AM - 5PM (Lunch 12 - 1)		ED	ED	ED	ED	ED	

Approved by _____

Exhibit 59

STATEMENT OF EARNINGS

NAME   John Day

PAY PERIOD   August 15 - August 31, 1985

WAGE RATE $10.00 per hour

	HOURS	WAGES
REGULAR		
OVERTIME		
O.T. TAKEN OFF		
O.T. PAID (X 1½)		
OTHER EARNINGS		
GROSS PAY		

DEDUCTIONS

ADVANCE	
TAX	
NATIONAL INSURANCE	
PENSION	
HEALTH	
OTHER	
TOTAL	

NET PAY

Issued by _____

Exhibit 60

PAY STATEMENT

NOTE: Retain this record of your earnings and deductions as reported to the government.

EMP. NO.	HR	RATE	PAY	HR	RATE	PAY	TOTAL EARNINGS	PENSION	NAT. INS.	TAX	HOSP INS	GR	CD	AMT	TOTAL DEDUC- TIONS	NET EARNINGS	TOTAL PENSION TO DATE	CK NO.	PAY PERIOD ENDING
	REGULAR			OVERTIME							MISC			DEDUCTIONS					

1. Pension _____

2. Bonds _____

3. Union _____

4. _____

5. _____

BANK: _____

PAY TO THE ORDER OF _____ $ _____

PAYROLL ACCOUNT   Cheque No. _____

Date _____

_____ /100 DOLLARS

(For) Employer _____

Received wages in full for the above payroll record.

Signature _____

Exhibit 61

SCHEDULE OF OVERTIME

The Month of ———— 198 ——

WEEK	S	M	T	W	T	F	S	TOTAL	REGULAR	OVERTIME
FIRST										
SECOND										
THIRD										
FOURTH										

OVERTIME: For example, ALL HOURS IN EXCESS OF 8 IN A DAY OR 44 IN A WEEK, WHICHEVER IS THE GREATER.

Calculations
Done by ————————

Reviewed and Approved by

————————

Exhibit 62

1985 - 1986 Vacation Schedule

Name	Week Commencing (Monday) 1985: JANUARY				FEBRUARY				MARCH				APRIL					MAY				JUNE				JULY					AUGUST				SEPTEMBER					OCTOBER				NOVEMBER				DECEMBER					1986: JANUARY				FEBRUARY				MARCH				
	7	14	21	28	4	11	18	25	4	11	18	25	1	8	15	22	29	6	13	20	27	3	10	17	24	1	8	15	22	29	5	12	19	26	2	9	16	23	30	7	14	21	28	4	11	18	25	2	9	16	23	30	6	13	20	27	3	10	17	24	3	10	17	24	31

Exhibit 63

THE ACCOUNTING FOR PAYROLL

GENERAL CONSIDERATIONS

A diagram such as the one shown below suggests the interrelationships within the payroll accounting system of a given Firm.

Schematically, a Simplified Payroll System is presented below:

THE PERSONNEL DEPARTMENT
OR
PERSONNEL SUPERVISOR
CHANGES IN PAYROLL

A. Payroll records should be updated

B. The Payroll is processed regularly

C. Payroll costs information transferred to the general/payroll accounting clerk.

Payroll Costs	Payroll Reporting	Payroll Cheques
To General/Payroll Accounting Clerk	To Management and Outside Agencies like Government, etc.	To Company's Employees

Exhibit 64

Needless to say, the payroll accounting function is one of the most important and sensitive parts of the machinery of accounting and those who are activating it must reveal, to a very great extent, a sound sense of responsibility, security and confidentiality. Along this line of thought, some of the most relevant aspects of the payroll work can be brought into attention.

First and foremost there is a need for company regulations for the reporting of hours worked. This ensures the hourly payroll security. As known, the basic document is the TIME CARD for reporting the hours worked and this document must be preserved in a safe place once completed and accounted for.

Whenever TIME CLOCKS are used, special attention should be given to avoid the possibility of an employee misusing someone else's card. In some enterprises, the foreman or manager in charge may be required to report the time worked by the employees under his supervision, instead of using time cards. Also, whenever employees are transferred from one place of work to another, the person in charge of such supervision must accurately report these movements of personnel. This will create the possibility for a proper cost accounting to payroll. It must also be stressed that all the time cards related to "transfers" of employees within a firm should always be approved by the supervisor in charge, prior to the submission of these cards to the payroll department for accounting purposes. In this way, any false reporting of hours, rates, absences with pay, fictitious information and the like, can be eliminated or avoided. Special attention should be given to the reporting of overtime hours for the salaried employees, and all the related hourly reports should be O.K.'ed or confirmed in any enterprise, in order to avoid later disputes.

THE PAYROLL EXPENSES AND LIABILITIES ACCOUNTS

GROSS EARNINGS (WAGES, SALARIES)

Gross Earnings constitute the amounts due to employees before certain amounts are withheld (deductions made). These amounts are calculated by multiplying the numbers of hours worked by the hourly rate of pay. Office employees are paid a straight salary of so much a week, a month or a year. Where employees are paid based on an annual salary, their gross earnings are computed as a fraction of the annual amounts each time the payroll is registered or accounted for (journalized). Salaries are considered an administrative expense paid to those who carry out administrative work in their office, and are charged to the Profit and Loss Account (debited).

The time cards kept for each and every employee are the basis for calculation of the gross earnings for hourly rated employees. This does not exclude the Company's policy in force to have time cards for some other categories of employees.

Wage or salary expense is equal to the gross amount of the payroll, which is substantially larger than the "take-home" pay received by employees.

Factory employees are usually paid on an hourly basis, on a piece-rate basis or some combination of the two. Based on a usual worker's contract of work, the employee is required to work a minimum of 40 hours weekly, for example, consisting of five days of eight hours each. The related calculation is made using an ordinary rate. Above this usual time, any calculation made is based on an overtime rate as stipulated, as expected, in the contractual agreement of employment and in the spirit of the law.

Wages expense are charged (debited) to and included in the so-called Cost of Goods Sold (Trading Account). Wages are paid to those occupied in producing goods or carrying out work on goods.

THE GENERAL TERM IN USE TO INDICATE THE CALCULATION OF AMOUNTS PAYABLE TO EMPLOYEES IS KNOWN AS PAYROLL.

Salaries are usually paid on an actual time-worked basis. Wage and salary costs constitute one of the largest business expenses and proper and up-dated records of such costs must be kept.

The pay period or the period of time related to the amount earned may be different from the accounting period.

EMPLOYER'S CONTRIBUTION TO NATIONAL INSURANCE FUND.

In certain cases, the employer is required by law or contractual agreement(s) to contribute towards the total cost of certain benefits. In particular, for example, this applies to National Insurance Fund.

Because the employer must contribute to the cost of National Insurance Fund, provision must be made for his expense, at the completion of each accounting for a payroll period.

COMPANY'S OWN PENSION SCHEME

Based on a certain rate established by a firm, an employee may contribute to the pension scheme or pension fund (private) a certain amount called superannuation. This is an additional pension to the state pension, and is related to the number of years that the employee has contributed to the company's fund.

It has to be noted that some superannuation schemes are compulsory, based on the company's policy(ies). The employer will contribute with his cost to such schemes, on behalf of the respective employees and based on the same policy(ies) in force.

The superannuation often takes the form of a lump sum payment received by the employee upon his or her retirement.

PAYROLL LIABILITY ACCOUNTS

The recording of each payroll creates liability accounts, represented by the various deductions from employees such as Income Tax, National Insurance Contributions, etc. Eventually, these liabilities must be paid. The actual dates vary, but essentially, payments are made monthly. These amounts withheld or deducted (the difference between gross earnings and take-home pay) are usually paid or remitted monthly by the employer to the Government, namely the Taxation Office on one hand, and in some instances to the insurance companies (private), banks, unions, social clubs and/or other outside agencies, on the other.

It has been emphasized that any person who fails to withhold or remit an amount which he/she has deducted or withheld is liable to a penalty. In this regard, every employer and payor who is withholding or deducting taxes or other amounts, must keep records and books of account, and allow inspection and verification at the request of the Taxation Office.

NET PAYROLL-DUE TO EMPLOYEES

Payroll cheques constitute the most sincere expression of the employee's merits at the place of work and they also represent the employer's recognition of the employee's performance, as expected.

Payment by cheque provides a receipt for the employer. A special stub or pay slip attached to the cheque provides the employee with the basis on which gross pay has been calculated and the details of the various deductions.

Undoubtedly, it is advantageous when payments are made by cheques to prepare the payroll work on a bookkeeping machine or by computer. The net pay or net earnings is calculated by subtracting from gross earnings or gross pay all kinds of deductions (compulsory and voluntary ones).

The following formula applies:

NET EARNINGS = GROSS EARNINGS — ALL DEDUCTIONS

RON'S AUTO REPAIR SERVICES LTD.

THE PAYROLL JOURNAL
W/S1

(WAGES SUMMARY)

FOR THE MONTH OF JANUARY 1987

DATE 1987	EMPLOYEE	TAX CODE	GROSS	PENSION	SEC. INS.	INCOME TAX	ON ACCT.	TOTAL DED.	NET PAY	CHEQUE NUMBER
Jan 31	**Management**									
	R. Smith	4	2000.00 ✓	25.00	50.00	325.00	—	400.00	1600.00	19
			(450)							
	Co.'s Contrib.			25.00 ✓	70.00 ✓					
				(DR 452)	(DR 452)					
	Shop									
31	B. Collins	1	1400.00	10.00	40.00	350.00	100.00	500.00	900.00	17
31	N. Thomas	3	1500.00	15.00	45.00	240.00	100.00	400.00	1100.00	18
	TOTAL		2900.00 ✓	25.00	85.00	590.00	200.00	900.00	2000.00	
			(409)							
	Co.'s Contrib.			25.00 ✓	110.00 ✓					
				(DR 410)	(DR 410)					
	Office									
31	R. Heart	5	1200.00 ✓	5.00	30.00	165.00	—	200.00	1000.00	20
			(451)							
	Co.'s Contrib.			5.00 ✓	42.00 ✓					
				(452)	(452)					
	GENERAL TOTAL		6100.00	55.00	165.00	1080.00	200.00 ✓	1500.00	4600.00 ✓	
	Co.'s Contrib. **TOTAL**			55.00	231.00					
	Due to Taxation Off. Account Number			110.00 ✓ (207)	396.00 ✓ (207)	1080.00 ✓ (207)	(112)		(206)	
	DEBIT/CREDIT		DR	CR	CR	CR	CR		CR	

Exhibit 65

ADVANCES TO EMPLOYEES　　　　Account No. 112

DATE 1987	PARTICULARS	FOLIO	DEBITS	CREDITS	DR. OR CR.	BALANCE
Jan 14	B. Collins	C/D1	100.00		DR	100.00
15	N. Thomas	C/D1	100.00		DR	200.00
31		W/S1		200.00		0.00

MANAGEMENT SALARIES　　　　Account No. 450

DATE 1987	PARTICULARS	FOLIO	DEBITS	CREDITS	DR. OR CR.	BALANCE
Jan 31		W/S1	2000.00		DR	2000.00
		G/J4		2000.00		0.00

OFFICE SALARIES　　　　Account No. 451

DATE 1987	PARTICULARS	FOLIO	DEBITS	CREDITS	DR. OR CR.	BALANCE
Jan 31		W/S1	1200.00		DR	1200.00
		G/J4		1200.00		0.00

WAGES · SHOP　　　　Account No. 409

DATE 1987	PARTICULARS	FOLIO	DEBITS	CREDITS	DR. OR CR.	BALANCE
Jan 31		W/S1	2900.00		DR	2900.00
31	A/E9	G/J2	500.00		DR	3400.00
31		G/J4		3400.00		0.00

ACCRUED PAYROLL　　　　Account No. 211

DATE 1987	PARTICULARS	FOLIO	DEBITS	CREDITS	DR. OR CR.	BALANCE
Jan 31	A/E9	G/J2		500.00	CR	500.00

Exhibit 66

EMPLOYEES' BENEFITS · OFFICE   Account No. 452

DATE 1987	PARTICULARS	FOLIO	DEBITS	CREDITS	DR. OR CR.	BALANCE
Jan 31	Management Pension	W/S1	25.00		DR	25.00
31	Management Insurance	W/S1	70.00		DR	95.00
31	Office Pension.	W/S1	5.00		DR	100.00
31	Office Insurance	W/S1	42.00		DR	142.00
		G/J4		142.00		0.00

EMPLOYEES' BENEFITS · SHOP   Account No. 410

DATE 1987	PARTICULARS	FOLIO	DEBITS	CREDITS	DR. OR CR.	BALANCE
Jan 31	Pension	W/S1	25.00		DR	25.00
31	Ins.	W/S1	119.00		DR	144.00
31		G/J4		144.00		0.00

NET PAYROLL DUE (CLEARING)   Account No. 206

DATE 1987	PARTICULARS	FOLIO	DEBITS	CREDITS	DR. OR CR.	BALANCE
Jan 31		C/D1	4600.00		DR	4600.00
		W/S1		4600.00	DR	0.00

PAYROLL DEDUCTIONS & BENEFITS   Account No. 207

PAYABLE TO THE TAXATION OFFICE

DATE 1987	PARTICULARS	FOLIO	DEBITS	CREDITS	DR. OR CR.	BALANCE
Jan 31	Pension	W/S1		110.00	CR	110.00
31	Ins.	W/S1		396.00	CR	506.00
31	Tax	W/S1		1080.00	CR	1586.00

THE PAYROLL FUNCTION IN A COMPUTERIZED ENVIRONMENT

As we are living in a world of rapid technological changes, we also feel the need to adapt or integrate the existing conventional systems to computer ones. It is for this reason that a separate part of this manual is reserved to cover the pros and cons of introducing computers into the business life. One should bear in mind that any business entity will adopt those systems and procedures as seen fit to its own specific needs or type of operation, in spite of the fact that principles on which the accounting machinery operates remain the same.

When the accounting system relies upon a computer, the gross pay and deductions are calculated automatically. All the related details of calculations are printed, and the cheques or payments made are also prepared automatically.

A computerized payroll program gives reports in the form of a printout of the payroll, pay slips, bank credit slips, and if needed, a list of cheque payments. At the end of each taxation year, the payroll program can print the necessary data for employees and for the Taxation Office.

Some of the reasons for having a computerized payroll system, either within the company or outside it (at a specialized agency), are as follows:

1 - It can increase substantially the productivity and efficiency in generating the required information.

2 - The availability of capable or trained personnel who can reconcile the manual payroll system against the computerized one obtained from the payroll unit.

3 - The computer's capability to store and retrieve large amounts of data, thus increasing information.

4 - The promptness of information released by the computer unit.

5 - The relative reduced costs for using the computer unit vis-a-vis the prompt availability of useful and needed information for various business purposes like the reporting and record-keeping ones.

6 - In the light of growing need for more detailed information required by the management for decision-making and the development of the company's operations, there is also a greater desirability to develop its system of internal documentation by using the computer generated data.

Along this line of thought, some benefits resulting from using a computerized payroll system should be stressed:

- The computer constitutes a basis for comparisons of calculations in order to eliminate errors or to notice errors and subsequently making possible, promptly, the eventual corrections or adjustments.

- It represents a counter-control of the correctness of the accounting clerk in charge of operations and helps to eliminate eventual fraud and negligence.

- It makes it possible for management to obtain timely information for decision-making and various analysis and reports, upon request.

- It offers accurate cumulative records for later use by other parts of the company and for various purposes like budgets, costing, forecasting, reports, etc.

- It facilitates control and serves as a stronger or more powerful measure of any internal control. Also it safeguards the company's information, especially within the competitive world.

In spite of the noticeable and useful advantages the computerized payroll system presents, there are also certain possible negative implications to individuals and society, such as the following:

- It causes a reduced level of employment in certain industries, and in certain areas, due to increased productivity, production and efficiency of operations.

- Computer-based systems are considered by some as impersonal systems, dehumanizing and depersonalizing human activities.

- The right of privacy can be seriously affected due to the enormous capability of the computer to store and retrieve information. The very existence of widely integrated systems of information makes possible and increases the chances for misuse of computer-stored information. It is only through severe legislation that this danger can be greatly reduced.

- Computerized crime fraud or errors may result from computer usage.

- The higher dependency upon computers may have drastic consequences following any malfunctioning of a computer-based system.

- The tendency towards mechanization compells people to conform to the system.

- Since the computer cannot reason, the ability of people is the key factor for directing and operating the information process.

Note: Only to a certain degree and extent, do these disadvantages apply to various firms.

In any selection of a computerized system, certain categories should be evaluated, including their composite elements:

- Initial costs
- Continuity costs
- Expansion costs
- Operating costs
- Hardware
- Programming
- Magnetic stripe
- Printer

- Ease of operating
- Service and Maintenance
- Terminal
- Systems support
- Out-Put
- Overall Impression related to Demonstration
  by salesperson

Management concerns before deciding to introduce the computerized payroll system are as follows:

- Insufficient controls
- Complexity of data processing
- Lack of needed standards
- Possibility of fraud
- Inadequate return of investment, etc.

A System Design, Development and Documentation must be in place. It should include detailed specifications for the following:

- Outputs
- Inputs
- Files
- Procedures

These will be used in the next stage — the programming stage — leading to the final one, that of implementation. The feedback will be obtained through testing and revision.

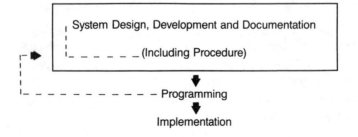

200

PROCEDURES INVOLVED IN THE DATA PROCESSING CYCLE

Certain inter-related steps constitute the data processing cycle of processing the payroll information of a company's employees:

1) **DATA ORIGINATION**

   The time cards are usually the coarse data. These are the so-called raw data for processing payroll.

2) **INPUT**

   The source data is processed into so-called input to the data processing system. In order to record data, the following apply:

   a) Editing - e.g., selecting the data necessitating processing. In this phase, information will be coded alphabetically, numerically or alphanumerically, this, in order to reach the highest degree of efficiency in processing.

   b) Verifying - e.g., verifying the accuracy and validity of the data. For example, checking if the overtime of an employee as indicated on his time card and continued by the company's supervisor is right.

   Input to payroll system includes, for example, employee name, social insurance number, regular hours worked, overtime hours and taxes.

3) **DATA MANIPULATION (PROCESSING)**

   This constitutes in fact the actual performance on the data submitted for processing and includes the following:

   a) Classifying. The data is classified by department, for example. It is considered a particular category or class.

   b) Sorting. The information is sequenced in a predetermined order. This is usually accomplished by electromechanical or electronic sorting techniques.

   c) Calculating and Recording. Calculations of gross pay, various deductions and net pay for each of the company's employees.

   d) Summarizing. The data is centralized in a meaningful way, as the company's management directs it or it requires certain information in respect to the total payroll paid as wages or salaries; from such kind of reporting, other useful detailed data can be obtained and presented in a certain structured and selected form.

4) **DATA REPORTING OR OUTPUT**

   The employee's paycheck is the main output of the payroll outcome. Together with the summaries of prepared data, it constitutes the needed or required output information.

   Output information includes, also, for example, withholding statements, payroll records, and reports to certain government agencies.

5) **DATA STORAGE**

   The data processing cycle comes to a close by having the available data stored for future retrieval needs. This operation can be accomplished electromechanically or in the electronic computer memory.

A Final Step: THE AUDIT

A constant review of all related performances by the computer unit or regular audits on data processing should be in place. The aim is to obtain certain benefits like the ones listed below:

- Reduced fraud, errors and omissions
- Improved controls
- Increased confidence and satisfaction
- Reduced operating costs
- Improved equipment use
- Improved efficiency and productivity
- Reduced time and costs, etc.

SELECTIVE AND SUGGESTIVE PAYROLL AUDIT SCHEDULES

The selective and suggestive payroll audit schedules that are presented in the subsequent pages of this Part were built up during the process of work and as the need arose during the performance of certain tasks and for practical and useful purposes in the field of audit.

As such, these useful schedules can be made use of as a practical and guiding light and in a flexible way, depending on one's concrete scope as may be often found in an audit program.

Key Points For Consideration

One of the main concerns of any auditor at the place of the client's offices, for payroll purposes, is to gain familiarity with the firm in general, and with all the related payroll matters and documentation, information, in particular. In this respect, my suggestion is to build-up, as expected, his or her own payroll plan of audit and verification. First of all, one should read the payroll procedures manual of the firm, if available. This will, with certainty, become a very useful and important tool since it includes both the questions and the related answers to most, if not all, important payroll matters that will , eventually, come to light during the audit work at the place of business. Thus, a person involved in control and verification, will gain insight into the company's state of affairs in respect to payroll.

The auditor will learn how the enterprise is eventually divided or segmented (depending on its size) into various sections, departments, units, individuals; and these, in turn, based on the specific functions assigned, tasks, or types of occupations.

One can learn who are the incumbents of the various positions at different echelons within the organization framework;

The auditor will find out who are the various heads, supervisors or managers, and foremen at various levels and what are their interrelationships within the organization and with their subordinates.

It has to be established who is in charge of the preservation of the confidential employees files and other personnel records and documentation supporting the various rates and payments made. Finally, how does the filing system work in the firm under consideration.

There is a need to know who is in charge of the authorizations of various rates of pay, gives approval for hiring of new personnel, the terminations or dismissals, the overtime requests, changes of rates of pay, schedules of work, planning of shifts and the authorizations in this respect, vacation time and planning, etc..

Whether or not the methods of bookkeeping/accounting and employment practices are set up to date and based on the required rules and procedures, becomes very important in running an efficient organization.

The auditor has to find out if all the matters regarding payments of various benefits, annual vacations and overtime rules are known to the existing clerical personnel involved in payroll calculations and related authorizations and decision-making process.

It has to be also assessed if the payroll staff is familiar with categories of employees referred to by the Law, and/or with the various related regulations regarding employment practices. In this respect, it has to be established if the staff is familiar and does keep abreast of new developments or changes in the related field of legislation.

One should also become familiar, before any control and verification takes place, with all kinds of payroll and related forms in use and what procedures are in force at various places within the organization and in respect to payroll.

In most organizations which are already established and with proper accounting systems in place, there is a separate listing kept of all the company's employees, by place of work, or units, or by type of work, with the related type or amount of remuneration (per hour, day, week, place, etc.). Such a record should be kept up to date for any accounting purpose.

The vacation time schedule should be examined and known how it is followed up; How are all the company's payroll records preserved for control and future verification, where is the place where such records are kept, if it is a safe one and who can gain access to it.

A binder with all the related and current payroll legislation should be kept in the organization, together with all the related payroll instructions and payroll related matters. This must be available for immediate use and up-to-date.

An auditor should also learn the specific company's management policy in force with regard to payroll procedures to be observed by staff involved.

Finally, one should know how the machinery of accounting works in respect to payroll and payroll related matters.

One should also agree that there is an interrelationship between the payroll accounting unit and the other units within the accounting department. It is for this reason that such an interrelationship should be examined.

The familiarity gained by the auditor with all the above points, as described, will make possible for him to draw a chart in order to illustrate the procedure for payroll in the respective firm under examination for audit.

The Accounting Firm _____

A Suggested
Audit Program

Client _____

Audit Date _____

Segment of Audit	For Current Working Papers			
Payroll Test	Time		Done	
	Planned	Actual	By	Index
Audit Objectives: 1. The internal control measures and the accounting procedures implemented, are conform the established procedures, as formally required and described in the Manual				
2. Such measures and procedures are operating effectively and are properly to provide a) adequate accounting control over labour costs and related allocation, in the accounts, and				
b) the gathering of necessary data for the various payroll written information required by law				
Audit Procedures: 1. Review of client's internal procedures;	·······	·······	·······	·······
2. For the interim period choose: Bi-weekly payroll (factory) X pers. monthly payroll (salaried) X pers.	······· ·······	······· ·······	······· ·······	······· ·······
A. Verify gross earnings with rate authorizations and time cards information (when applicable)	·······	·······	·······	·······
B. Verify payroll deductions based on the tables in use.	·······	·······	·······	·······
C. Verify net payroll against the journal or other records of disbursements.	·······	·······	·······	·······
3. For the chosen period, verify the allocation to the general ledger of related accounts and the necessary transfer of funds to the payroll bank account, if any.				
4. Test verification additions of payroll journal for the chosen period under audit.				
5. Present your conclusion on the audit as performed	·······	·······	·······	·······

Prepared By _____ Date _____

Approved By _____

Exhibit 67

The Great Western Company Ltd.
Audit
Summary of Factory Payroll Distribution Entries

Re: The Fiscal Year Ended December 31st, 1988

Schedule No.:_____
Done By:_____
Date:_____

Note: This Schedule will be performed for all months of the year.
The information will be in respect to the following classification:

Direct Labour Variances and
Indirect Labour-Factory Overhead

Direct labour to Work In Process at Standard

Re: Direct Labour Variances:
Pay rates
Interim rate changes
Make-up pay
Defective materials
Spoiled work
Re-work
Waiting for materials
Machine breakdown
Excess Set-ups

Re: Indirect Labour-Factory Overhead
Supervision
Indirect labour
Repairs
Maintenance
Overtime premium
Shift premium
Vacation and Holiday pay
Total Indirect Labour
Grand Total - Factory labour at actual

Exhibit 68

The Great Western Company Limited
Audit
Accrued Payroll Taxes
Re: For the fiscal year ended December 31st 1988

Schedule No.:_____

Done By:_____

Date:_____

Particulars	Payroll		Taxes	
	Contributions Made		Unemployment Ins.	
	Employer	Employee	National	Provincial
Balance as at December 31st 1987 To Accrue for the current year Totals at credit				
Remittances Made & Reports Filed				
Re: first quarter January	xxxxxx	xxxxxx	xxxxxx	xxxxxx
second quarter April	xxxxxx	xxxxxx	xxxxxx	xxxxxx
third quarter July	xxxxxx	xxxxxx	xxxxxx	xxxxxx
fourth quarter October	xxxxxx	xxxxxx	xxxxxx	xxxxxx
Totals at debit	xxxxxx	xxxxxx	xxxxxx	xxxxxx
Balances as at December 31st 1988	xxxxxx	xxxxxx	xxxxxx	xxxxxx
See related schedules	(•••••••••)	(•••••••••)	(•••••••••)	(•••••••••)

Notes: - The following adnotations (markings of above) may apply:

- Including deductions & costs paid to Government Office for Nov.

- Copies for governmental reporting reviewed;

- The monthly payments made by cheques representing the related remittances of the respective amounts, were examined;

- Subsequent copies of returns filed in January 1989, were examined;

- Payments made by cheques, were examined;

- The examination and inspection of the respective returns filed during the subsequent month of January 1989 and the tests made of 1988 accruals, confirm that the accruals for the respective year under consideration for audit, are correctly stated.

(Initialed) by _____(auditor)

Exhibit 69

The Great Western Company Ltd.
Audit
Accrued Liabilities - Summary

Re: The fiscal year Ended December 31st, 1988

Schedule No.:_____
Done By:_____
Date:_____

Particulars	Index	Final Dec 31, 1987	Per Books Dec 31, 1988	Adjustments DR. or CR.	Final Dec 31, 1988
Accrued factory payroll		xxxxxx	xxxxxx	xxxxxx	xxxxxx
Accrued payroll taxes:					
- Employers		xxxxxx	xxxxxx	xxxxxx	xxxxxx
- Unemployment		xxxxxx	xxxxxx	xxxxxx	xxxxxx
Accrued interest payable		xxxxxx	xxxxxx	xxxxxx	xxxxxx
Totals:		xxxxxx	xxxxxx	xxxxxx	xxxxxx

Note: Our review disclosed no material unrecorded accrued liabilities.

Exhibit 70

The Great Western Company Ltd.
Audit
Accrued Expenses

Schedule No.:_____

Re: The fiscal Year Ended December 31st, 1988

Particulars	Balance Dec 31 87	Balance Dec 31 88
Accrued Payroll:		
Factory Payroll-Net for the period ended		
December 31, 1988 and Paid January 6, 1989.	xxxxxx	xxxxxx
Salary Payroll - Month of December 1988 and		
Paid December 30, 1988	xxxxxx	xxxxxx
(see schedule)		•••••••
Accrued Salesmen's Commissions:		
December commissions less paid on account		
(see schedule)		•••••••
Payroll deductions		
Income taxes of the employees including December		
payroll for the period ended December 23, 1988		xxxxxx
Unemployment Insurance		xxxxxx
Pension Plan		xxxxxx
Union Dues		xxxxxx
Group Medical Insurance		xxxxxx
(see schedule)		•••••••
Additional information		
Unemployment insurance		xxxxxx
Pension Plan		xxxxxx
(see schedule)		•••••••

Explanatory notes for certain marks of above figures;
   - agreed to commission information presented (reports) and our sample
     verified against December 1988 sales figures

   - conform payroll summaries and payment made in January 1989 as re-
     corded in the cash disbursements book.

Done By _____

Date _____

Exhibit 71

The Great Western Company Ltd.
Audit

Re: The Fiscal Year Ended December 31st, 1988

Done By:_____
Date:_____

Note: The audit tests were performed in respect to a certain
number of employees (........).

This schedule will contain the following information:

The employee number;

Rate;

Total hours worked;

Gross pay;

Income taxes;

Unemployment Insurance;

Pension Funds

Other Deductions;

Total Deductions;

Net Pay;

Cheque Number;

Our Observations:
An indicator mark for above shall be made in respect to the following:

-per authorization-Individual Employment Cards

-total per time cards

-calculated

-calculated from appropriate deductions source

-cancelled cheque examined and agreed

Exhibit 72

The Great Western Company Ltd.
Audit
Payroll Test

Re: Audit of the Fiscal Year ended December 31st, 1988

Procedures:
In accordance with our Audit Programme, we have selected 20 Employees paid bi-weekly.

The period selected was May.

After indicating all the related details on the schedule, the figures were traced and agreed to appropriate services performed.

Observations:
No exceptions were noted.

Conclusions:
In our opinion such procedures and measures are operating effectively and are adequate to provide.

a) proper accounting control over labour costs and the distribution thereof in the accounts, and

b) the accumulation of the necessary data for the various payroll related matters required by government regulations

By:_____
Date:_____

Exhibit 73

Notes To The Attached Schedules

1. Working on such orders were completed as at _____.

2. Additional expenses incurred in connection with preparing new building for occupancy and moving in equipment, (see schedule _____).

Except as noted, all variations in the above figures appear reasonable and in line with normal seasonal variations.
See schedule _____ for tests of payroll records.

3. Tie-in of Direct Labour with cost of sales:
   Direct labour   (number of employees)
       with cost of sales per
       Add: Increase in labour in Work in Process ....
       Less: Decrease in Labour in Final Goods ....
       Add: Labour in Inventory Adjustment ....
       As above ....

Done By: _____
Date: _____

Exhibit 74

214

Schedule No. _____

Done By _____

Date _____

Re: Company's Operational System

The employees who are working in the productive sector of the company are paid on a piecework basis. The work performances are known from the employees work reports which are reviewed and approved by their respective supervisors.

Such records of work performance are further transferred into the production records in order to prove that the work paid for agree with the number ordered on each production order. Certain necessary allowances are authorized by special day work tickets issued by the supervisors. In this respect it can be mentioned that supervisors also issue day work tickets indicating the specific accounts to which indirect labour is to be posted or recorded. The company employees involved in the production sector and performing piece work, make use of their clock cards at a company time clock placed at the plant main entrance. The payroll unit of the accounting department is dealing with the issuance of the respective cheques. The company's controller signs the cheques presented to him and presents them to the Head of the Administration Office who is acting as the firm's paymaster. All of the payroll work is based on a punch-card system characterized by a high degree of accuracy.

Re: Testing of Factory Payroll

The factory payroll for the period under consideration tested, which is _____ was chosen for the factory payroll test and examination. The total number of employees working in the productive sector is _____. The selection for testing was made for a number of _____ non productive workers and employees involved in a supervisory capacity.

Regarding the productive sector, the reports of piecework performances were reviewed in respect to their approval by the supervisors. Also the notes were verified based on the standard cost books and computations checked in order to prove the total related gross earnings. These information are compared to the payroll journal or register. The allowances, if any, or the recorded normal working time was verified against the day work tickets of performances. The total weekly hours was further compared with the total hours indicated on the employees' clock card. The respective rates used for payments made were compared against the related information on employees' files used and preserved in the payroll unit of the accounting department. The figures representing the totals in respect to allowances and daily work performances were calculated again as for verification purposes, and compared against the payroll journal. In the same way, the records of work for those involved at at the supervisory level and indirect work were verified, namely a comparison was made of the total hours indicated by the daywork tickets against clock cards. The various income taxes as deducted from employees' gross earnings were verified in respect to the related documentation for exemptions and the tax tables for the deductions at source.

The company's various related contributions of costs payable to the various governmental authoritive agencies, were verified by using the rate of _____ applied on a gross earnings and up to a certain "ceiling" or maximum amount. This calculation was further verified in relation to the employees' earnings summary of record for the respective and related period under consideration.

Deductions other than those for income taxes were verified in respect to authorizations kept on employees files in the payroll unit of the accounting department.

The respective payroll journal was verified in all respects (adds and cross-adds) and the totals were also verified against the monthly summary of payroll. Further to this, the related summary was verified (adds checked) and traced to the transfers of all the totals from the columns of the payroll register or journal, to the various accounts of the company's General Ledger.

It can be emphasized, that our verification did not reveal any irregularities.

Re: Various Contracts in Force, e.g. Union Contracts.

In this respect it can be mentioned that the union contracts in existence were reviewed. We have noticed that no changes were made in the contracts various provisions. None of the contracts in force is to be subject to renegotiation or review or modification, before the year of _____.

Based on the information obtained from the Head of the factory administration and the Director of Personnel Services, it was found that no disputes or litigations are under way or, eventually, to occur.

Re: Inspection of Pay-off

We have conducted a close observation of the distribution of paychecks to the company's employees, from certain selected departments of the firm, like _____, on the day of _____.

In this respect, we did not inform anyone about our intention for observation. We have compared the payments against the payroll journal prior to the time of cheques been handed-out. Certain cheques, as the ones mentioned below, were unclaimed and kept under our attention, until subsequently handed out or delivered to the employee.

_____

_____

(Note: For the unclaimed cheques the following information should be provided: clock number, name of employee, reason for non-delivery, date of subsequent delivery of the respective cheques)

Exhibit 75

A SUGGESTIVE QUESTIONAIRE

for

A PAYROLL PROCEDURES MANUAL
IN A GIVEN ENTERPRISE

The following steps should be taken by any other auditor, for payroll procedures familiarity with the accounting system and related payroll matters.

-Establish 'WHO IS WHO' in the organization and the interrelationships amongst the various incumbents occupying the different positions;
- Read the firms established rules and company's policies in respect to payroll and related matters, if any;
- Find out what business forms are in use within the company, in respect to payroll;
- Read the established duties and related responsibilities for the personnel involved in the payroll unit of the accounting departments;
- Draw a flow chard reflecting the stream and directions taken by different business payroll forms, documentation, records and related information, for the respective enterprise.

The following questions may also apply:

- What is the pay period ending: weekly, bi-weekly, semimonthly, monthly, etc..?
- Where are the payroll records kept?
- Who is responsible for the safe preservation of such records?
- Who is authorizing the pay rates and eventual changes of such rates?
- Who is in charge of hiring and dismissal of payroll personnel?
- Who is the paymaster of the firm?
- Who is authorizing the daily time working records of the various departments?
- Who is in charge of the various payroll calculations?
- What accounting system is in use, in respect to payroll?
- Who is in charge for the accounting for payroll and the various reconciliation of the accounts?
- What are the distribution of duties or separation of duties for safeguarding the payroll funds?
- How often is the payroll work inspected by management?
- What is the system of internal controls in respect to cash and related payroll matters.
- If the bank account reconciliations are performed monthly, and irregularities eliminated on time?
- What is the companies procedure regarding the unclaimed cheques?
- How often an audit takes place in respect to payroll and related matters?
- How the various auditors past recommendations were followed up and solved favorably?

Many other useful questions can be rightly asked, depending on the specificity of the company's operations and the state of the internal control system in use.

Exhibit 76

PART FIVE

A SIMPLIFIED GUIDE FOR INVENTORIES

CONTROL AND MANAGEMENT

CONTENTS

General Considerations 221

Inventory Management 222

An Useful Questionnaire 226

The Physical Inventory System:
-   A Sampling Record 227

Purchases of Goods taken into Inventories 228

Inventory Control..229

The Recording of Incoming Goods 230

The Purchase Cycle..231

The Physical Inventory System and Sound Control over the Inventories 232

The Needs for Determining the Cost of Ending Inventory
-   Evaluation at Cost..234
-   Evaluation at Market Value 236

Certain Accounting Considerations regarding Purchases of Goods 239

Inventory in the Automotive Industry 242

Inventory in Restaurants 244

Certain Important Guidelines for Marketing of Inventories.....................................245

Self-testing Questions regarding Inventory Calculations 248

List of Exhibits

GENERAL CONSIDERATIONS

This useful Guide can serve many people involved in working with inventories of various kinds of products, in various positions, and at different levels of small, medium or large companies to be found in different parts around the world. It will help, especially, those who are striving to gain the necessary practical skills or knowledge of handling inventories and inventories-related matters. But most of all it is designed for those occupied in the process of control and management of inventories in any organisational structure.

Entrepreneurs, managers, and all those aspiring to reach managerial positions will, undoubtedly, refer to this Guide constantly as a useful tool at their place of work.

Inventories of goods either to be used in the manufacturing sector, in the process of production - its various stages, or for re-sale, constitute one of the most important and valuable categories of current assets, in most companies around the world. As such, inventories are shown or recorded in the respective balance sheets, at their lower of cost, or near realisable value. It is also assumed that inventory of goods, either for production purposes or for re-sale, for example, will be used up or sold, as the case may be, during one year of a given firm's course of operations (current year) which is also considered a fiscal year for government-reporting purposes.

This present Guide should be used keeping in mind that specificity of one's firm's business operations and it should always be adapted to suit one's particular needs and/or interests. It should also be seen as merely a guide and not as a substitute for one's need to complement his or her knowledge, by seeking the assistance through advices and consultations, of a professional in the field.

A dictionary of accounting terms may also prove to be useful whenever the need may arise in order to clarify some specific notions or related technical terminology in use.

The process of accurate recording of the related transactions for purchases of goods and inventories during a given period, should facilitate, at a later date, adequate reporting and interpretation of the specific and related data. Such records are becoming valuable, especially when audit, control and inspection or verification of prior years' firm's activities will take place.

As one experienced business man once stressed:
> '...good management of an inventory has to do with reaching the best compromise between the opposing pressures for higher and lower inventories ... It makes better sense to employ a more precise system fo control on the important items than on the unimportant many'.

INVENTORY MANAGEMENT

Special Considerations

Successful Inventory Management should start with those handling of basic stock, namely with the assortment of merchandise which takes into account the largest portion of the volume. A proper selection of basic stock means savings of capital investment, reducing amounts of costs by simplifying inventories, cutting down in product handling and eliminating waste in administration time.

By concentrating on basics, one may hope to increase the buying power and this in turn may lead to better buying clauses obtained from suppliers for the firm including better prices.

A substantial amount of capital of a retailer, for example, can be found tied up in inventory of goods for re-sale. Thus the need by the company that its management be knowledgeable in handling properly the inventories in order to achieve the best operating figures expressed in terms of profits.

It is for this reason, especially, that proper Inventory Management Systems be in place.

Sound physical control over the inventory has to do with the proper receiving of goods in stock and adequate storage and handling. This will contribute to the possibility of elimination of shortages and overages, lost and damage goods, etc.

A proper way of controlling the inventory should include the following measures:

– proper storage of goods, depending on the features of the products;

– authorization for any withdrawal from the stockroom;

– inventories kept at an established minimum without adversely affecting sales;

– inspection of all incoming goods and verification of quantities, descriptions and quality, as ordered from the suppliers;

– matching of incoming invoices against the delivery slips (confirmed) before filing of them for later accounting and control purposes;

– a subsidiary ledger of accounts payable should be kept up-to-date and all suppliers accounts should be reconciled on a regular basis or on set or planned dates;

– each item should be stored in a specific area of the stock room;

– the existing facilities for storage should ensure safeguarding and control.

Any business enterprise carrying goods for sale, should know and provide the minimum and the maximum quantities for certain needed items in stock and also account for the span of time between the ordering and the actual receiving of the goods. This will have a beneficial impact in the sense that a business will be able to determine the needed order, when to order, and the sequential movement of the items in the inventory.

By having adequate records of the 'movements' of items in stock, it can be easily established the following:

– the quantities available in stock;

– the funds invested in the item during a certain given period of time;

– how the item is 'moving' (selling) by amount, and the related trend, if any;

– whether or not there is any problem in inventory levels;

– the right time of reordering.

The physical count of all the inventory items should take place, if possible, at least once a year, especially for financial statement purposes and tax reasons.

Any possible comparison between the physical count and the inventory records will make possible adjustments in order to account for any eventual discrepancies in stock and safeguard the respective goods against damage, theft and accumulation of slow moving and/or obsolete items.

A good and sound system of internal control will make possible that the function of record-keeping be segregated from the control of inventory. This means separate persons involved in different tasks, at the place of work. There should always be supporting evidence of purchases and sales of goods in order to compare the figures against the actual count that took place. The inventory count should be performed by a clerk other than that in charge for the record-keeping.

223

A merchandise inventory constitutes the total items of tangible personal property that a business firm has available for sale. It is also considered a current asset since it is assumed to be converted or sold for cash within the next current year after the fiscal year.

An adequate business management and organization has to include also good handling of the merchandise inventory along the following lines:

- To realize sales, one should have the right item in stock ready for sale at the right time for the right customer.
- Financial 'wisdom' must be revealed since most of a firm's cash is usually tied-up or invested in the inventory of goods for resale.

It has to be emphasized that slow moving items in stock will have a negative impact on the cash flow needed to finance the necessary or immediate expenses and the acquisition of new inventory items.

The ideal situation of course, is to have the best suitable 'mix' of items to generate maximum sales figures and good profit from sales. In this respect, it is essential to have a sound inventory control system in place. This will serve to easily trace currently required items in suitable quantities and in a diversity of prices, brands, and the like, based on the consumers' expressed demands.

Physical and financial control over the inventories involves the following conditions:

- an adequate system of recording goods on hand and on order with their related ratios of sale;
- the best possible 'mix' of profitable items of merchandise for sale (given an enterprise budget for inventory in stock);
- a properly planned or targeted sales figure supported by an adequate level of saleable inventory in stock.

These above mentioned conditions are interrelated and have a tremendous impact on the company's financial well-being.

The inventory of a business enterprise should include all goods and property of the business available for sale, regardless of where the goods are located at the time of the inventory, namely:

- goods in transit - one must include proof of clear and good title to the purchaser.
- goods on consignment-property of the consignor.

Damaged and obsolete goods should be separately listed, kept separately, and should not be included in inventory since they are not saleable.

The cost of an inventory item includes the invoice price by supplier, less the discount taken, plus any eventual and incidental costs incurred to place the goods into a saleable state. Such incidental costs are, for example, import duties, freight-in, insurance, etc..

Efficient and wise management of any business has to do also with adequate control and management of inventories.

Amongst the relevant functions of management in a given enterprise, are those of purchasing, costing/pricing, personnel and recordkeeping/accounting.

It can be stressed that sound management is the foundation of business success.

Planning, directing, delegating, organizing and controlling, and coordinating are some of the most important and traditional management functions fulfilled by the manager/owner of a business, for example.

People involved in control and management of inventories also, should reveal certain qualities or good criteria for judgement of their abilities in this respect, namely:

- A sound sense of responsibility;
- Accurate knowledge gained through studies and experience at work;
- Good skills of cooperation with others (inside and outside the firm);
- Clear expressions;
- Confidentiality on business matters;
- Ability to reach decisions independently;
- Leadership skills;
- Planning and organizing;
- Good judgement for analyzing problems at work;
- Communication and inter-personal skills;
- Directing and controlling;
- Etc.

QUESTIONNAIRE

(e.g. in a manufacturing enterprise)

– Are those products characterized by a low volume of turnover reviewed at certain planned intervals, with an intention to discountinuance?

– Is the company planning to have too large an assortment and different items for economical production or sale?

– What useful and proper steps is the company taking to attain a maximum output while utilizing its high volume machinery and equipment to the optimum?

– Is there any excessive material 'blocking' the smooth level of production?

– Are volume-cost relationships analyzed and known to the people involved in the accounting area for inventories?

– Is there a minimum in-process inventory kept in all the various departments and work units?

– Does the inventory levels reflect the adequate coordination with the production plans and related sales requirements?

– Is the needed quantity of each item in inventory precisely made known and can such items be found in time of need in order to be transferred into the production sphere?

– What kinds of inventory records are kept within the organization, its various departments and work units, and this in respect to the inventory consumption?

– Are such inventory records analyzed and comparisons made against actual inventory figures, periodically or at the minimum once a year or at the end of the company's fiscal period?

– How are the inventory levels established?

– How are the economic order quantities planned?

– Are low volume products 'excessively' controlled or too much time spent on their record-keeping and inspection?

– Is there an adequate financial accounting in place in respect to inventories? Is it an economical and flexible one as well as being consistent with accepted principles of accounting theory and practice?

– Are the accounts for inventories properly classified by the company's list of accounts in current use?

– Are the journal entries and the related adjustments, as necessary, made during the fiscal period? Are they adquately substantiated and supported by authorized documentation?

– Are the books audited or examined in respect to inventories also, at least once during the fiscal period under consideration, for the given company?

– Are interim-profit and loss statements produced and made available for management analysis and control?

– Does the information in the financial statements facilitate management control and management decision making process?

THE PHYSICAL INVENTORY SYSTEM

No.	Alarm Clock set		Reorder time: days		
Product Classification	Product Description	Cost	Retail	Min.	Max
Date	Reference	IN	OUT	BALANCE	
Bal. fwd.					

Exhibit 77

PURCHASES OF GOODS
TAKEN INTO INVENTORIES

The reference made throughout this book on purchases of goods and inventories, is to include all kinds of goods either purchased and stocked for re-sale (trading firm) or ready to be transferred and used in the process of production (manufacturing type of firm). Therefore, the so-called purchases and/or inventories of other nature (like assets as machinery, equipment, automobiles, etc.) are totally excluded from our presentation.

Inventories, as current assets are listed in the records of a firm and/or presented in the balance sheet statement. It is assumed that such assets have the capability to be converted easily into cash within the current (next twelve months) period or year of operations of the firm.

Any shortage of goods purchased, or damaged goods received, are documented in this respect by certain specific memos (descriptive) and debited to the suppliers' account.

The suppliers' invoices are recorded at their purchase price and cost value but at the same time, the firm is making use of a Purchase Returns and Allowances account, in order to indicate the amount of returns (control account) in relation to the total cost of purchases (control account). Such an account serves management as information of any returns level above the expected or normal one, and thus making possible useful analysis and corrective actions.

In any calculation of the cost of purchases received by the firm, the freight-in, transportation-in, duty costs, brokerage fees, and other related costs of bringing in the goods to the firm's warehouse, are combined with the Purchases account in finding the delivered cost of purchases.

INVENTORY CONTROL

(e.g. in a manufacturing type of business)

The issue of inventory control is rightly considered as one of the most important in any business of any size and in any industry around the world.

Anyone involved in any critical examination of a business' state of affairs, will also apply the inventory control criteria in such an examination. This in order to identify the eventual weaknesses and make possible to take corrective or remedial steps towards the needed improvements in this area. In a manufacturing kind of business, for example, the production of various goods should be properly co-ordinated in all the firm's departments and units of work, and a minimum in-process inventory be evident.

In this line of thought, it has to be stressed also that adequate means of co-ordinating production levels (planned) with inventory levels, while taking into account the sales department(s) requirements are needed.

Needless to say, when inventories are too high, the company will be negatively affected since this constitutes excess idle capital and takes away valuable and costly space. It also represents an increase of risk of spoilage and obsolences of items carried in stock. On the other hand, those companies that are revealing too low inventories, increase their risk of running out of much needed items in stock and may lose sales orders. Consequently, the planning of economic production levels or targets of production is adversely affected.

Therefore, wise management of an inventory can be shown by finding one best way to obtain a compromise between higher or lower inventories tendencies, or reaching a 'happy medium' level of inventories of various items needed in the given company under consideration.

It is, especially, for this reason that any company should strive to have a more accurate system of inventory control, particularly on the important items.

THE RECORDING OF INCOMING GOODS

The goods ordered, purchased and received by the company are recorded in the company's purchase journal of the respective period, and based on the necessary legal documentation for incoming goods, as ordered.

The monthly total value-at cost or purchase price (as agreed) is posted or transferred to the Purchases of Goods or Inventories account (control account), as the accounting system requires, and at the same time an indication is made, as a credit to the Accounts Payable account (control account), in the company's General Ledger of accounts.

It has to be emphasized that a correct and complete accounting procedure requires that the individual amounts comprising such a total, be posted to the respective related individual (suppliers) accounts, in the Subsidiary Ledger of Accounts Payable of the firm.

In order to highlight the process of purchasing that may take place in a given company, the purchase cycle is described, in the subsequent pages, step-by-step. Also, a brief comment on the accounts payable voucher system and the debit memorandum, is made.

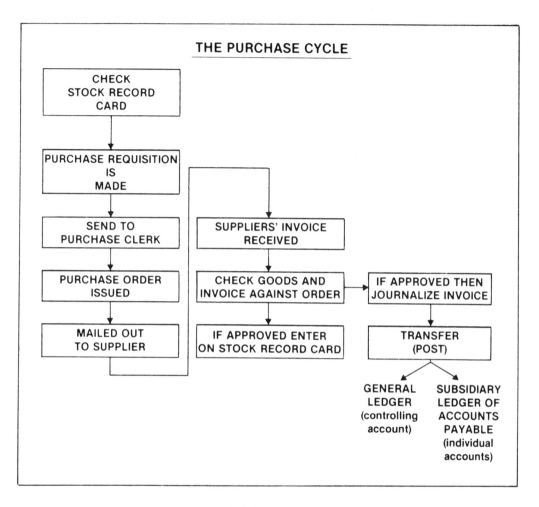

Exhibit 78

THE PHYSICAL INVENTORY SYSTEM

AND

A SOUND CONTROL OVER THE INVENTORIES

First of all, a business must know and provide the minimum and the maximum quantities for certain needed items in stock and also know the lag time between the ordering and the actual receiving of the goods. This will assist the business in determining when to order, how much to order and the sequential movement of the items in the inventory.

A perpetual method of inventory control, whenever possible, should be in operation. It will record on a unit basis, the receipt and sale of merchandise ('ins' and 'outs'). In this respect, it has to be mentioned that various sizes of small business will adopt different kinds of inventory control in order to suit their particular needs and their existing state of facilities including the availability of adequate personnel.

Thus, the perpetual inventory method keeps a continuous record of the cost of units added to stock and the cost of units sold. It is found more likely in use in a business dealing in merchandise of high unit value.

A relevant illustration is provided below. It is suitable for the smaller retailer who has complemented the inventory cards record with a daily or weekly sheet to include reorder information of certain items.

No. 4	Alarm Clock set		Reorder time: 5 days		
Product	Product	10.00	22.00	30	70
Classification	Description	Cost	Retail	Min.	Max
Date	Reference	IN	OUT	BALANCE	
Bal. fwd.					50
			2		48
June 4 1987			3		45
5			6		39
6			1		38
8			3		35
12			4		31
18		100	1		130
25	P.O. 501*		2		128
29		1**			129

* purchase order number
** item returned by customer in good state, added to stock.

Exhibit 79

One can find the 'ins' from the packing slips and from the already verified supplier's invoice, and the 'outs' from the sale tag or sale invoice.

In this way, by having adequate records of the 'movements' of items in stock, we can easily establish the following:

- the quantities available in stock
- the money invested in the item during a certain period
- how the item is 'moving' (selling) by amount, and the related trend, if any
- whether or not there is any problem in inventory level
- the right time of reordering

The so-called basic book used by some small businesses is considered a useful and auxilliary control tool to the perpetual unit control. It helps to identify what items comprise the bulk of the sales ('basics').

Another way of controlling diversified items is by classification: e.g. colour, style, size, etc..

In this respect, a proper coding system should be in place in order to facilitate control.

The physical count of all inventory items should take place, if possible, at least once a year especially for financial statement purposes.

Any possible comparison between the physical count and the inventory records will make possible adjustments to the books for any eventual discrepancies in stock, and safeguard the respective goods against damage, theft and accumulation of slow moving or obsolete items.

The periodic inventory method does not record from day-to-day the cost of goods in stock or the cost of goods sold; instead, at the end of each period, the goods on hand are counted and priced at cost; the total amount of ending inventory figured out in this way is used in the calculation of Cost of Goods Sold and also appears in the Balance Sheet as a current asset.

When such a method is in use, the ending inventory is established by taking a physical count of all the items in stock, in good condition for sale, and with the related quantities in stock and later priced at cost to obtain the total value of the inventory in stock at the end of the period under consideration.

Sound physical control over the inventory has to do with the proper receiving of goods in stock and adequate storage and handling. This will help to eliminate shortages or overages, lost and damaged goods, and the like.

An adequate way of controlling the inventory should include the following measures:
- proper storage of the goods
- authorizations for any withdrawal from the stockroom
- inventories kept at an established minimum without adversely affecting sales
- inspection of all incoming goods and verification of quantities, descriptions and quality, as ordered
- matching of incoming invoices against the delivery slips (confirmed) before filing them for later accounting and control purposes
- a Subsidiary Ledger of accounts payable should be kept up-to-date and all suppliers' accounts should be reconciled on a regular basis or on set or planned dates
- each item should be stored in a specific area of the stock room
- The facilities for storage should ensure safeguarding and control.

METHODS FOR DETERMINING THE COST OF ENDING INVENTORY

The following are the alternative methods (currently in use) available to a firm:

A. EVALUATION AT COST
- Specific invoice prices.
- Weighted average.
- First In, First Out.
- Last In, First Out.

B. EVALUATION AT MARKET VALUE
- The Replacement Cost Method.
- The Net Realizable Value Method.
- The Net Realizable Value Less Normal Profit Method.

These different methods can change the cost of goods sold figures and therefore the resulting gross profit.

A. EVALUATION AT COST

Under the methods included here, the beginning inventory is 100 units costing $9.00 each, total purchases are $9600.00 and 250 units remain at the end of the month. Note that costs change for different orders.

1. LAST IN, FIRST OUT (L.I.F.O.)

Under this method, the ending inventory is costed at the cost of the oldest units.

Purchase Date	Quantities Purchased	Cost Per Unit	Total
Beginning Inventory	100	9.00	900
1/4/1987	150	7.00	1050
1/18/1987	200	11.00	2200
1/25/1987	365	10.00	3650
1/29/1987	300	9.00	2700
			10500

If 250 units remain at the end of the month they will be considered the oldest ones. The value of inventory will therefore be 1950:

Exhibit 80

Beginning inventory of	100 units at	9.00	=	900
Plus: Purchase of 1/4/1987	150 units at	7.00	=	1050
				1950

The cost of goods sold will be 8550:

C.G.S. = Goods available for sale -
       Inventory as at 1/31/1987
    = 10500-1950
    = 8550

2. FIRST IN, FIRST OUT (F.I.F.O.)

When this method is used, ending inventory is costed at the cost of the most recent units.

Using the previous example, inventory at 1/31/1987 will be 2250.00

1/29/1987   250 units at 9.00 =   2250.00

The cost of goods sold will be 8250.00

C.G.S. = Goods available for sale - Inventory as at 1/31/1987
        = 10500-2250
        = 8250

3. THE AVERAGE COST METHOD
Under this method, inventory is costed at the average cost.

In the previous example, the average cost is:

$$\frac{\text{Total Available for Sale}}{\text{Total Units Available for Sale}} = \frac{10500}{1115} = 9.42 \text{ (approx.)}$$

The 1/31/1987 inventory will be 250 units at 9.42 per unit or 2354.00
The C.G.S. will be 8146.00

The following picture summarizes the results when using the 3 cost methods:

		L.I.F.O.	F.I.F.O.	Average Cost
	Beginning Inventory	900	900	900
Plus:	Purchases	9600	9600	9600
Equals:	Goods Available for Sale	10500	10500	10500
Less:	Inventory at the End	1950	2250	2354
Equals:	C.G.S	8550	8250	8146

NOTE: In an inflationary period the L.I.F.O. method undervalues the inventory since it uses the oldest costs. When prices are rising, the last-in,first-out method, by assigning the more recent and higher costs to the units sold, will cause the reported profits to be lower than would be shown under either first-in, first-out or weighted average methods.

Exhibit 81

235

B. EVALUATION AT MARKET VALUE

1. THE REPLACEMENT COST METHOD.

This indicates the cost of eventual acquisition of items if they were to be purchased on the date of the reported inventory on hand.

2. THE NET REALIZABLE VALUE METHOD

When using this method, the inventory is valued – on the reporting date – by determining the estimated sale price per unit, minus all the related and incurred expenses, like sales commissions, freight-out, etc.

3. THE NET REALIZABLE VALUE LESS NORMAL PROFIT METHOD

This method is used when a normal profit per unit will be deducted from the net realizable value.

An adequate valuation of inventory is the crucial step in obtaining the cost of goods sold and subsequently in figuring out the net income of the period. Adequate valuation of inventory is also useful for Balance Sheet purposes.

It has to be emphasized that the gross profit method is an approximate valuation of the inventory(ies) without taking a physical count. This will facilitate the preparation of monthly financial statements for management decision making purposes.

Some small businesses use an inventory count stated at retail price and then reduce it to a cost basis by applying the prevailing ratio between cost and selling price during the period under consideration. When such a method is in use (retail inventory method), the following steps should be observed:

1. The record of the beginning inventory and of all purchases made during the period are kept at both cost and selling prices.

2. The cost of goods available for sale during the period is computed at both cost and selling prices.

3. By dividing the cost by the selling price using the information in step 2, the cost ratio is obtained.

4. The sales of the period are deducted from the goods available for sale (at selling price) and the result indicating the ending inventory at selling price, is compared with the physical count taken at selling price.

5. The ending inventory at selling price is converted to a cost basis by multiplying it by the cost ratio obtained in step 3.

In order to obtain accurate figures of the cost of goods sold and thereby reach a correct result of net income for the year, an adequate costing of inventory is a must.

The FIFO method of inventory costing, when used, will show higher reported profits, especially during a continued period of rising prices.

As already described above, the inventory costing under FIFO method is based on current costs since the older costs were already used to calculate the units sold. In contrast with FIFO method, LIFO method useds recent cost prices to units sold and stocks the units or goods on hand, at older prices (at cost).

When a physical count of the inventory is not possible, certain firms are using the gross profit method. By this method, an approximate costing of inventories is obtained. This method is most likely used when monthly or interim financial statements are needed by management for their current business decisions and for internal control purposes. It is also useful when a theft or fire occurs and there is a need to approximate the units or items on hand.

As we already described above, the perpetual method of costing the inventories requires the existence of permanent records that indicate continuously the movements of stock, namely the 'ins' and 'outs' of units and the existent amount of units on hand or in stock. Undoubtedly, one will agree that this method is more costly since it requires permanent personnel and it is more costly when using more paper.

Note: In order to reduce the inventory expressed in terms of prices at retail, to a cost basis, a certain ratio between cost and selling price (of current period) is applied.

The amount of ending inventory is indicated on the Income Statement (at credit) and also on the Balance Sheet (at debit) in respect to goods of a merchandising type of business.

It has to be emphasized that, when the periodic inventory is in practice by the firm, the need is always to take a physical or actual count of the inventory at the end of the period under consideration, and this for financial statements purposes, as required by the income tax regulations. Simply stated, it means the listing of all the merchandise items in stock owned by the firm and multiplying the number of units of each item by the related respective cost per unit. The aggregate of these values, at cost, will give us the total amount for inventory at end of period.

The beginning inventory is a constitutive part of the cost of goods sold and it appears (at debit) in the Income Summary account. It is merely an addition to the Purchases account in the total 'picture' of determining the results of operations of a certain given period.

The function of recordkeeping should be segregated from the control of inventory. This means separate persons involved in different tasks, at the place of work. There should always be supporting evidence of purchases and sales of goods in order to compare with the actual count taken. Such an inventory count should be performed by a clerk other than that in charge for the recordkeeping.

Outside accountants when engaged by the firm, will indepedently verify and inspect the inventory count.

It is highly recommended that independent accountants will be retained by the firm in order to perform annual audits and examinations or reviews of the company's yearly operations and related records, on a yearly, monthly or other selected periods basis. Such accountants or auditors will be able to make suggestions or recommendations to the management of the firm in respect to improvements of the internal control measures and the system to include also considerations in respect to purchases and inventories as well. This will help detecting ahead of time any eventual irregularities and make possible preventive actions taken by the firm's management.

CERTAIN ACCOUNTING CONSIDERATIONS
REGARDING
PURCHASES OF GOODS

The invoices for purchases are recorded at gross value, at cost.

The following are certain related accounting entries, most commonly in use in various companies around the world:

DATE	PARTICULARS	DEBIT	CREDIT
	Purchases	xxxxxx	
	Accounts Payable		xxxxxx
	To account for purchases of goods		
	from _____ terms _____		
	Accounts payable	xxxxxx	
	Purchases Returns and allowances		xxxxxx
	Damaged goods returned to _____		
	supported by debit memo no.: _____		
	Accounts Payable	xxxxxx	
	Purchases Discounts		xxxxxx
	Bank Account (Cash)		xxxxxx
	Paid _____ invoice of _____		
	less discount taken _____		
	Accounts Payable	xxxxxx	
	Purchase Discount Lost	xxxxxx	
	Bank Account (Cash)		xxxxxx
	Paid _____ invoice of _____		
	less returns		

Note: Discounts lost will appear in the section of operating expenses.

Usually, when a company is in strong cash position, it could easily decide to take advantage of the cash discounts offered to it on purchases of goods. This may, in certain cases, cause a reduction in the interest the firm may earn on bank savings deposits.

Exhibit 82

When a Voucher Register is in use in a certain firm, certain accounting entries, like the ones presented below, are made:

DATE	PARTICULARS	DEBIT	CREDIT
	Purchases	xxxxxx	
	Vouchers Payable		xxxxxx
	Vouchers Payable	xxxxxx	
	Purchases Returns and Allowances		xxxxxx
	Vouchers Payable		xxxxxx
	To cancel old voucher and to set up		
	new voucher for balance		
	Vouchers Payable	xxxxxx	
	Bank Account (Cash)		xxxxxx
	Purchase Discount taken		xxxxxx

Exhibit 83

A Partial Income Statement of a certain firm, and for a certain given period of time, as presented below, will bring into relevancy the various components of the 'picture' of cost of goods sold, and its place in the establishing of the gross profit on sales.

THE FIRM _____

PARTIAL INCOME STATEMENT

For the Year Ended _____

Gross Sales (before returns, allowances and discounts)			xxx
Less: Sales discounts		xxx	
Sales allowances		xxx	
Sales returns		xxx	xxx
Net Sales (after returns, allowances, discounts)			xxx
LESS: **COST OF GOODS SOLD:**			
Inventory at start of period		xxx	
Add: Purchases of goods	xxx		
Freight-IN	xxx		
Duty and brokerage fee	xxx		
Delivery and transportation-in	xxx		
Cost of goods	xxx		
Less: Purchases returns	xxx		
Purchases allowances	xxx		
Purchases discounts	xxx	xxx	
Net Purchases		xxx	
Cost of goods available for sale		xxx	
Less: Inventory at end of period		xxx	
COST OF GOODS SOLD:			xxx
GROSS PROFIT ON SALE			xxx

Exhibit 84

INVENTORY IN THE AUTOMOTIVE INDUSTRY

Parts are one of the main sources generating income in this type of business. One can find the units out from stock and transferred or charged to customer's original repair order for a certain indentifiable job.

Parts and accessories constitute the inventories dealt with by the respective departments, in a functional structure of an automobile repair shop. One should try and become familiar with the organization chart of such a business, divided into its various departments.

The account classifications and book of accounts will indicate, separately the inventories at cost for categories of goods like Accessories, Gas and Oil and Grease, and Parts.

The information in respect to incoming stock can be found in the related Purchase Journal of the firm and for each of the categories of the inventories mentioned above.

An account peculiar to this kind of business is Inventory-Repair Work-In-Process Labor.

The material units transferred out of stock into the repair job is recorded on the back of the customer Repair Order and also on the information sheet to be posted to the inventory control card (specifying also the job number). This becomes part of the system for obtaining the cost of a certain related job performed for a customer. In the Inventory control cards and purchase records, prices are shown at their net value (after deducting the discount obtained from supplier). This represents an Inventory practice specific to this type of business. The respected Inventory of parts is controlled by indicating on the card the number of the work repair order.

After comparing the standard and actual cost of each job, the management can analyze the difference and, whenever possible, take corrective action in respect to each eventual variance.

In such a type of business, inventory control and an up-to-date stock purchase control is of great assistance to management since it presents certain noticeable advantages:

– It indicates the units in stock available at any moment, for use;

– It makes easily possible the re-ordering process of parts, etc.;

– It identifies the specific parts in stock available and also those items unavailable;

– It has a reference to the related order and invoice of an item needed to be reordered;

– It eliminates unnecessary overstocking and idle capital investment;

– It facilitates an adequate stock turnover;

– It serves as a shelter against obsolescence, and

– Waste of time is eliminated.

By investing wisely in Parts Inventory, the owners can obtain a profit as a return on their investment.

The inventory turnover (the cycle of sell-out and replenishment), when higher, it means greater profits on investment, periodically.

Every manager should strive to have the right parts and accessories in the right number of units required, and at the right time. A well balance of Parts and Accessories inventories at all times is highly desirable and is an indication of good control and good management over the inventories.

An adequately operated stock purchase control will have the following advantages for a given business or this sort, namely:

- It will help maximizing sales figures at end;
- It eliminates unnecessary investment of operating capital and overstocking of goods;
- It eliminates understocking;
- It assists the business to reach an adequate stock turnover for a more profitable operation;
- It saves space, time and effort, etc.

The Parts Inventory Control Card will have the following information:

- Part number;
- Part name;
- Monthly sales record;
- Category (how fast the part is moving from stock);
- Floats;
- Unit packs (how many units are in a package to order);
- Card numbering sequence order;
- Trade conditions and net prices, and
- Location.

In the body of a control card, the following information can be found:

- Date;
- Quantity ordered;
- Backorder;
- Reference number;
- Quantity received;
- Quantity sold and total sold to-date;
- Balance.

INVENTORY IN RESTAURANTS

It has to be stressed from the beginning that the state of accounting records in restaurants is very important. In this line of thought it can be said that there is a growing need for good control and management over inventories and over other related costs as well.

In this type of industry, the real need is for effective operational control in order to, especially, eliminate waste.

In a typical restaurant business, the storekeeper should obtain, normally, a requisition confirmed or approved by the chef. This for all the transfers made in respect to food supplies.

Special care should be taken in the estimating or costing of a closing inventory. This in order not to distort the end results figures expressed in terms of profits or losses, which appear on the financial statement.

It is highly desirable that diligent and careful management practices prevail regarding inventories handling and related matters, as a substitute for an elaborate costing system.

THE REPORTING SYSTEM (re: inventories of goods)

- The daily reports of liquor are made available by the bartender in charge who is handling the stock and its replenishment;

- Daily report of meat check-outs are submitted by the storekeeper in order to indicate the purchases various needs;

- At end of period and for financial statements purposes, a complete count and inspection and verification of all the inventories available are taking place. This in respect to the following known categories, namely:

> FOOD;
> LIQUOR and
> SHOP SUPPLIES like paper, etc.

The resulting ending figures in this respect are shown or presented fairly, at cost or purchase price on the company's balance sheet as at end of its fiscal period under consideration. The figures are, obviously, supported by the necessary legal documentation like invoices, etc.

CERTAIN IMPORTANT GUIDELINES
FOR
MANAGEMENT OF INVENTORIES

- The personnel involved in handling inventories and inventories related matters should gain familiarity with the company's overall aims and objectives, in general, and with the policies, systems and procedures in respect to inventories, in particular;

- Also, one should know 'WHO IS WHO' within the organizational structure of the firm and what is the interrelationship amongst the various incumbents within the same framework of the given firm; Their various duties and responsibilities should be known;

- Good management of inventories will, undoubtedly, help to generate more and more sales for the company. The related prices should be estimated, effectively;

- As we are living in an increasingly complex and inter-dependent world, a highly competitive one, experiencing rapid technological changes, the objective of any firm should be to obtain maximum sales and profits from the existing products in stock or available; One should procur and have in stock the required products, in very diversified lines in respect to prices, colour, style and brands. This will try to answer the existencies of more sophisticated customers;

- A proper inventory management has also to do with an adequate system of recordkeeping for all items available in stock by a firm, those on order, and ensure that an indication is made regarding the related rates of sales;

- Within the limits of a certain budget and the available finances, an ideal mix or a well diversified range of items should always be maintained;

- One best sales program should be in place and supported by a realistic need for an adequate stock to achieve the target of sales;

- A sound and fair inventory management should include both financial and physical control over the existing and planned sales for the firm under consideration;

- Minimum and maximum quantities for each and every specific item should be established and based on prior periods figures while taking into account the existing trends and customers' aspirations; Also familiarity with the time needed to obtain the replenishment of stock from various suppliers, from the point of time of re-ordering such items;

– Depending on the availability of the needed technical personnel, the specificity of the company's various operations, and other factors or criteria for judgement, certain methods for inventory calculations, control and related adequate procedures should be selected, to suit the firm's particular needs and/or interests;

– Flexibility should be one of the characteristics of good management in order to make possible adjustments of various kinds, as the need may arise from time to time, in the light of new intervening circumstances;

– Continuous research and absorption of knowledge from the immediate environments and markets, regarding the new products, the new trends, changes in customers desires and tastes and the possibility of procurement of the material and other items to complete the stock, should take place in the firm; The overall impact by the government various regulations and the state of the national and international state of the economy should not be ignored;

– Through good working conditions and good team cooperation and harmonious interrelationship amongst the various departmenst and people who are occupying the different positions within the organization, an open line of communication should be maintained. This will make possible to sense the eventual danger signals in inventory management;

– Making use of the existing learning programs, business seminars and courses, the availability of technical assistance in its various forms, like management consulting, interaction with accountants and auditors outside the firm, should be of permanent concern for the management; This will, with certainty strengthen the internal control system and stimulate a sound management decision process in respect to inventories, and towards the attainment of the company's aims and its objectives, in general.

SELF-TESTING QUESTIONS

REGARDING

INVENTORY CALCULATIONS

A. The Splendid Company Inc. is trading one product only, at a very reasonable cost.

The volume of sales during the year of 1987 was 600,000.00 at a unit price of 9.00.

The inventory at January 1, 1987, amounted to 26,000 units valued at cost of 80,000;

Purchases for the year were as follows:

    40,000   units at 2.00
    50,000   do at 3.50
    27,000   do at 3.70 and
    15,000   do at 3.90

Instructions:

1. Complete the December 31st, 1987 Inventory information, using the three known methods of inventory calculations;

2. Prepare the Income Statement information for each of three methods of inventory calculations (only to Gross Profit sales calculations)

3. Comment on the differences in using the different methods of pricing inventories.

B The starting inventory balance of a certain finished product owned by Ranger Company Inc. on May 1st, 1988, and the acquisitions of this product made during the month of May same year, were as follows:

May 1	Starting	inventory	220	units	@ 2.00 =	440.00
May 5	First	acquisition	1500	do	@ 2.05 =	3750.00
May 12	Second	do	700	do	@ 2.14 =	1498.00
May 20	Third	do	580	do	@ 2.19 =	1270.00
May 29	Fourth	do	400	do	@2.23 =	892.00
		Totals	3400			7850.00

At May 31 inventory at end of day comprised 389 units. Find out the cost of ending inventory, based on each of the following methods of pricing inventory:

    a. Average cost;

    b. First-in, first out;

    c. Last-in, first-out.

LIST OF EXHIBITS

Exhibit Number	Description	Page Number
77	- The Physical Inventory System: An Example	227
78	- The Purchase Cycle	231
79	- An Inventory Record for a Product: A Relevant Illustration	232
80	- Inventory Evaluation at Cost	234
81	- Inventory Calculation Using the Average Cost Method	235
82	- Accounting Entries for Purchases of Goods in Use	239
83	- Accounting Entries Related to a Voucher Register	240
84	- A Partial Income Statement Related to Inventory Calculations	241

PART SIX

BUDGETING

AND

CASH FLOW PROJECTIONS

(Including Selective Illustrations)

CONTENTS

Introduction 253

The Important Steps..255

Budgets for Small Businesses
  –   Important Considerations 256

Budgets and Cash Flow Projection Patterns
  –   Selective Illustrations 263

Cash Flow Projections: Their Usefulness 283

Budgets, Cash Flow Projections and Forecasting into the Future 287

Summing-Up 289

List of Exhibits

INTRODUCTION

Needless to say, budgets and cash-flow projections, including all their related matters, are of vital importance for survival in any kind of business enterprise around the world and in any field of work.

This Part can serve as a useful guide also in respect to planning the timing of eventual changes that should take place in the company's future activities or business operations, like placing new products on the line, expansion, etc., without creating difficulties in handling the existing cash resources.

The cash-flow budget offers the following, in many enterprises:

- a statement of cash earnings, indicating the relationship between the business plans and the cash balance;

- sound forecast information, as basis for comparison with the actual results; this, in turn, will make possible to sense adverse trends and take corrective and necessary steps on time, before it too late to redress an undesirable situation;

- a communication instrument to the creditor like the banker, in order to prove the possibility and the availability of funds to cope with the commitments for the undertaken repayments, e.g. on account of loans, etc.

As already stated above, this selective general guide is designed to assist people from any country, regardless of their type of occupation and involvement in the business world, in the planning of their individual or business affairs, through budgeting wisely and cash flow projections schedules. This is not a complete solution to the problem of sharing information on this topic of paramount importance, so vital to almost anyone in our modern and complex business world.

It is highly recommended to anyone involved in budgets work that first and foremost to gain familiarity with certain specific topics, as related to one's specific business environment, namely:

- the functions of money;

- how governmental departments and agencies can influence income;

- financial institutions and the like.

As in respect to financial planning, the following statements can be advanced:

- one's ability to administer money is gained through experiences encountered in making related business decisions;

- money management is something characteristic to each individual, since personal values and resources, coupled with one's own standard of living, determines mainly one's financial requirements;

- financial planning can have only favourable effects on promoting better relationships and a higher degree of satisfaction and benefits for those involved in this specific technical work;

- human resources combined with material resources can increase income.

As one expert on the topic explained, a budget is a realistic plan for income distribution and for handling carefully a cash-flow-designed plan of earned money, what is preserved, and what is gone in the form of various expenditures or investment(s).

As we mentioned before, budgeting and profit planning apply to any size of business organisation. There is always a need to examine the entire aspects of the business enterprise in order to facilitate control of the difficult situations that may arise during the period under consideration and to account for the various variances which may occur. As one of the experts in the field stated: 'Budgeting is conceived to be the preparation of a budget and its fullest use not only as a device of planning and co-ordinating but also for control'. One should strive to gain knowledge of the firm's aims and objectives and on all the factors which may or can affect the harmonious integrations of the business, in order to achieve these aims and objectives. In this respect, any analysis will, perhaps, consider the alternatives available for both short- and long-term commitments or requirements. The planning of allocating the available resources by management should extend over all sections and segments of the company's operations, departments, units, etc. This on one hand, and on the other, over sales, costs, financing, and the like.

THE IMPORTANT STEPS

1. Aims and objectives outlined in detail
    Numerous companies have a deliberate policy of listing or enumerating their stated aims and objectives along the business lines for short or longer terms. Examples to be mentioned here are sales figures, new items to be created or produced, gross margin and operating costs estimated, etc.

2. The underlying assumptions
    These will include the statements indicating what actions will be taken in order to meet the stated aims and objectives. It will also include the descriptions of the circumstances or conditions under which the targets will be reached, even additional steps or costs necessary in this respect.

3. Sales projections by products and by month, etc.
    In this respect an analysis will be necessary regarding the past performances and especially considering all the eventual noticeable and recorded variances together with the underlying causes for such variances. This will be of much help in taken all the possible or contemplated steps to eliminate prospective difficulties in fulfilling the aimed targets.

4. The inventory and receivable projection schedules
    Here, we should translate all the sales forecast figures into actual cash received in same period under consideration considering also the allowable time for collection of receivables.

    Next step will be to project the needed purchases of materials to reach the projected levels of sales, based on the existing inventory figure and the sales forecast; the payments schedules can then easily be projected based on monthly purchases and the related assumptions of above work.

5. Summary of cash receipts and cash disbursements
    The figures for cash receipts will be quite easily obtained from cash sales collectible of receivable figures already estimated. Other cash sources can be added. Cash disbursements will include payroll costs, commissions for sales, general and administrative expenses, production costs, etc.. Interest costs and taxes due should be added.

    Having all these figures, one can figure out the net cash surplus or deficit for the related period under consideration.

6. An overall review of the existing budget
    The very purpose of preparing a cash flow budget is to be able to assess the probability of net cash position of the business, based on the underlying assumptions made. All the possible fluctuations should be assessed to facilitate corrective actions.

7. Recording the actual results of cash transactions.
    The information obtained from the bank will serve a basis for a useful comparison and to sense various trends, if any. Thus corrective steps may be taken, before difficulties brings the business to an undesirable position.

BUDGETS FOR SMALL BUSINESSES
Important Considerations

Any business strives not only for surviving but also for growing and for better results and more profits. In a way, budgets come to light in order to formalize the company's operations. It is highly recommended that any business will set up its own budget, right from the start of its operations. It is only in this way that owners and managers will be able to depict any eventual problems of financial nature that may arise and thus be able to take any corrective steps, from the start. All expenditures and income of any kind should be estimated at realistic levels and seen as targets to which everyone in the company feels committed subject to change only, if newly unpredictable events occur. Any desirable level of profit cannot be reached at random, namely without a system of control in place, or a budget. Once structured, budgets must be monitored and constantly adjusted, whenever necessary. The procedures adequate for setting up the budgets and follow-up their performances lies with the company but there are certain factors of influence that must be taken into account, like the type of industry, the kind of business, its structure and its main people at the managerial levels. Not all operating expenses can be controlled with the same degree of strength and to the same extent. Some expenses are even uncontrollable. It is worthwhile to brake down the targets into smaller units of time, like quarters or months. There are certain important components in the process of setting a budget, namely the following:

— allocating time for the development of aimed targets;
— enumerating in writing such targets;
— follow-up the progress to record changes, and
— taking corrective steps whenever necessary.

It is by this procedures that companies will increase their chances to redress, if not to avoid financial difficulties or real problems. Especially, it is during periods of uncertainty and poor economic conditions that budgets prove to be instrumental in taking corrective actions following managerial control.

Any successful budget has to do with managerial involvement at a higher level, clear delegation of responsibility to meet the targets, complete authority to implement them, and the establishing of means of monitoring such targets. In a larger company, everybody should feel responsible for the budget success, through involvement and authority for implementation. In other words, each person in the company should be made responsible for each target, believed to be a realistic one, and be entrusted with the authority to control the related expenditures in carrying out the task.

Certain discrimination should be made between forecasting and budgeting. A forecast is merely a prediction of what one assumes it will happen. By contrast, a budget refers to a commitment to what was already forecast, namely to attain a desirable outcome. There are several types of budgets, like the following:

— Cash budgets characteristic for newly created businesses and the growing ones;
— Capital budgets in use whenever capital expenditures are useful and important or of a recurring nature;
— Human resource budgets used as a tool of control in labor-intensive companies.

In general, the term budget is used to refer to an operating budget, where detailed sources of revenue or income are listed on one hand, and expenditure detailed, on the other. All these, broken-down in turn by units in operation (e.g., departments).

The so-called budget choices include the following concerns:

A. PLANNING
    1. Initiation and participation;
    2. Implementation;
    3. Timing.

B. CONTROL
   1. Revision;
   2. Fixed or flexible budgets;
   3. Incentives based on budgets;
   4. Evaluation criteria for performance;
   5. The degree of 'tightness' in the budget.

A. PLANNING

The scope of planning is to create an integration of the business's strategy with the structure, management, employees and the tasks outlined in the plan. It becomes an operational guide for the firm's activities, periodically.

   1. Initiation and Participation
      Budgets can be initiated at the top level, when owners and/or managers know better than the lower levels in the organization, as to what and how things should be done.
      Budgets can be initiated also at the bottom level when the firm should make use of operating management's knowledge and experience since they are the only ones involved in the day-to-day operations.

   2. Implementation
      To be effective, a budget should be a mixture of participation by all levels of the management, namely the initial budget outline coming from the top, with details formulated by the others involved, who will express their agreement and the undertakings or commitments.

   3. Timing
      Some budgets are based on calendar periods: months, quarters, for example. The range or extension of the budgets may vary, between three months to two years (in larger organizations). Again, it has to be emphasized that a budget should be structured from the start, especially in newly created businesses.

B. CONTROL

   1. Revision
      Whenever possible, budgets should be revised, under eventual newly created circumstances. This will make possible comparisons between the planned and performance figures.

   2. Fixed or Flexible Budgets
      Specific objectives are sometime delegated to individuals in order to accomplish their tasks. These come in the form of production standards, sales, quotas, or simply estimates known as variables. From time to time, these are compared against performances in order to take corrective actions or even revise plans, if necessary.
      On the other hand, in certain business environments, like manufacturing plants, flexible budgets are used as important tools for control This will involve using estimates as substitutes to provide a standard of comparison. Thus results will be compared with estimates in order to find out the variances or changes in costs, prices, etc.

   3. Incentives Based on Budgets
      Incentives are used by some companies as a motivational drive in meeting the company's objectives. Thus performances are rewarded whenever is proved that accomplishments are made, as desired, and even beyond the planned figures.

4. Evaluation Criteria for Performance

   The performances can be evaluated on different levels, for example:
   — contribution to overhead and profits;
   — contribution to department profit (after deducting the fixed costs);
   — contribution to corporate profit (after all kinds of costs are taken off).

5. The degree of 'tightness' in the budget.

   This is a controversial point of discussion and different companies have different policies or views about it.

Again, it has to be emphasized, that a professional accountant should be called upon to assist and provide advice on specific matters or questions within the area of budgeting-finance. Such a professional can be used as a resourceful person whenever necessary, especially during the development and the control of technical projects in use.

One may agree that successful financial management has to do, mainly, with the determination of the financial requirements of a business and also with the methods and sources of financing.

Depending on the size of the business operations and of a firm's complexity and organizational structure, that one may find himself involved in a greater or lesser degree and extent than expected initially, in working specific useful projects in this interesting area.

Certain mechanical methods should be in place in order to make proper determination of short and long-term requirements of a financial nature of a business.

It is widely recognized that by converting the financial planning work to budgets and cash flow statements, for example, one may be able to increase the chances of convincing the creditors of a firm that capital requirements, once obtained, will be managed wisely.

In this line of thought, it has to be recognized that is vital to keep abreast of economic and financial conditions of one's country, capital markets and money availability with the related costs, as important factors in the financial management of the business, especially in our modern and complex world.

The formulation of financial requirements of a business, considered in respect to the need for short and long-term funds, are of equally importance in the life of the respective business and play a vital role in its development and towards its growth.

The following points should be considered on this subject matter:

1) An operating and realistic budget system should be in place in any business, either small or large. Sound estimates can be derived from the available data provided by the accounting system at work, in any firm. In this way, accurate forecasts at close periodic intervals can be produced. In this line of thought, it can be mentioned that, practically, the forecasting of cash is made by using the framework of an income statement specifically designed for the firm, for a certain selected future period, and will include the best possible estimated figures for receipts and disbursements of expenditures of the period under consideration.

2) One's own experience and specific business knowledge on one had, and analyzed actual figures of the past performances on the other, constitute the solid basis to, logically, support the estimates.

3) Budgeting as a whole, or any kind of forecasting and cash flow projections, in any given business, should take into account all the fluctuations that take place during the entire cycle of the business operations.

Other important matters that should be contemplated, can be the following:

1) The availability of sources of additional funds, when necessary:

2) The suitability of the existing business or organizational structure to meet the financial needs.

3) The kind of financing required and how to obtain it.

Obviously, one should only search for possible sources of financing, only after the business has outlined diligently its financial requirements.

CAUSES OF VARIANCES

The difference between the planned figures and the actual ones, may result due to certain causes, like the ones presented below:

- Purchases of materials may decrease when sales decrease;
- Purchases of materials may increase when sales increase;
- Direct labour costs may decrease when sales decrease and inventory increase and thus production is brought to a lower level;
- Direct labour costs may increase when production increases as a result of the need to match the sales increases
- Insurances, business taxes, licences, may fluctuate as a direct result of changes in the respective rates (adjustments) or new additions, for example.
- Fuel costs in the factory overhead may change depending on the winter conditions
- Utilities costs may fluctuate depending on the heavy repairs or idle periods of production that brings increase or decrease in the power consumptions or simply because of the increased or decrease in the levels of productions;
- Maintenance and repairs of the shop machinery and equipment may increase or decrease in respect to costs depending on the efficiency of operations, degree of care by the employees, etc.
- Change in the inventory levels depends on the changes in the sales volume
- The sales may decrease as direct result of community strikes; Consequently, the cost of sales will decrease, if the consumers are affected in their buying power;
- Salaries of sales personnel and sales commissions will decrease, if sales decrease;
- Delivery, transportation-out and freight-out costs may decrease, if sales decrease;
- Increase in postal rates will bring increase in office expenses in respect to postage costs;
- A higher loan balance will bring higher interest costs;
- Increase sales may bring increase in accounts receivable balances;
- Increase purchases may bring down the bank repayments
- Inventory increased figure may come as a result of purchases slow down that did not level with the sales decrease
- Accounts payable may reveal a down figure as a result of less purchases made because of sales decrease;
- finally, income taxes will decrease as a result of lower earnings figure.

SUMMING-UP

Those who are successful in financial management are also capable of anticipating the eventual cash difficulties that may occur and work out an effective strategy that indicate the sources for cash in order to meet the necessary targets.

A cash flow forecast is instrumental for management planning. It measures the movements of cash transactions, the ins and the outs of cash in a given enterprise. Simply stated, is the difference between the incoming cash and the planned expenditures and outlays of cash other than expenses, like capital investments.

Those involved in financial management, face quite often the following questions:

- What is the real cash position of the firm? Can it be considered as of a satisfactorily level? Undoubtedly, a projected deficit will be the warning to negotiate an operating loan, while surplus will show that funds are available for investments ventures, either short-term or long-term ones.

- What period of time should be considered as suitable for creating the desired cash position?

- What is the extent of borrowing funds or the extent of their availability for, at least, short-term investments to start with?

- Should financing be needed, how much can it be considered at a satisfactorily level and what is the possibility of scheduling satisfactorily, the repayments of borrowed funds?

It is known that in many businesses, the cash flow forecast is made out usually for twelve months and it is subsequently to its creation that it is monitored or controlled in order to account for the arising variances, if any.

The related format can be adapted to suit the particular needs of a firm, thus reflecting the specific business operations.

The related theory advanced in this field should be studied in conjunction with the analysis of the practical budgets and the cash flow projection patterns that are to be found in the pages that follow.

It is, perhaps, in this way, that one may successfully 'defend' a business plan whenever presented to an interested party(ies).

BUDGETS AND CASH FLOW PROJECTIONS
PATTERNS

Anyone involved in working with budgets and cash flow projections should bear in mind the need to adjust the existing patterns, presented in this section, to the specificity of the business enterprise under consideration.

It is only through careful and diligent analysis and careful thought that new and suitable designs may come to light.

PERSONAL MONEY PLANNER
MONTHLY

REVENUE/NET INCOME:

Sources: Net Salary   _____

             Interest Earned   _____

             Dividends Received   _____

             Capital Gains   _____

             Rental Income   _____

             Commissions   _____

             Refunds Received   _____

             Gifts Received — Cash   _____

             Other Income (specify)   _____

TOTAL Income (Net)   ════════════

PAYMENTS:

Contributions to Savings (specify)   _____

Short-Term Investments (specify)   _____

Long-Term Investments (specify)   _____

Charitable Donations   _____

Income Taxes Arrears   _____

Associations Dues   _____

Memberships Fees   _____

Bank Loan Repayments   _____

Credit Cards Repayments   _____

Medical Insurance   _____

Exhibit 85

Professional Fees _____

   - Accounting _____

   - Legal _____

   - Consulting (Financial) _____

Bank Service Charges _____

Automobile Expenses:

   - Gasoline _____

   - Repairs _____

   - Maintenance _____

   - Insurance _____

   - Washing _____

   - License _____

   - Parking _____

   - Other (specify) _____

Food _____

Entertainment _____

Clothing _____

Personal Library-Additions _____

Newspapers, Magazines, etc. _____

Gifts _____

Rental of Personal Office Equipment _____

Home Mortgage _____

Property Taxes _____

Property Insurance _____

Home Repairs _____

Home Maintenance _____

Utilities:

- Natural Gas   _____

- Power   _____

- Other (specify)   _____

- Telephone   _____

- Water   _____

- Cable T.V.   _____

- Home furniture-additions   _____

- Home fixtures   _____

- Household help   _____

- Educational Seminars   _____

- Vacations   _____

- Sports   _____

- Hobbies   _____

- Health Care   _____

- Child/Dependant Care   _____

Personal Investments:

- Stocks   _____

- Bonds   _____

- Real Estate

TOTAL PAYMENTS   _____

FIRM'S NAME_____
PERIOD_____

PERSONAL OR BUSINESS PROGRAMME
AND
CORRESPONDING FINANCING

A. Programme:

    Acquisition of building   _____
    Acquisition of land   _____
    Acquisition of furniture   _____
    Acquisition of equipment   _____
    Acquisition of truck   _____
    Working Capital   _____
    Leasehold Improvements   _____

        TOTAL   _____

B. Financing:

    Supplier's loans payable   _____
    Mortgage loans payable   _____
    Proceeds from disposal of automobile   _____
    Working Capital   _____
    Bank Loan Payable   _____
    Additional Investment   _____

        TOTAL   _____

Exhibit 86
NOTE: A must equal B

PROJECTED STATEMENT OF INCOME

An Operating Forecast will be prepared using as a starting point the most recent operating statement for information on past accomplishments. We shall deal firstly, with sales or revenue other than from sales, to forecast. Subsequently, we shall list all kinds of expenses assumed to be incurred, in the process of generating the related revenue or sales, during the same period of time. In doing so, we shall make use of the best and most reliable data, available to us. Finally, it will be possible to establish the projected profit figure.

Note: The results should be broken in smaller periods of time, like months and weeks. This will facilitate control and comparison between the planned and actual figures, detect any eventual problems or difficulties that may arise during the business cycles, and take all the possible or/and necessary corrective steps on time.

FIRM _ _ _ _ _ _ _ _ _ _ _ _ _ _ _ _ _ _ _
(MANUFACTURING ENTERPRISE)

CASH FLOW PROJECTION

FOR THE PERIOD _ _ _ _ _ _ _ _ _ _ _ _ _ _ _ _ _
(Allocated by month)

	Planned	Actual
REVENUE: SALES OF GOODS		
Sales of goods - previous year	....	....
Add: Additional sales of goods - this year	....	....
Total sales of goods, as projected	....	....
CASH RECEIPTS		
Sales made by cash	....	....
Accounts receivable - trade, collected	....	....
Advances from shareholders (loans)	....	....
Proceeds from disposals of fixed assets	....	....
Total Cash-in	....	....
CASH DISBURSEMENTS		
Payments made to creditors - accounts payable	....	....
	....	
Payments made for direct wages and benefits	....	....
	....	
Manufacturing overhead expenses	....	....
Selling expenses	....	....
General expenses	....	....
Administrative expenses	....	....
Repayments on account of borrowed funds	....	....
Acquisitions of assets	....	....
Total Cash-out	....	....
Net Difference (Cash-in-cash-out)	....	....
Opening Cash Balance		
Closing Cash Balance (Net difference + Opening cash balance)		....

Notes (Observations) ....
....
....

Exhibit 87

FIRM _____
(e.g. RETAIL OUTLET)

CASH-FLOW PROJECTION

	Planned	Actual
Income (cash only)		
Sales of goods by cash	....	....
Accounts receivable - trade, collected	....	....
Proceeds from loans receivable	....	....
Proceeds from sale of fixed assets	....	....
Other cash received (be specific)	....	....
Total Cash-in	....	....
Expenses (cash only)		
Shop-rental of space	....	....
Office-rental of space	....	....
Equipment rental	....	....
Management salaries	....	....
Office salaries	....	....
Shop wages	....	....
Employees benefits-shop	....	....
Employees benefits-office	....	....
Professional fees	....	....
Utilities	....	....
Telephones and telecommunications	....	....
Shop repairs and maintenance	....	....
Equipment repairs and maintenance	....	....
Insurances	....	....
Business taxes	....	....
Licenses	....	....
General expenses	....	....
Interest on loans	....	....
Bank service charges	....	....
Advertising and promotions	....	....
Payments		
Purchase of fixed assets:		
- land	....	....
- building	....	....
- furniture & fixtures	....	....
- equipment	....	....
Payments made on term loans	....	....
Payments made on mortgages	....	....
Income taxes payments	....	....
Dividend payments	....	....
Payments on accounts payable - trade	....	....
Other payments (be specific)	....	....
Total Cash-out	....	....
Surplus of cash or deficit (cash-in minus cash-out)	....	....
Opening cash balance	....	....
Closing cash balance	....	....

Exhibit 88

FIRM_____

PROJECTED STATEMENT OF CASH FLOW

For the period

	PLANNED	ACTUAL	VARIANCE
INCOMING CASH:			
- Accounts receivable - trade			
- Government grants			
- Bank loans			
- Mortgage loans			
- Rental income			
- Other income (specify)			
TOTAL			
CASH PAYMENTS:			
- Purchases of materials			
- Direct wages			
- Employees benefits - labour			
SHOP OVERHEAD:			
- Utilities			
- Taxes (property)			
- Insurances (building, contents)			
- Other costs			
SELLING EXPENSES:			
- Salaries - sales personnel			
- Commissions sales persons			
- Advertising			
- Promotions			
- Travelling			
- Shows and displays			
- Other costs (specify)			
GENERAL AND ADMINISTRATIVE EXPENSES:			
- Management salaries, bonuses, etc.			
- Office salaries, bonuses, etc.,			
- Licenses			
- Taxes			
- Interest			
- Consulting fees			
- Legal fees			
- Accounting fees			
- Other costs			
Income taxes - provisions			
Capital investments			
Repayment of long-term debt.			
Repayment of current loans (bank, etc.)			
TOTAL			
CASH SHORT/OVER			
ADD: Balance of cash at start			
Balance of cash at end			

Exhibit 89

272

THE FIRM _____

A PRO-FORMA BALANCE SHEET

For the period

	PLANNED	ACTUAL	VARIANCE
CURRENT ASSETS:			
- Cash in bank account - business			
- Accounts receivable - trade (net)			
- Loans receivable/Advances			
- Other receivable			
- Inventories, at lower of cost			
- Prepaid costs			
TOTAL			
FIXED ASSETS:			
- Furniture, Fixtures & Office Equipment			
- Automobiles & Trucks			
- Shop (Factory) machinery & equipment			
- Less : Accumulated Depreciation			
TOTAL			
TOTAL ASSETS			
CURRENT LIABILITIES:			
- Bank loan payable			
- Mortgage payable			
- Accrued liabilities			
- Accounts payable			
- Income taxes payable			
TOTAL			
Long-term amounts payable			
Advances from shareholders (loans)			
Capital stock			
Retained earnings (deficit)			
TOTAL LIABILITIES & EQUITY			

Exhibit 90

PROJECTED ACCOUNTS PAYABLE

	Planned	Actual
Month	....	....
Projected purchases	....	....
Payments of current accounts	....	....
Payments on account: 30 days old	....	....
Payments on account: 60 days old	....	....
Payments on account: 90 days old	....	....
Payments on account: older than 90 days	....	....
Payments on account payable	....	....

Exhibit 91

PROJECTED CASH SALES AND ACCOUNTS RECEIVABLE

	Planned	Actual
Revenue sales	....	....
Projected revenue - sales	....	....
Cash sales	....	....
Collection re: 30 day old balances	....	....
Collection re: 60 day old balances	....	....
Collection re: 90 day old balances	....	....
Collection re: older than 90 days balances	....	....
Collection from accounts receivable	....	....

Exhibit 92

Certain assumptions and notes are usually enclosed to the financial statements, even to the projected ones, like the following:

1. Sales: Increase of approximately____% over the year of____

2. Accounts receivables: ____% of monthly sales will be collected during the following month.

3. Accounts payable: ____% of direct purchases will be paid during the subsequent month, after they occur.

4. Fixed assets: ____% depreciation calculation on the undepreciated balance. Net book value should be figured out and stated as such; Presentation should be made by categories of assets (class).

5. Debt: Borrowed funds from _____payable at _____per month plus interest at____% above the prime lending rate, over _____years.

Exhibit 93

CONDENSED PROFIT AND LOSS STATEMENT
FOR THE FISCAL YEAR ENDED _____

ıal

......
.....
.....
.....
.....
.....
.....
.....

REVENUE:

(Gross)   Sales of goods ....
Less: Discounts allowed...
            Refunds... _____

(Net)   Sale ....

LESS: Cost of Goods Sold
            - Inventories, at start..
            Add: Purchases of goods ....
                  Freight-in...
                  Direct Labour ....
                  Benefits costs... _____
                  Subtotal..
            Less: Inventories, at end.................................... _____

GROSS MARGIN (PROFIT)   ....

EXPENSES:
            Factory overhead..
            Selling ....
            General and administrative....................................
            Financial .... _____
            Total .... _____

NET OPERATING PROFIT (LOSS)

Add: Other income .... _____

NET PROFIT .- Pre-Taxes...
Provision for income taxes (deduct) .... _____

NET PROFIT (LOSS) FOR THE FISCAL PERIOD........................... ════════

Exhibit 94

STATEMENT OF INCOME AND RETAINED EARNINGS
YEAR ENDED _____
(with comparative figures at _____)

	1986	1985
REVENUE:		
Sales		
Cost of Sales..	_____	_____
Gross Profit	_____	_____
EXPENSES:		
Advertising..		
Bank charges and interest		
Depreciation..		
Office..		
Professional fees...		
Rent		
Subcontractors...		
Telephone...		
Travel...		
Vehicle	_____	_____
	_____	_____
Income before income taxes..		
Income taxes..	_____	_____
Net income for the year		
Retained earnings (deficit), beginning of the year	_____	_____
Retained earnings, end of year.....................................	======	======

Exhibit 95

FIRM'S NAME _____

MERCHANDISE BUDGET
(MONTHLY)

E.g., The Month of January 1989

	Planned Jan. 89	Last Year Jan. 89
SALES OF GOODS:		
— Cash Sales	_____	_____
— Credit Sales	_____	_____
TOTAL	_____	_____
INVENTORY END OF MONTH:		
— Raw Materials	_____	_____
— Work in Progress	_____	_____
— Finished Goods	_____	_____
TOTAL	_____	_____
MARKDOWNS		
— Total	_____	_____
— %	_____	_____
SHRINKAGES:		
— Total	_____	_____
— %	_____	_____
PURCHASES:		
— Raw Materials	_____	_____
— Finished Goods for Resale	_____	_____
INITIAL MARKUP MAINTAINED %	_____	_____
GROSS MARGIN:		
— Total	_____	_____
— %	_____	_____

Exhibit 96

OTHER USEFUL CALCULATIONS

- Total planned Sales/Average Inventory = Inventory Turnover Rate
- Planned purchases for a certain month can be calculated as follows:

- Sales ....

    Add: - Markdowns ....

       - Shrinkage ....

       - End of Month Inventory ....

       - Subtotal ....

    Deduct:- Beginning of month inventory ....

    Planned Purchases ....

- Planned gross profit for a certain moth can ve calculated as follows:

    - Planned Sales ....

    Deduct: - Cost of Sales
            (based on initial markup) ....

          - Cost of Markdowns ....

          - Cost of Shrinkag ....
    - Gross Margin

    Then Gross Margin/sales X 100 = Gross Margin rate (%)

- The Return on Inventory Investment can ve calculated as follows:

    Gross Margin/Average Inventory at Cost

- Production requirements for any given month can be calculated as follows:

ESTIMATED SALES DURING THE MONTH ....

ADD : PLANNED INVENTORY END OF
    THE RELATED MONTH ....

LESS: PLANNED INVENTORY BEGINNING OF
    SAME MONTH ....

Exhibit 97

STATEMENT OF INCOME

FOR THE MONTH OF _____

REVENUE:
SALES
Less: **Cost of Goods Sold**
Purchases of merchandise
Fregiht-in
Wages & Benefits
Subcontracting work
Subtotal _____
Less: Inventory-end _____   _____

GROSS PROFIT

OVERHEAD
Management
Office Salaries
Rental of Space
Depreciation
Advertising
Legal Fees
Utilities
Repairs & Maintenance
Taxes
Employees benefits
Loan Interest
Bad Depts.
Telephone
Insurance
Automobile
Stationery & Office
Postage
Interest & Service Charges _____   _____

NET LOSS   ═══════

APPROVED BY MANAGEMENT

Exhibit 98

FIRM

BUDGET OF STOCK AT RETAIL VALUE

THE PLANNED FUGURES BASED ON THE PREVIOUS YEAR ONES

MONTHLY PROJECTIONS

	PLANNED THIS YEAR	PREVIOUS YEAR
- Sales (Net)	_____	_____
- Ending Inventory	_____	_____
- Markdowns	_____	_____
- Shrinkage	_____	_____
- Purchases	_____	_____
- Initial Markup	_____	_____
- Gross Profit	_____	_____

NOTES: The above information are presented both in absolute figures and in related percentages for the respective related figures.

The actual figures of last or previous year data will serve as a basis of calculations for the current year planned performances, namely for the planned month-end stock or inventories.

Exhibit 99

FIRM_____

PLANNED INVENTORIES AT END-OF-MONTH

Previous year
Actual stock ratio

Stock/sales ratio
Industry

Planned
Stock/sales ratio

Planned sales

Planned inventory
End-of-month

NOTES: -   This information is based on the actual figures of last (previous) year data;

-   The stock at the end of the month divided by sales during the month will give us the stock/sales ratio;

-   The planned end-of-month inventory will be calculated by multiplying the planned stock sales ratio by planned sales of the related or respective month;

-   Certain needed information, like the actual stock/sales ratio by industry(ies) can be found in the trade publications of a given country.

Exhibit 100

Great Manufacturing Co. Inc.

Statement of Cost of Good Manufactured

For the Year of _____

Stock in process of work, at start of period
Raw materials use:
    In stock, at start of period:
    Acquisitions made
    Deduct: Allowances and returns _____
    Freight-in _____

    Cost of raw materials ready for use
    Deduct: Stock at end of period _____

Cost of raw materials consumed
Direct wages and benefits
Overhead costs (total) _____

Total manufacturing cost

Total cost of items in process during period _____

Less: Stock in process at end of period _____

Cost of goods manufactured _____

Exhibit 101

281

It has to be stressed that effective administration on the job of the various tasks entrusted for performance, depends on one's personal gained skills, as revealed along technical, human and conceptual levels.

CASH FLOW PROJECTIONS:
THEIR USEFULNESS

Good experience shows that those who are ignoring the need for financial planning and forecasting or projections of any kind, will sooner or later encounter serious financial difficulties.

The benefits of cash-flow projections and budgeting wisely can be emphasized in the following statements:

— a statement of cash earnings could indicate the relationship between the business plans and the cash balance;

— sound forecasting information, as basis for comparison with the actual results attained, will in turn make it possible to sense adverse effects and trends and take corrective and necessary steps on time;

— a communication instrument to the creditor like the banker, in order to indicate the possibility of having available funds, during the future periods, in order to cope with the eventual commitments for repayment of loans, etc.

Budgeting and cash-flow projections drawn from various periods of time, affect any business enterprise anywhere in the world, at one time or another, depending on the needed arising circumstances.

A wise and pondered manager will, more likely, examine all the facets of his business enterprise and constantly control and assess the eventual difficult cases he may be confronted with during the daily business operations, and also account for the variances which may be recorded at a later date. This in turn will facilitate the possibility of taking corrective steps, whenever necessary, and before it is too late.

An authority on the subject matter once stated that 'Budgeting is conceived to be the preparation of a budget and its fullest use not only as a device of planning and co-ordinating but also for control'.

There are certain factors responsible for good managing of budgets and cash-flow projections, namely:

— Complete knowledge of company's aims and objectives;

— The supporting ideas, assumptions and other relevant considerations of such aims and objectives, in respect to their implementation;

— A good projection of the estimated figure of sales volumes for all the company's goods;

— Projection schedules of inventories and receivables;

— Cash receipts and cash disbursements summary figures;

— A complete review of the entire projection;

— Accounting for the results obtained and their analysis; also an outline of the necessary corrective steps be taken.

There are several types of budgets, like the following ones:

— Cash budgets characteristic for newly created business enterprises and the growing ones;

— Capital budgets in use whenever capital expenditures are useful and important or of a repetitive nature;

— Human resource budgets used as a tool of control in labor-intensive companies.

Important matters, like the ones indicated below, should be considered:

—   The availability of sources of funds, whenever necessary;

—   The suitability of the existing business or organizational structure to meet the financial needs or requirements, and

—   The kind of financing required and how to obtain it.

Successful financial management in respect to budgets and cash-flow projections should also include the managers' capability of anticipating the eventual cash difficulties that may occur and work out an effective strategy that will provide or indicate the sources for cash in order to meet the necessary targets.

A cash flow forecast is a very important tool for management planning.

—   What is the real cash position of the firm? Is it a satisfactory one?

—   What period should be considered as suitable to generate the needed cash?

—   How to obtain the necessary funds, from what available sources? This in the case of short-term or long-term needs or requirements.

—   How much to borrow and how to structure the repayments?

We have presented certain useful tables for a better guide to management of budgets and cash-flow projections. The respective formats should be adapted to suit one's particular need in the respective firm and to reflect the specific or particular business operations in use.

BUDGETS, CASH-FLOW PROJECTIONS AND FORECASTING INTO THE FUTURE

Based on proper record-keeping work and business information and related documentation made available through the internal system of the mechanism of accounting, a proper set of forecasts should be drawn by the technical staff of a business in cooperation with the business management. These will be presented in the form of a set of pro forma financial statements, to include a projected balance sheet statement and a projected statement of income or earnings, for a selected future period of operations. It will also, possibly, include a projected cash flow projection of various aspects of business activities. The availability of such statements, as mentioned above, will, more likely, lend credibility of company's operations, to outside users of such business information and will also serve as a precious yardstick for measuring the actual performances against the projected figures. Furthermore, it will make possible to take corrective steps and make adjustments for improvements of performances.

Budgets constitute an integral part of Financial Management along with other facets of it. Budgets are also considered planned targets and controls that are designed to ensure that plans are attained. In this respect, a reasonable degree of accuracy can be achieved when using, on one hand, relevant and accurate data from the past performances in respect to sales, costs, etc., and obtaining information about the future regarding changes in prices of various products and/or services to be used by the firm, on the other.

It can be emphasized that the size of the operations of a business enterprise will have an impact on the degree of information and one needs to include in a budget. Thus the complexity or sophistication in an eventual resulting presentation.

Undoubtedly, a budget will also reveal the skill and degree of knowledge of a manager responsible for its presentation. A manager at a retail business, will have to acquire and communicate for building-up of a budget, along the following:

- Sales;
- Operating costs and cost of goods sold;
- Inventory;
- Cash;
- Advertising and Promotions, and
- Profit Planning.

Budgets, as 'plans translated into monetary terms' should be realistically stated and allow for changes, whenever needed in respect to the various units or departments of a business.

By depicting eventual variances or deviations of the actual performances against the planned figures, a manager will be able to make the necessary adjustments and/or take corrective steps in order to avoid stock-outs or surpluses.

LIST OF EXHIBITS

Exhibit Number	Description	Page Number
85	- A Monthly Personal Money Planner	265
86	- A Personal or Business Programme for Corresponding Financing	268
87	- A Monthly Cash - Flow Projection in Use	270
88	- A Cash - Flow Projection e.g. Retail Outlet	271
89	- A Projected Statement of Cash - Flow for a Given Period	272
90	- A Pro - Form Balance Sheet	273
91	- Projected Accounts Payable (Table)	274
92	- Projected Cash Sales and Accounts Receivable (Table)	274
93	- Certain Useful and Related Notes	275
94	- Condensed Profit and Loss Statement	276
95	- Statement of Income and Retained Earnings	277
96	- A Monthly Merchandise Budget	278
97	- Other Useful Calculations (Schedule)	279
98	- Statement of Income: An Illustration	280
99	- A Budget of Stock at Retail Value	280
100	- A Planned Inventories at End of Month	281
101	- Statement of Cost of Goods Manufactured	281

SUMMING-UP

The structuring of a budget has its start with a detailed sales budget schedule for a certain selected period, and broken down into weeks, months, years. This forecast will be prepared by the type of products, by departments, by salesmen, by sales territories, etc. A realistic budget should always taken into account the past performances and related analysis with all its causes for any inadequacies, as sensed in the past. At all the stages of preparation of profit planning there must be an open line of communication between different sections of operations. Any sales forecast is based on the firm's actual capabilities of reaching its objectives in regard to different volumes of production.

Once this is attained, the next step is to construe a cost budget for the already selected volumes of production (for sales). In this respect, there are two types of costs to be considered:

— The fixed costs and the variable ones.

The fixed costs will change little with the increasing levels of production, while variable costs will vary more or less depending on the levels of production (units).

The next and the last one is the estimating of various overhead expenses, to include administrative, selling and general expenses. Once these steps are taken, a profit and loss budget can be scheduled, to indicate profits for the various selected periods and at different levels of production.

There are two ways of calculations of the estimates in a profit and loss budget, namely the accrued versus cash basis of calculation.

The accrual way may well consider delays in payment of customers accounts and the credit available for suppliers of goods and services and the sales on account incurring an obligation. On the other hand, a cash flow projection will indicate in detail the receipt of cash (actual) and the payments of credits (actual). The various detail budget schedules will constitute the profit planning build-up.

Wisely managing your budgets and cash flow projections implies the following carefully planned steps:

1.   Outline your aims and business objectives in detail;
2.   Phrase the underlying assumptions in carrying out these aims and objectives;
3.   Project your sales volume by products involved;
4.   The inventory and receivable projections schedules;
5.   Summary of cash receipts and cash disbursements;
6.   An overall review of the completed budget;
7.   Recording the actual results and indicating the corrective actions be taken.

At the very basis of the entire work of cash flow budgeting we can find the desire by any individual or business to ensure maximizing the sales and thus the profits, while ensuring that at any given point in time there is enough cash to cope with current payments reflected in the incoming bills. Thus it can be rightly said that cash management is vital in its role of keeping alive the business. The core components in cash management are measurement and action. That means, that on one hand we have to develop a sound system for forecasting the cash needs and on the other we have to take action in advance by deciding what should be done. Lastly, to take the necessary steps to ensure that all anticipated expenses are met.

By having a cash-flow budgeting, it means that we have a system in place of measuring the projected figures of cash inflows and outflows, and see, practically, how the management plans to attain the needed financial objectives of a given period.

Needless to say, adequate budgets should always be generated and used as useful tools in the hands of the business managers.

Monitoring the daily activities and various operations, while using the budgets as a guide, constitute one of the keys to successful business operation.

In order for a budget to lead to acceptable or expected reasonable good results, at the least, certain prevailing conditions should be met, namely:

—   A proper record-keeping and accounting system should be in use;

—   Management interest, motivation and enthusiasm along with the required or needed technical skills, general and specific knowledge of his business and good experience, are a must;

—   An adequate budget system drawn on the basis of the company's interests and specific needs.

PART SEVEN

BUSINESS WRITING SKILLS

A SELECTIVE GUIDE

This presentation of selective business letters of special skills, although limited, it is not aimed at a gifted and fortunate few.

Thinking precedes writing, and to think is the hardest thing to do. It is one's own experience and observation that is 'translated' into sentences by the delicate power of the mind.

It has to be mentioned that it is through rigorous self-training and continuous improvement that one can reach a desirable level of business writing skills.

CONTENTS

Introduction 295

Certain Important Highlights...297

A. The Solicited Letters of Inquiry 299

B. The Unsolicited Letters of Inquiry 301

Letters of Recommendations 315

Contractual Agreements 319

List of Exhibits

LIST OF EXHIBITS

Exhibit Number	Description	Page Number
102	- A Solicited Letter of Inquiry	300
103	- An Unsolicited Letter of Inquiry	301
104	- An Example of Personal Resume	304
104A	- A Related Reply (to the above)	305
105	- Another Relevant Letter of Inquiry	306
106	- A Related Reply (to the above)	307
107	- An Exemplification of an Agreement with its Relevant Terms and conditions	309
108	- A Letter of Recommendation	315
109	- An Example of a Business Prospect (in support to the above)	317
110	- A Distributorship Agreement: An Illustration	320
111	- A Contractual Agreement Re: Business Partnership	322
112	- Another Relevant Example of a Contractual Agreement	323

INTRODUCTION

Like in many other fields of study, in the area of business writing skills, there is no royal road to gain the needed knowledge, and what lies ahead is learning through both theory and practice, mostly practice.

As people's background, experiences and needs or interests differ, so the path of learning varies.

With patience, perseverance and careful and constant review of what is done, one can attain good results. There is no paved way to reach the sea of knowledge and it is my firm belief that by revealing strong will and determination, while making use of other people's good experience, one may hope to reach its splendid shores.

This collection of selective business letters of special skills, although limited, is not aimed at a gifted and fortunate few. As someone once stated, "great poets are born and not made, but good writers can be made or rather can make themselves."

Thinking precedes writing, and to think is the hardest thing to do. It is one's own experience and observation that is 'translated' into sentences by the delicate power of the mind. Seeing, feeling and thinking are the greatest elements of the writer's art. On the other hand, writing is said to be hard since the words are numerous and tricky.

It is through rigorous self-training and continuous improvement that one can reach a desirable level of business writing skills.

As someone once stated "The vehicle of expression is quite as important as the thing said."

In this line of thought, the following statements can be made, if one is to reach a better and higher level of skillful writing, namely:

- A business letter is an invitation for a prompt reply. Any delay may cause a loss of business or affect a good opportunity.

- A successful business letter has to be precise, clear, concise, meaningful, free of any ambiguities. It must be explicit and specific, with direct and short sentences.

- Good business language, good command of one's words, free of errors, will undoubtedly lead to desirable results or, at least, please, the receiver.

- Writing is also an expression of one's personality as developed, or in the process of development.

- A well-written letter will, in most cases, lead to the build-up of a good or favourable business relationship.

- The form and style of business letters are of paramount importance.

- The body of a letter, namely the message one wishes to convey, is considered to be the most important part of a letter.

- The quality of any business letter is a reflection of one's ability to write it.

- The ability to express thoughts clearly and concisely are skills of utmost importance in the business world.

- In order to reach, successfully, the desired level of professionalism in writing, one should try to enrich and improve not only the command of the great arsenal of methods and techniques of modern times in this respect, but also to acquire the best and most selective principles of skillful business communications.

- A reasonable person will think before he writes, and when he writes, and then, think about how he can refine or improve the sentences of the letter.

- Clarity and coherence are essential elements of written communication.

- One should try and be as expeditious as possible, and this can be easily attained if proper things are put in proper places.

- To be efficient and effective, one should be concise and say the things in the shortest and most direct way.

- The sentences of a letter should be brief and clear, and relevant ideas brought to light in a meaningful and concise way, as one would like to convey them to an audience.

- Action verbs, avoiding too much use of the passive voice should prevail.

- A direct, specific line of thought must be revealed, and an appropriate tone should be used.

- To obtain action, to create good will, and to provide information or reasoning, are the main aims of a business letter.

- The forms and mechanics of a business letter must be learned and one should constantly strive to improve his skills.

CERTAIN IMPORTANT HIGHLIGHTS

RE: **LETTERS OF INQUIRY**

The practical letters that follow reveal good command of technical notions and certain specific terminology used in some particular fields of work.

The application for an instructor' position with a reputable College of Business reached its objective, as the related reply indicates.

A newly created publishing firm expressed an interest in having an estimate for printing books by a reputable printing house of a University.

The estimate obtained together with the proposed arrangement for payments and credit, represent excellent illustrations of good letters that reach their objectives of 'getting business'.

RE: **LETTERS OF RECOMMENDATIONS**

A letter of recommendation to a bank manager on behalf of a company that applied for a certain credit line is presented also in this Part. The prospect of potential development of the company in question was instrumental in obtaining a favourable decision from the bank. Needless to say, a good correlation or positive interrelationship amongst various factors may, in many instances, lead to a desirable decision.

RE: **CONTRACTUAL AGREEMENTS**

A written agreement is presented by an existing publishing firm to a freelance sales representative in the field of bookselling. It is construed on the premise that the freelance may suggest additional clauses, alter the existing ones or simply accept the agreement as is. In fact, the purpose of the paragraphs, as presented here, is to offer a skeleton or framework in order to facilitate the inclusion of other eventual clauses, as the parties involved in the transaction may decide to include.

In another respect we may face the need to study a partnership type of agreement. In this line of thought, it has to be mentioned that in addition to the already existing standard partnership agreement to be found in any of the modern western countries, for example, the prospective partners of a business may set up and agree to additional selective clauses which are considered legally binding upon the parties involved. An illustration of such a case is presented in the subsequent pages.

Yet, on another level, a certain contractual agreement is prepared by a management consultant on behalf of two parties who are selling-buying an existing business in the field of food services. It constitutes an important step before a legal and final arrangement amongst the parties is to be reached and also prepares the parties for a smooth transition of the business and change of ownership.

Like in many other fields of study, in the area of business writing skills as well there is not a royal road to gain the needed knowledge, and what lies ahead is learning through practice, mostly practice.

As people's background, experience and needs or interests differ, so the path of their learning varies. With patience, perseverance and careful and constant review of what was done, one can attain good or fruitful results.

THE SOLICITED LETTERS OF INQUIRY

_____
_____
_____

_____
_____
_____

Dear Sir: _____

This letter is in regard to your request for information on the _____ model
number _____ serial number.

This machine was built in _____ with an estimated life of _____ years or longer
providing that it is properly maintained.

The structural design, function, and capabilities of the model are the same as the current
production model.

The current cost of the _____ model and its optional walkway is _____ FOB.
This price does not include any thread, cams, needles or bobbins. The selling price of the
_____ model is _____ FOB. This price includes approximately _____
in supplies.

The dimensions of the machine are _____ inches (_____ cm) wide, _____ inches
(_____ cm) high, and _____ inches (_____ cm) deep.

The walkway measures _____ inches (_____ cm) high, _____ inches (_____
cm) wide, and _____ inches (_____ cm) deep.

The machine weight excluding walkway, is approximately _____ lbs. The walkway weight is
approximately _____ lbs.

The cost of shipping the machine to _____ is _____ approximate. The
cost of crating the machine is _____ approximate. The total shipping cost is _____
approximate and does not include any import duties.

All prices are in _____ currency.

FOR ANY FURTHER INFORMATION REGARDING THE MACHINE, PLEASE FEEL FREE TO
CALL US AT _____

Sincerely yours,

_____
Sales Manager

Exhibit 102

_____

THE UNSOLICITED LETTER OF INQUIRY

_____
_____
_____

_____

_____   Date:_____
_____
_____
_____

Dear Sir:

<u>Re: Instructor Position</u>

Please consider the attached information in the light of your interests. Also, may I ask you to transfer this information to other departments for their eventual consideration.

Sincerely yours,

_____

_____

Encl.

Exhibit 103

RESUME OF

_____

PERSONAL DATA

Addresses	**Residence**

_____
_____
_____

Business

_____
_____
_____

Mailing

_____
_____
_____

Social Insurance No.   _____

Date of Birth   _____

Marital Status   _____

Citizenship   _____

OCCUPATIONS

- **President and Executive Director**
  Publishing Firm (see business address)

- **Writer** of Business Education Books
  General Interest

- **Independent General Accountant and Business Consultant**
  (see business address)

- **Training Officer** through public lectures and business seminars of Practical Business Knowledge Series

- **Instructor/Teacher** of Business Education Subjects
  Specialties
  - _Bookkeeping-Accounting_
  - _Marketing-Salesmanship_
  - _Communication-Writing Skills_
  - _Business Law_
  - _Economics_
  - _Business Organization_
  - _Management_

PUBLICATIONS

1988 _____
1988 _____
1988 _____
1987 _____
1986 _____

UNPUBLISHED WORK

- _____
- _____
- _____
- _____

EDUCATION & QUALIFICATIONS

- Bachelor of Education in Business Education
  University of _____
  − Accounting Specialist
  − Marketing Specialist

- Bachelor of Arts Social Sciences
  University of _____ & University of _____

- School of Commerce and Finance
  − Accounting Specialist
  − Marketing Specialist

- Qualified Instructor/Teacher of Business Education
  Recognized by the Ministries of Education of _____,
  _____, and _____.

EXPERIENCE

Teaching

- _____ Boards of Education
- _____ Board of Education
- _____ Institute of Technology

Practical

- Independent General Public Accountant in _____ (1981 − 1988)
- Senior Auditor/Accountant for Public Chartered Accountants
  Firms in _____ (1970 − 1980)
- Senior Accountant/Auditor-Central Institutions (1956 − 1970)
- Founder of _____ (1987)
  Publishing Firm of Business Education Books with special
  representatives in major cities around the world

OBJECTIVE

Sharing my knowledge and experience with others, through creative writings, working and teaching/instructing in the field of business education.

Note

Personal publications, as listed above, are presented annually at International Book Fairs around the world and some Colleges and Universities are listing them as desirable readings for their courses.

Exhibit 104

_____
_____
_____

CONFIDENTIAL   Date:_____

Mr._____
_____
_____

Dear Mr._____:

                      RE: Competition No._____

I am writing regarding your recent candidacy for a position at our College of Business.

Due to the number of unusually well-qualified applicants who responded to our advertising, the selection of the successful candidate for this position has been painstaking and time-consuming. Thus the delay in replying to your letter. Please accept our sincere apologies.

We would like you to contact us at your earliest convenient time, in order to arrange an interview.

May I take this opportunity to thank you for the interest you have shown in the College.

Sincerely yours,

_____
President

_____

Exhibit 104 A

_____
_____
_____

_____
_____   Date:_____
_____
_____

Dear Sir:

We are a new publishing firm and we would like to do business with your reputable printing house.

Could you, please, provide us with an estimate based on our specifications, per attached.

We are indebted to you, for your prompt attention to this matter.

Sincerely yours,

_____
President

_____

Exhibit 105

_____
_____
_____

_____
_____
_____

Our ref:_____

Dear Mr. _____:

_____

280 x 216 mm   256 pages   _____

We have pleasure in submitting our estimate for producing the above.

Printing and Binding

Reproducing from crc supplied, in black ink only, on
paper as below. Fold, slot and gather text, glue into
covers, trim flush and pack. Delivery ex works.

_____ copies at one time   _____
_____ copies at one time   _____
_____ copies at one time   _____
_____ copies at one time   _____

Amending pages   per page   _____

Paper

Supplying 90gm2

_____ copies   _____
_____ copies   _____
_____ copies   _____
_____ copies   _____

Covers

Reproduce from colour separated artwork supplied,
printed 2/1 on 280 gm2 artboard, varnished 1/0.

_____ copies at one time   _____
_____ copies at one time   _____
_____ copies at one time   _____
_____ copies at one time   _____

Any corrections or ammendments to the above specifications would be reflected in our final charge.

Prices quoted are conditional upon any sheets, covers, or any other materials or items, supplied to us for inclusion in this work, being usable as received and any rectification that is necessary may be the subject of an extra charge.

Subject to there being no change in the cost of paper or other materials, these prices are firm for production until _____.

I hope this estimate is of interest to you and look forward to your further instructions.

Yours sincerely,

_____

_____

Exhibit 106

———————————————————

—————————————————

———————————————

———————————————
———————————————
———————————————

Our ref: _____

Dear Mr. _____:

———————————————

Re: _____

This agreement is an addition to our Standard Terms and Conditions, details of which are on the reverse of this letter.

1. The printing and binding of the books are as set out in our Estimate number _____, dated _____.

2. ____ confirms that the artwork delivered on _____ and _____ is suitable for filming for acceptable quality book production. Any adjustments needed will be notified to you and quoted separately.

3. The production schedule is based on delivery to you of ___ copies of each title by _____. The balance to be held in stock until _____.

4. Artwork will be delivered back to you on _____ following filming.

5. Payment schedule will be as follows:

   i. ____ per cent, _____ as deposit when the artwork is returned to you on _____.

   ii. ____ per cent, _____ on _____ when all the books will be completed, ____ per cent or the finished books will be ready for collection on that date.

   iii. ____ per cent, _____ on _____ no books will be delivered on that date.

   iv. The balance of the account due, to be paid on _____ when the balance of stock will be ready for collection.

   v. The Printer will store, on request, the _____ per cent balance of books for a period of up to six months from _____ without charge. The balance of the account, however, will still be due for settlement on _____.

_____
Commercial Director

and

_____
President

TERMS OF BUSINESS

In these Terms, the Printer means _____.

1. AGREEMENT. These terms which supersede any earlier terms of business of the Printer shall override any terms or conditions stipulated incorporated or referred to by the Customer whether in the order or in any negotiations and unless otherwise agreed in writing by the Printer all work done by the Printer shall be upon the terms specified in the Printer's last estimate for the work including these terms as supplemented if at all by the Printer's Acknowledgement of Order.

2. ACCEPTANCE. Permitting the Printer to start work on the basis of the Production Schedule submitted with the Printer's Acknowledgement of Order will be treated as acceptance of these terms in default of any prior acceptance thereof.

3. PRICE. *(a)* Quotations are based on the current costs of materials and are subject to increase at any time to meet any increase in such costs. Estimates not based on sight of complete copy, including illustrations, are provisional.

(b) In the case of a price quoted other than in sterling the Customer shall indemnify the Printer to the extent that the amount received by the Printer in payment of the price or any part thereof converted into sterling is less than the sterling equivalent of the price of the relevant part thereof converted at the mean rate of exchange between the bid and offer price as at 11:00 am on the date of the Printer's first written estimate on which the contract price was based as perceived by Barclays Bank plc.

4. VALUE ADDED TAX. Value Added Tax or similar tax payable shall be charged whether or not included on the quotation or invoice. Unless otherwise stated, all prices quoted are exclusive of VAT which must be added where applicable.

5. PRELIMINARY WORK. A charge shall be made for specimens and other work produced at Customer's request, whether experimentally or otherwise.

6. COPY. A charge may be made to cover any additional cost involved where copy supplied is not clear and legible.

7. PROOFS. Proofs for all work may be submitted for Customer's approval and the Printer shall incur no liability for any errors not corrected by the Customer in proofs so submitted. Customer's alterations and additional proofs necessitated thereby shall be charged extra. When style, type or layout is left to the Printer's judgement, changes therefrom made by the Customer shall be charged extra.

8. DELIVERY. *(a)* Unless otherwise agreed the Printer will give the Customer prior written notice of intended delivery. Delivery of work shall be accepted when tendered and except as provided in Clause 8*(c)* all risk will pass to the Customer upon delivery to the Customer.

(b) Unless otherwise agreed delivery will be at the Printer's works. The cost of delivery to any other address will be the subject of an extra charge and the Printer has absolute discretion to nominate carriers.

(c) In cases where work is delivered other than at the Printer's works the Customer shall bear all risk of loss or damage to the work from the moment of delivery to the carrier at the Printer's works.

9. PAYMENT. If a credit arrangement has been agreed the term shall run from the date of dispatch of proofs or copies. Otherwise payment shall be due 30 days from the date of dispatch. Overdue accounts shall attract interest at the rate of 4% above the ⎯⎯⎯ Bank Base Rate from time to time from the due date to the date payment is effectively received in full both before and after judgement. All costs and expenses incurred by the Printer in connection with any late payments shall be a debt due under this contract and shall attract interest accordingly. Should the work be suspended at the request of or delayed through any default of the Customer for a period of 30 days the Printer shall then be entitled to payment for work already carried out, materials specially ordered, and other additional costs including storage.

10. VARIATIONS IN QUANTITY. Every endeavour will be made to deliver the correct quantity ordered, but estimates are conditional upon margins of __% for work in one colour only and __% for the work being allowed for overs or shortage (__% and __% respectively for quantities exceeding _____) the same to be charged or deducted.

11. LIABILITY. *(a)* The Printer will take reasonable care and exercise reasonable skill in carrying out the work in accordance with the specification.

(b) The Printer excludes liability to the Customer for any loss or damage to the work following delivery at the Printer's works to the Customer or the carrier and for any loss of profit third party claim or consequential loss whether due directly of indirectly to negligence of the Printer or any other reason.

(c) Subject to sub-clause *(b)* the liability of the Printer for negligence or any breach of any term condition or warranty whether express or implied and whether arising by statute or otherwise shall be limited to the contract price for the work hereunder.

(d) The Printer shall not be liable in respect of any claim unless the requirements of clause 12 hereof have been complied with except in any particular case where the Customer proves that (i) it was not possible to comply with the requirements and (ii) advice (where required) was given and the claim made as soon as reasonably possible.

12. CLAIMS. Advice of damage, delay or partial loss of goods in transit or of non-delivery must be given in writing to the Printer and the carrier within three days of delivery (or, in the case of non-delivery, within ___ days of date of intended delivery) any claim in respect thereof must be made in writing to the Printer and the carrier within seven clear days of intended delivery. All other claims must be made in writing to the Printer within ___ days of delivery. The burden of proof of when and where damage, loss or delay was incurred is on the Customer. Where there is doubt such damage, loss or delay shall be assumed to have occurred after dispatch when goods are at Customer's risk.

13. STANDING MATERIAL. *(a)* Materials owned by the Printer and used by it in the production of intermediates shall remain its exclusive property. Such items when supplied by the Customer shall remain the Customer's property.

(b) Work may be effaced from intermediates immediately after the order has been executed unless written arrangements are made to the contrary. In the latter event rent may be charged at the Printer's current rates.

14. CUSTOMER'S PROPERTY. *(a)* All property supplied to the Printer by or on behalf of the Customer shall while it is in the possession of the Printer or in transit to or from the Customer be deemed to be at the Customer's risk unless otherwise agreed (and the Customer should insure accordingly).

(b) The Printer shall be entitled to make a charge at the Printer's current rates for the storage of any Customer's property left with the Printer before receipt of the order or after notification to the Customer of completion of the work.

15. MATERIALS SUPPLIED BY THE CUSTOMER. *(a)* The Printer may reject any paper, plates, or other materials supplied or specified by the Customer which appear to it to be unsuitable. Additional cost incurred if materials are found to be unsuitable during production shall be charged.

(b) Where materials are so supplied or specified, the Printer will take every care to secure the best results, but responsibility will not be accepted for imperfect work caused by defects in or unsuitability of materials so supplied or specified.

(c) Quantities or materials supplied shall be adequate to cover normal spoilage.

16. RESERVATION OF TITLE. *(a)* Notwithstanding delivery of any of the work the property in the goods delivered shall remain with the Printer until receipt by the Printer of payment in full for the work delivered.

(b) The Customer shall (unless otherwise agreed by the Printer in writing) ensure that all goods which are in the possession or control of the Customer and the property in which remains with the Printer are stored separately or marked so that such goods may be readily identified as the property of the Printer.

(c) The Customer may sell goods from any consignment notwithstanding that the Printer has not received payment in full for such consignment and in such event:

(i) such sale shall be deemed to have been effected by the Customer as agent for the Printer subject to sub-Clause 16 *(c)* (iv) below;

(ii) the Customer shall hold on trust for the Printer and shall account to the Printer for the proceeds of sale of such goods;

(iii) until payment to the Printer in full for the consignment from which such goods were sold the Customer shall maintain such proceeds in a separate bank account and such proceeds which shall not be overdrawn nor contain other monies except the proceeds of sale of goods sold by the Customer from any other consignment of goods supplied by the Printer and not paid for in full by the Customer, and

(iv) the Customer shall fully indemnify the Printer against all costs, claims, damages and expenses howsoever arising from the sale of any goods for the Customer pursuant to the provisions of this clause.

17. TERMINATION. *(a)* The Printer may terminate this Agreement forthwith by written notice:

(i) in the event of any breach by the Customer of this Agreement or of any other contract between the Printer and the Customer which remains unrectified _____ days after notice of such breach.

(ii) in the event of the Customer becoming insolvent, committing an act of bankruptcy having a final judgement entered against the Customer which has remained unsatisfied for more than _____ days or being a Company being deemed to be unable to pay its debts within the terms of _____ having a receiver appointed in respect of any of its assets or having a winding up petition issued against it.

(b) Termination by the Printer shall be without prejudice to all accrued rights of the Printer and all costs and expenses of such termination and recovery of payment or goods shall notwithstanding termination be a debt from the Customer to the Printer.

(c) In the case of contracts for printing periodicals either party may terminate the contract by thirteen weeks' written notice to that effect to the other party in the case of monthly or more frequently produced periodicals or by twenty-six weeks' written notice in the case of a contract for any other periodical. (Notice may be given at any time but where possible should be given immediately after completion of work on any one issue.)

(d) In the event of termination the Printer shall:

(i) be entitled to charge for work already carried out (whether completed or not) and materials purchased for the Customer, such charge to be an immediate debt due to it, and

(ii) in respect of all unpaid debts due from the Customer have a general lien on all goods and property in its possession (whether worked on or not) and shall be entitled on the expiration of 14 days' notice to dispose of such goods or property in such manner and at such price as it thinks fit and to apply the proceeds towards such debts in such order as the Printer thinks fit.

18. ILLEGAL MATTER. *(a)* The Customer will draw the attention of the Printer to any material which is or may reasonably be considered to be defamatory and the Printer shall not be required to print any matter which in his opinion is or may be of an illegal or libelous nature or an infringement of the proprietary or other personal rights of any third party.

(b) The Printer shall be indemnified by the Customer in respect of any claims or complaints arising out of any illegal or libelous matter or any infringement of copyright, patent, design, or of any other proprietary or personal rights contained in any material printed for the Customer. The indemnity shall extend to all costs, damages and penalties and any amounts paid on a lawyer's advice in settlement of any claim.

19. FORCE MAJEURE. The Printer shall be under no liability if it shall be unable to carry out any provision of the contract for any reason beyond its control including (without limiting the foregoing) Act of God, legislation, war, fire, flood, drought, failure of power supply, lock-out, strike or other action taken by employees in contemplation of furtherance of a dispute, or owing to any inability to procure materials required for the performance of the contract. During the continuance of such a contingency the Customer may by written notice to the Printer elect to terminate the contract and pay for work done and materials used at contract rates, but subject thereto shall otherwise accept delivery when available.

20. Law. These conditions and all other express terms of the contract shall be governed and construed in accordance with the laws of _____.

21. Assignment. The benefit of this Agreement may be assigned at any time by the Printer. The obligations on the Printer hereunder may be performed by subcontractors nominated by the Printer and unless otherwise agreed no transfer of the business or any part thereof of the Printer or any subcontracting or assignment hereof shall constitute a breach of any term or duty owed hereunder by the Printer to the Customer. The Customer shall not assign this Agreement without the prior written consent of the Printer.

Exhibit 107

As one writer once stated, 'great poets are born and not made, but good writers can be made or rather make themselves'.

Seeing, feeling and thinking are the greatest elements of the writer's art. Writing is said to be hard since the words are numerous and tricky.

LETTERS OF RECOMMENDATION

(Recommendation to a financial institution in support of a client's application for a loan)

TO WHOM IT MAY CONCERN

This is to confirm that I am Mr. _____ personal and business accountant since _____. In this capacity, I witnessed Mr. _____'s business progress, both as a General Manager and Entrepreneur in the field of manufacturing of transmissions and installations.

The development both economical and financial of his enterprise since _____ made possible an yearly allocation of $_____ as Mr. _____'s management fee.

His knowledge on technical and management lines in the field is widely recognized within the business community.

I would also like to emphasize that Mr. _____'s integrity and honesty are beyond question.

For any further reference, please, do not hesitate to contact the writer.

Submitted by,

_____
Chartered Accountant

Exhibit 108

BUSINESS   PROSPECT

STRICT   CONFIDENTIAL

RE: _____

The management commits itself to take the following steps, in order to progressively reach an improved cash flow 'picture':

- management will concentrate on the collection of accounts receivable and all amounts, as collected, will be promptly deposited into the bank account in order to reduce the overdraft figure;
- all current payments of any liabilities will be financed from collections of accounts receivable and not from approved line of credit;
- all kinds of inventories will be reduced to the minimum, based only on immediate needs to cover the existing orders;
- all new orders will be approved based on customers advances (on account) of at least _____% of the total estimated sales price;
- all suppliers will be paid _____ on account of the existing debts with the remaining balance to be liquidated gradually based on the company's future record of improved cash flow and progress-to-date. This will be done by mutual agreement and understanding with the suppliers regarding the company's new strategy for development;
- search for new and better manpower, trained and suitable for the specific profile of the company; also adding new technical staff in the production section;
- analysis of the existing levels of expenses, and studying the possibility of lowering the levels of such expenses to the minimum while obtaining the best efficiency and productivity of operations;
- engagement of an accountant to constantly monitor and advise on all the steps taken on a daily basis regarding collections, etc.;
- the bank branch will receive a monthly listing of receivable, payables and inventories on hand together with a verbal briefing of the company's state of affairs and prospective development for the coming months, by the General Manager.
- if, and only if, the management confirms that the steps recommended above will be taken in entirety, the my personal recommendation or suggestion to the Bank Manager is for an approved line of credit of _____ as of today's date, and to be increased by _____ to _____ and subsequently   reduced during the months of the spring season, as the company's well-to-do will be reflected in increased revenue.

It has to be emphasized that an existing order of large amount, sound and verified, based on solid and concrete contractual agreement, makes possible the bank's decision for advances or a credit line (see attached).

_____
Chartered Accountant

Exhibit 109

One should bear in mind that any practical letter should reveal good command of technical notions and of specific terminology used in the respective field of work under consideration.

Undoubtedly, the application of such notions and terminology should be made with special care depending on certain and related circumstances and/or the cases involved.

CONTRACTUAL AGREEMENTS

AGREEMENT

THIS AGREEMENT MADE THIS _____ DAY OF _____

BETWEEN:

_____

_____

- and -

_____

_____

(hereinafter called the Distributor)

DISTRIBUTORSHIP AGREEMENT

1.   The Distributor shall have exclusive sales rights to the following publications:

_____

_____

2.   The area of distribution will be the Province of:

_____

3.   This agreement shall remain in force until cancelled and may be cancelled for cause as set forth in this agreement.

4.   During the life of this agreement, _____ will refer to the Distributor all inquiries originating from the Distributor's market area and will not solicit business for items listed in Paragraph 1.

5.   _____ and the Distributor shall reply with reasonable time to each party's correspondence, communication, letter, cable or telegram. Reasonable request for information shall be supplied with dispatch.

6.   The Distributor will have to sell _____ during the following period and this agreement shall be renewable yearly, provided _____ are sold yearly.

7.   This agreement is subject to automatic cancellation, without notice, in the event of default of any payment for a period of sixty days from due date.

8.   The Distributor shall on each purchase order specify preferred method of shipment, carrier and routing. _____ shall not be liable for any expense incurred in forwarding, when shipment of orders executed in accordance with the Distributor's specified instructions. Unless specified on the purchase order, _____ shall forward the order, using the routings of its own discretion.

9.   _____ shall not be liable for publications damaged in transit. The Distributor shall inspect the publications immediately upon delivery by the carrier, and make claims against the carrier for loss, shortages or damages, if any, in accordance with the carrier's normal practice.

10.   Trademarks, registrations and patents of _____ shall not be infringed upon. All technical information, documents, drawings, blueprints, customer lists, and the like,

furnished to the Distributor by _____ remain the property of _____ and shall be considered "Confidential", and shall not be divulged to any other party. Upon termination of this agreement, such Publications and any other material supplied must be returned to _____ within ten days.

11.   The Distributor's purchase price shall be _____ for the publications, the said cost to be FOB _____ with a minimal order of _____ publications.

12.   In order to assist the Distributor, _____ will provide all existing promotional material at cost or no cost, at their discretion.

13.   The Distributor, during the term of this contract shall not sell or attempt to sell within the territory allotted to it, any publications in direct opposition to those publications supplied to it by _____.

14.   The Distributor covenants that it will not, during the term of this contract or within one year after termination of it, either directly or indirectly, either on his own behalf or on behalf of anyone else, solicit orders for, or sell, or otherwise deal in any publications similar to the publications of _____ described above.

        IN WITNESS WHEREOF _____ has set its corporate seal attested to by its proper officer on behalf of the company and the Distributor has set his hand and seal on the day and year first above written.

SIGNED SEALED AND DELIVERED   )
)
)   _____
)
)
)   Per: _____
)
)
)   Per: _____

Exhibit 110

321

AGREEMENT

between

Mr. _____

and

Mr. _____

Re: Business Partnership

1.   The above named parties agree to establish a business partnership as described below:

_____

_____

2.   The starting date is considered to be _____.

3.   The profit or loss to be established on December 31st of each and every year will be shared on an equal basis (50% each).

4.   It is agreed that the Firm's name will be _____.

5.   The Partner's contribution into the business will be that listed in attached Schedule 'A' part of this agreement.

6.   The work sharing load to be carried out by the Partners will be as stated below:

_____

_____

7.   This agreement can be terminated at either party's written request if submitted to the other party 30 days prior to the termination date, as requested. In this case, the arbitration for the liquidation of assets and the process of correct termination will be entrusted to an outside party, by mutual agreement.

8.   No commitment of any kind that has financial implications or legal consequences will be undertaken by any of the named partners without the written agreement by the other partner.

9.   The Firm's Accountant as appointed is _____.

10.   The Firm's Attorney as appointed will be _____.

11.   The daily business decisions to be made should be carried out under the supervision of either one of the partners in such a way required by the law, the various regulations and the ethics of the profession.

12.   In order to ensure a smooth development of the business operations, any misunderstanding between the partners will be clarified as soon as possible. In the event of further disagreement, an outside party will be asked for mediation.

Mr. _____   Mr. _____

Exhibit 111

AGREEMENT

between

_____

and

_____

The above named parties to this agreement express their consent, fully and unequivocally, on the following clauses:

1.   This agreement will be enforced as of _____ for one year only and may be renewed at either party's request.

2.   _____ obtains the right to use the _____ leased premises without any restriction, in consideration for a monthly total rent of _____ to include various costs like business tax, telephone, utilities, repairs and maintenance of shop and of existing equipment in use by _____.

3.   A prepaid security deposit of _____ will be advanced by _____ (no interest bearing).

4.   This agreement may be terminated at either party's written request and notice given at least one month in advance.

5.   A mutual exchange of information regarding planning of advertisement must take place in order to avoid any conflict of interest regarding business promotion, etc.

6.   Each party is fully responsible for carrying its own business and for observing the Law, the rules and the various related regulations.

7.   _____ will consult with _____ regarding his desire to place his business sign in a mutually convenient place.

8.   The equipment used exclusively by _____ will continue to be _____ cared for _____ and/or maintenance by him.

9.   _____ will build a Canopy or install it in order _____ for it to be common use like all the existing equipment. This is to be done no later than _____.

10.   _____ will operate a Pizzeria in such a way as to not affect _____ licence rights to operate its business.

11.   _____ will be responsible for any damage(s) he or his associates directly or indirectly many cause to the existing equipment during his hours of operating the business.

      This extends to all kinds of existing assets on the Company's premises, as listed and leased.

12.   The insurance policy will be regularly reviewed in order to include any additional equipment on the premises and for both businesses with the extra billing to be sustained by the respective owner of the added equipment.

13.   An inventory and complete description of all existing assets on the premises will be taken to reflect the ownership. This will be done by both parties in order to make possible the supervision and safeguarding of the both businesses' assets.

14. The liquor licence of _____ will be extended to _____ in certain conditions set up by mutual agreement and to be part of a separate agreement.

15. Each party will notify the other in case of any additional equipment brought on the company's premises.

Dated at _____ this day of _____.

_____   _____

Witness   _____

Exhibit 112

PART EIGHT

THE 'KNOW-HOW' TO PREPARE

AND

OBTAIN A BUSINESS LOAN

CERTAIN USEFUL GUIDES

CONTENTS

Introduction 327

The Importance of Small Businesses in a Country's Economy...............................328

In Search for Finances 331

The 'Key' Players or Interested Parties involved in a
    Small Business Loan Transaction 337

Professional Assistance and Counselling along Financial Lines 339

The Relevant Documentation and Information in support to an
    Application for a Small Business Loan 341

A Firm's Prospects for Development:
    It's Detailed Business Plan..343

The Methods and Transactions of Controlling your Cash 350

Towards an Effective Financial Control...351

A Lender's Assessment Consideration of a Client File
    regarding an Application for a Loan 353

The Financial Analysis: Certain Useful Ratios and Related Calculations 359

Approval or Rejection: The Leading Factors for Success 365

A Suggestive Management Questionnaire for Effective Financial Planning............369

INTRODUCTION

This Guide came to light following the growing need experienced and expressed by many individuals and firms to obtain either a personal or a small business loan, for a certain immediate purpose, e.g. to establish a new business enterprise or to develop/or expand an already existing one. Such a need is felt, constantly, everywhere and especially by smaller firms, in different industries around the world.

As preparation for such a matter constitutes the main factor related to success in submitting an application for a loan, the subsequent pages of this useful and interesting Guide, will deal with some of the most relevant aspects connected with such kinds of requests.

Private individuals, owners, managers and executives at various levels within different types of business organizations and in all areas of occupations, will find the information contained in this Guide, very precious for their work of preparation, in order to obtain a small business loan and, especially, during the process of dealing with outside financial institutions for the same purpose of borrowing funds to serve their various particular needs and interests.

Undoubtedly, professional assistance and counselling offered by the existing specialized offices, like legal, accounting and financial ones, may prove to be vital, especially, during the first years of business operations, when the need to gain familiarity with banking operations is a more ardent one.

One may also benefit from other people's good and wide experience in the area of handling the daily or current financial operations and other similar and related transactions, which are very useful in dealing with bankers and other lenders, at different levels.

Trying and preparing the various necessary information and documentation, as required by outsiders, mainly by financial institutions, like banks, in support of an application for a small business loan, is not an easy task to perform. Special care and attention to details are much needed. It is for this reason, especially, that a step-by-step approach is used in this Guiding Manual, in order to facilitate one's process of learning the various topics of interest, and help gain insight into the subject matter under consideration.

THE IMPORTANCE OF SMALL BUSINESSES IN A COUNTRY'S ECONOMY

Each and every year, more and more people decide to set up and run a business of their own with the strong belief and determination that their potential capabilities and the acquired skills, will make possible their successful development and attainment of their goals. In many countries around the world, such small businesses constitute the backbone of their respective economies.

It is widely known that Governments of different levels, in many places around the world, play an important role in encouraging such a trend of economic formation. This, either through grants and/or free professional and technical advices available through Government Advisory Offices or other related agencies.

On the road to successful development of their objectives, business firms should take certain necessary steps, as described, briefly, in this Manual.

It has to be emphasized from the beginning, that it is through good Financial Planning of one's business enterprise that it can be found one best way of getting the most from a lender, like banks, for example.

In this line of thought, it should also be stressed that, favouring a good lender/borrower business relationship, and according to the bank's or other lenders' best interests, a business management team should monitor and control its normal activities and operations. This can be revealed through good management techniques of handling the cash flow, and the accounting procedures in place, as part of a sound internal control system in operation in a given company under consideration.

As this present topic of concern is a delicate one, one in charge of running a business should first of all consider the financial implications and the responsibilities involved in carrying on a business for profit, as reflected in the company's business plan.

In this respect, it is highly recommended that one in charge of managing a business, in our modern and changing world of rapid technological innovations and progress, reveal confidence in the business prospects for development, leading towards a satisfactory level of profits, year after year.

Any lender-bank, for example, will be very glad to know that a prospective customer interested in borrowing funds, knows about the handling of his business as much as possible, so that the chances of successful development do exist. Examples of such aspects are the knowledge of the businessman or management of the enterprise about the credit term available from the company's suppliers, his personal needs, his projected cash-flow requirements and what kind of finances he is in need for short-term or long-term and how he is ready to repay the eventual debt.

As one may agree, success cannot simply come from working at random, without a plan and without the needed resources, especially the technical and the financial ones. It is through diligent and careful planning that a business can hope and reach the splendid shores in the realm of success. Any plans drawn in a rush will more likely, not stand the test of time and may lead to business failure, sooner or later, as many of us witnessed already during our business life.

A borrower should try and familiarize himself firstly with all the available kinds of finance — their sources, their cost or terms or conditions to obtain them and their main features or characteristics.

It has to be emphasized that any business, regardless of its size, or nature of operations, should endeavour to organize its finances in an utmost efficient way. This can be attained, with best chances for success, when an efficient and well-trained management of the business runs the daily company's operations.

Since present governments of the western hemisphere countries, through their agencies, are committed to supporting the growth and development of small business enterprises, owners and managers of all levels and of various areas of occupations, should direct their attention to the various advertised business enterprise allowance schemes available through the existing financial institutions. The interested firms, should, through their representatives, investigate and research the financial markets within their immediate environment, study the available financial products offered by such institutions, and compare their advantages, the costs of borrowing funds involved, the various terms and conditions in force. This, prior to the presentation of a formal request for a small business loan.

One might easily agree that good knowledge of handling human resources and gaining insight into the banking or financial work intricacies can only be of help. At the same time one's pleasant personality and reputation in the respective field under consideration can have a tremendous impact in one's interrelationship with the financial personnel of various institutions.

IN SEARCH FOR FINANCES

Various private individuals and small business firms around the world, try and seek to obtain different sizes of funds from various lenders-banks or other financial institutions, for different purposes, like the following:

— financial working capital, through overdrafting;

— short or long-term funds;

— speculative purpose(s);

— to finance contractual agreements;

— acquisition of other business(es);

— farming purpose(s);

— to finance importation or exportation of goods;

— prospective good venture(s);

— etc. .

MAIN FINANCIAL INSTITUTIONS

Commercial Banks;
Mutual Savings Banks;
Savings and Loans Banks;
Credit Unions;
Life Insurance Companies;
Pension Funds;
Mutual Funds.

Regarding the common sources of short-term financing, the following can be mentioned:

— Accounts payable and accrued liabilities;

— Single payment note-unsecured;

— Lines of credit — unsecured;

— Revolving credit arrangements — unsecured;

— Commercial paper;

— Accounts receivable — secured;

— Factoring — secured;

— Inventory liens — secured;

— Trust receipts — secured;

— Warehouse receipts — secured.

The major banks around the world, amongst other important financial institutions, are stating, unequivocally, that their staff resources are ready and well-prepared to consider and deal with their customers' borrowing requirements and other more immediate matters needed to be solved. They also claim of being able to give competent advices to all new or prospective customers from different areas of occupation, and to assist them under current or newly arising business circumstances, especially in their search for finances.

As a wide range of financial services are largely publicized by such financial institutions, it is highly recommended that any interested party become familiar with the available and detailed information and reading material regarding offers made by banks, for example. This prior to approaching a prospective lender, in search for a loan.

One will, undoubtedly, find out, sooner or later, about the need to prepare a business plan, cash-flow projections and budgets, together with other relevant documentation and information about the business state of affairs and its prospect for development, in support to an intended application for a business loan.

Certain major financial institutions are well-equipped with Business Information Offices designed to assist small businesses become more familiar with certain banking operations, like assistance to obtain Government Grants for Small Businesses. Such advisory services in operation with the major lending institutions will be able to help businesses in their search for new ideas, get the needed financial help in respect to such activities like exports, and also regarding creation of jobs and training. These along many other possibilities and assistance especially to find out how to explore all the resources available to small businesses, and whether or not a particular business may or may not qualify to obtain finances.

Many people around the world try to put to use and test their potential capabilities, skills and abilities in order to start a business on their own, for the purpose of making a profit.

In their endeavour to establish a particular and adequate form of business organization, these people are embarking on the way of searching and selecting from a comprehensive range of loan finance products especially designed to meet their specific needs and requirements, as offered or made available through negotiations, by the various existing financial institutions or lenders of all kinds, as known in different countries around the world.

Lately, certain major financial institutions brought forward new schemes available to anyone, in order to assist in obtaining a business loan. This, in addition to the already existing forms of loans. Among such newly offers can be cited A Personal Pension Loanback Scheme and various Business Development Loans, which can be obtained subject to certain qualifications and conditions, an individual or business firm must meet.

A Personal Pension Loanback Scheme, as advertised by banks, is regarded as a useful and beneficial method of financing a bank loan or part of a loan, by repaying the capital sum borrowed from a future lump sum provided by a Personal Pension Plan. It is further claimed by such banks, that, on a comparative basis, such a method works like an endowment mortgage. Such a scheme is designed for self-employed and/or professional people who intend to obtain funds for any business need, e.g. to buy into a practice or to expand and/or develop an existing business. In this respect, it is advisable that the interested party to such a scheme, will prepare details regarding certain information like size of loan, banking, employment, income, personal pension plan, and life assurance details. The familiarity one will gain with these matters, will facilitate the answers to certain eventual questions that may arise regarding the main benefits resulting from using such a scheme, the limits of borrowing, the modality of repayment, the stipulated clauses, the required interest rate, the insurance considerations, etc.

The advertisements displaced by banks and other major financial institutions and agencies around the world, to the attention of small businesses, regarding the availability, under certain conditions, of Business Development Loans, invite attention since it is claimed by such entities that this kind of loans represent a direct avenue to borrow money to inject into one's business; the interest, the term and the monthly repayments, as further emphasized by the same banks, are all fixed and help firms to structure their budgets. It is also stressed that such loans should be considered an efficient modality to finance acquisitions of important assets or to set up permanent working capital.

Another form of advertised loan designed to ease the financial difficulties experienced by many in various fields of occupations, is the so-called BUSINESS STARTER LOAN. Under such a scheme, certain small amounts are available, at a certain fixed rate, and repayments can be made periodically during a shorter or longer period of time, and up to maximum of five years, usually.

Obviously, secured loans will be offered by lenders at a lower rate of interest than the unsecured ones. Certain specific arrangements can also be made, by which the respective business can hold the entire capital and interest repayments over several months, at the discretion of the lender, and based on the negotiation terms, as part of the contractual agreement between the lender and the borrower. The borrower, may be granted the possibility or clause to repay the entire loan altogether, earlier than the agreed term, and without any penalty involved, but subject to a certain handling fixed fee or charges.

Yet, another form of finances that came to light in U.K., and made known to the public at large, is the so-called INSURANCE ENHANCED FINANCE, as a new concept in corporate finance. It is claimed, as stated officially through the media, that such a form of finance is designed to offer small to medium sized companies a better financial package — it provides EXTRA FINANCE through insurance backing. This, without restructuring one's existing banking facilities.

Needless to say, a wise business person will always ponder the cost of such a type of loan and the related tax advantages, if any, that can be generated through such forms of finances.

In presenting his case, a business firm's representative should contact directly, face-to-face a lender's business office manager or counsellor and obtain all the necessary information and details prior to the formulation and submission of an application for a business loan.

It is highly advisable that in all the circumstances of borrowing funds, a business will seek to insure the loan. This in case of any eventual sickness or accident. Such kind of arrangements can take place through the same bank the loan is negotiated or obtained.

It has to be stressed that in the art of management in general, and of financial management in particular, the learning by young managers from their business leaders or supervisors is a paramount and decisive factor that will shape their future business behavior and also exercise a tremendous impact on their business decisions taken at various levels in a firm.

Academic achievement alone is not enough, but when coupled with good experience and good and adequate training on the job, it can bring one to splendid heights and noticeable accomplishments in relation to difficult tasks.

THE 'KEY PLAYERS' OR INTERESTED PARTIES INVOLVED IN A SMALL BUSINESS LOAN TRANSACTION

The following constitute the possible parties involved in the work and process of obtaining a small business loan:

— an individual applicant or owner or his business firm's representative;

— a firm's auditor or accountant;

— a firm's financial consultant;

— a borrower's legal counsellor;

— a lender's legal office;

— a lending institution or its representative;

— a government agency or its legal representative, if a certain government grant is given to the respective business enterprise involved in a small business loan transaction.

PROFESSIONAL ASSISTANCE AND COUNSELLING ALONG FINANCIAL LINES

One of the most immediate help or known assistants to a businessman or to a company's management is the accountant or auditor engaged by the firm, with certain assigned tasks or responsibilities for financial and accounting reporting on, at least, yearly basis, and to serve, if required, in an advisory capacity, whenever necessary to the firm under consideration.

As far as the search and the process of obtaining the needed finances are concerned, a good accountant will assist the business enterprise with the following:

— When required, the accountant will draft a sound and fair presentation for the bank manager, in support to an application for a small business loan;

— If possible, and whenever desirable, the accountant will make a special reference or recommendation to the banker, on behalf of the business, and related to an application for borrowing funds;

— The accountant can also assist the business by drafting loan proposals and programmes of financing;

— He can also assist the business in preparing cash-flow projections for the future business operations; also prepare budgets for the same business under consideration;

— The accountant can serve as an auditor and assistant on certain aspects of the administration work involved in company's various activities, and on important payroll matters.

However, a business enterprise may ask and obtain assistance from his bank manager who is expected to get involved in the process of tax planning and relevant related matters.

Whenever necessary, an accountant tax specialist may be asked to assist the business management or owner of an enterprise, on certain tax matters since a clear knowledge of all taxation implications related to bank transactions or loans, should be known, from the start, in a lender-borrower relationship. Therefore, taxation planning constitutes an important aspect of the business and it is expected that the bank manager get involved in this area, from the start. His acquired knowledge in this respect will assist him in the process of assessment of a client's application file and in order to ensure the potential ability by the borrower to repay his debt.

In respect of the documentation and execution of the formalities related to a loan transaction, it is desirable that legal assistance be sought from a legal office, by the small firm, should such help not be possible to be obtained from the respective bank handling the application for a small business loan.

In addition to the professional office mentioned above, there are the so-called or known Enterprise Agencies in certain countries around the world, like in U.K. and others (under various names) as well which serve an important and vital role. They are set up by the existing Governments in order to provide useful guidance, advices and counselling to small businesses, on specific matters of concern, like training, finances, marketing, management, etc.

THE RELEVANT DOCUMENTATION AND INFORMATION IN SUPPORT TO AN APPLICATION FOR A SMALL BUSINESS LOAN

An applicant for a business loan should try and put together the best package of business and personal information as expected or required by the financial lending institution, in support of his application. This is vital in his strive for successful consideration of the respective application since the lender has to become familiar and gain insight into the respective business operations and its prospects for development and potential ability to repay the loan obtained.

The following represent the constitutive elements of a client's file in support of his eventual application for a business loan, namely:

— A formal and detailed application form obtained from the lender and completed by the applicant. Such an application may include the following kinds of details, like;

— Business details;

— Proprietor's details (director, partner, etc.) including financial details;

— Other details like:

  — Purpose of the business loan;

  — Amount required;

  — Date required;

— Documentation to be enclosed:

    — Cash-Flow Forecast;
    — Debtors and Creditors Aged Listings;
    — Business Plan;
    — Financial Statements;
    — Eventual recommendations or references from the Auditors and/or other offices;
    — Proposed Programme of Financing;
    — Other Business Management Information and details like information regarding the key people involved in the management of the firm and whether or not they are insured.

It has to be stressed that it is in the firm's best interests to co-operate with the lender's representative in supplying all the needed and auxiliary information and required documentation by the lender. This in order to facilitate the processing of the respective application for a business loan and in accordance with the lender's policies and related procedures in use.

In his endeavour to prepare for such an important submission, the applicant should try and seek assistance from his accountant and legal advisor or from a small business advisor — the legal lender's representative usually, at no cost.

A FIRM'S PROSPECTS FOR DEVELOPMENT: IT'S DETAILED BUSINESS PLAN

Practical work carried out in various firms and in different areas of occupation revealed that good knowledge of a company's products and their related business operations together with the transactional proceedings involved, constitute a must for any incumbent of a firm, especially for any business manager, towards progress and success since this plays a major role in the process of fulfillment of the managerial tasks, especially the most important and difficult ones.

THE COMPANY _____

ADDRESS _____

THE BUSINESS PLAN

Prepared by _____

Date _____

A complete and sound Business Plan should include the following data or information:

— Identification of the business firm;

— Background of the business: Personal and specific business details;

— Object and objectives of the business: Its various products and/or services provided described;

— Related Market and Marketing information to include the state of business competition;

— Financial Implications to include all aspects of business finance, financial projections in support of the stated financial needs, and details regarding the requirements for finance.

SPECIFIC IDENTIFICATION OF THE BUSINESS FIRM

Here, the following should be included:

— The legal and formal name of business;

— The address of the Head Office of the established business, its branches, if any, and the company's warehouse and other facilities in existence, if at a different location than that of the Head Office;

— Mailing address if other than the business address, telephone, telex, facsimile numbers and other related or necessary addresses for communication purposes;

— The date business started and the date of incorporation of the respective business, if limited company; the name and address of the main shareholders and executive directors of the business; (if possible, enclose the copy of the incorporation papers)

— The form of business organisation (sole proprietorship, partnership, corporation, etc . . .)

— The main business activities or operations, described in detail.

BACKGROUND OF THE BUSINESS: PERSONAL AND SPECIFIC DETAILS ABOUT THE BUSINESS IN OPERATION

— The names, positions and brief descriptions of the duties and responsibilities of the key management people in charge of conducting the business operations, with their related yearly income;

— The eventual stated need for additional personnel, general and technical, due to expected growth of the business operations and for increase of its activities; it should be clearly and completely indicated the particular skills and knowledge required to fill in such positions, date positions will be created and the related remuneration or kind of compensation associated with such positions;

— What plans are in place in case the existing management people become incapacitated to work and carry on their stated duties;

— Full description of the business location and its premises; If possible, a copy of the lease agreement should be included with these papers; if leased premises are considered inadequate, then plans which are in existence to compensate for lack of space in the future;

— The past history and development of the business since its start, to include the noticeable changes and accomplishments as recorded by the business during the years in operation; also any plan(s) for future, in this respect;

— The past financial data and history of finance of the company (up to 5 years). All the financial statements and the main supporting documentation should be included with this business plan;

— The names and addresses of the business connections with professional agencies, like bankers, accounting and legal offices.

THE AIMS, GOALS AND OBJECTIVES OF THE FIRM

Complete and detailed descriptions of your business aims, goals and objectives should be included in this plan.

An up-to-date catalogue, if any available, should also be enclosed in order to highlight the business products and/or services provided; promotional brochures and other relevant material regarding brands, colours, designs and various specifications should be presented together with this business plan;

Pertinent information or details regarding the eventual new products and/or services under development or of future creation;

The state of research and development, if any, in respect to the above.

**RELATED MARKET AND MARKETING INFORMATION,
TO INCLUDE THE STATE OF BUSINESS COMPETITION**

The description of your marketing research and investigation, as made by you or your business representative;

The descriptions of market fluctuations in respect of the company's sale of products and/or services provided during the period since its start, and the state of the existing market competition and its competitors;

The factors responsible for business success or business failure(s) during the stated periods of business operations;

The available orders and contractual agreements in force, and the stated levels of sales as anticipated or projected for the coming or future periods;

Marketing strategies and techniques as developed and to be put to use in the future, together with their related costs or estimates to acquire and activate them for the benefit of the company.

THE METHODS AND TECHNIQUES OF CONTROLLING
YOUR CASH

In this respect, it has to be stressed that monthly current bank account(s) reconcillations constitute a must.

Poor cash control is in almost all cases, and in any business of any area of occupation, responsible for business failure(s).

Undoubtedly, the ability to control cash can be gained through the time, when one is exposed to various cash operations and activities and these, coupled with good training and/or experience on the job.

Aged accounts receivable and aged listing of accounts payable, respectively the lists of debtors and creditors should be drawn up monthly and immediately analysed by management. Such analysis may reveal a slow collection process or bad debts or doubtful collectable amounts and the need for immediate payment in order to benefit from discounts based on payment within a stated period of time.

Whenever control of the stock takes place and increases or decreases of certain items are made, this will exercise an impact on the levels of increases or decreases in the availability of cash.

In this line of thought, it is wise to establish always alternative sources of supply of materials and seek better terms from various existing or prospective creditors, taking advantage of purchases in bulk if certain discounts are offered, and creating the best 'mix' of inventory of goods in stock, while diminishing the slow-moving items on hand and eliminating the obsolete ones.

Whenever needed, amended cash flow and amended budgets should be structured based on the company's available and up-to-date information. It is only in such a way that any eventual corrective steps can be taken before it is too late.

As useful and important cash flow indicators, the following can be mentioned:

— The available or existing current bank account balance, plus the balance of cash float, on hand;

— The credit terms obtained from various suppliers and other creditors as recorded in a company's contractual agreements;

— The credit terms and related length of time allowed or granted to a company's existing clients, based on the policies in force;

— The eventual substantial amount of outflow of cash used for acquisition of assets, of payments made on account in this respect, etc.

— The eventual incoming of a substantial amount of cash from disposal of assets, etc.

— The capital amounts injected or advanced by shareholders into their business or simply raised through sale or shares and/or interest in the respective firm under consideration.

TOWARDS AN EFFECTIVE FINANCIAL CONTROL

A lender will be very much interested to know whether or not the borrower has instituted already an effective financial control since this is considered an important matter to successful handling of the business finance of an enterprise. The same business in question should reveal its ability to take prompt measures or actions, in the right direction, in case certain unforseeable circumstances arise during the normal course of business operations. This will be possible, especially when up-to-date information of financial nature is available through proper recordkeeping and accounting and supported by a sound internal control system.

Therefore, it is imperative for a business to become familiar with the basic elements of financial control, in addition to good professional advise. Wise and sound financial decisions can only be made when supported by correct data or complete information, as needed, and used in the right way.

Potential financial difficulties can be foreseen even before they occur, if a business, for instance, is doing the following:

— Depict rising costs during the normal course of its activities, that threaten the profit margin;

— Institutes and continuously improves and handles properly its accounting and financial records, for all the business aspects and its functional operations;

— It compares constantly the progress to-date against the formulated business plan and controls regularly the flow of cash.

In this direction, there are certain necessary ingredients for successful and effective financial control. They are of paramount importance, namely the following:

— A business is required or recommended to know permanently its current financial state of affairs;

— It should prepare monthly forecasts positions;

— It should seek and make, whenever necessary, adjustments to the existing profit and cash flow forecasts;

— Select the best course of action amongst the available alternatives or options, in order to correct the eventual arising circumstances of financial problems, and

— Constantly, review its business performances and make a constructive and self-critical assessment of them and the business progress to date.

It has to be emphasized that any manager who may wish to claim responsibility for the successful accomplishments at the place of work towards reaching the company's goals and objectives, cannot do so without a careful planning of his work. This task is a vital one in any organizational setting around the world. Thus the universal validity of the planning process.

A LENDER'S ASSESSMENT CONSIDERATION
OF
A CLIENT FILE
REGARDING AN APPLICATION FOR A LOAN

The lender's guiding factors and the yardsticks used by him in assessing the merits of his client's case regarding the application for a business loan, will more likely, have to do with the following considerations:

— the purpose of the borrowing funds;

— the kind of customer he is dealing with;

— the size of the business loan involved;

— the potential ability of the customer to repay the funds borrowed;

— the degree of reliability of the data submitted by the applicant and included in such documentation like:

  — Cash-Flow forecasts;

  — Budgets of sales;

  — Costs and profits;

  — Break-even analysis;

  — Capital Investment appraisal,

  — Etc. .

— the required or contemplated terms of loan;

— securities and guarantees offered and possible to be accepted by the bank;

— the past history of the business in operations, if any;

— information regarding the key people involved in the management of the firm's operations;

— the fairness and soundness of the firm's financial statements;

— the results of lender's financial analysis of the accounts;

— the strength of the company's internal control;

— the nature of the business, its products or services provided and considered within the context of the market competition and consumers' needs and demands;

— length of time in business and owner's experience and background;

— the length of the business relationship with the lender and other financial institutions;

— credit-rating agencies' reports;

— auditor's unqualified reporting and his eventual recommendation;

— business insurance and key people's life insurance, if any;

— other pertinent information necessary or required by the bank, at its discretion and depending on certain circumstances, like banking changing policies or rules, in respect to certain categories of loans and/or customers.

There are certain aspects of financial performances that may be revealed when financial statements figures are provided for analysis. Such information is of great importance to the banker since it constitutes his basis of assessment of the client's case.

Regardless of the client's size of business, in searching for a loan there are always certain major considerations that come under the banker's immediate attention, like the following ones:

PROFIT TRENDS. Only by having the firm generating profits, and this on a continuous basis, the business can survive the economic cycles and its forces at work within the competitive market and be able to repay its debts to the lender. Undoubtedly, the borrower's permanent operations, constitute somehow, one of the best securities in the eye of the banker or other lender involved in the transaction.

It has to be emphasized that there are certain factors which may affect the profits, gross margin and/or net profit of a business enterprise, for example:

— the competition aspect of the business and its saleable products;

— changes in fixed assets balances;

— fluctuations in the volume of sales;

— the level of various overhead costs,

— etc. . .

CASH-FLOW PROJECTIONS. Needless to say, any private individual or business firm should endeavour to increase its working capital, during the life of its business and try and give rise to the creation of sufficient funds, beyond the increase in its working capital. It is in the way that the banker may see profits made and his interest of securitisation of the debt ensured.

MAIN RATIOS AND RELATED CALCULATIONS. Any wise banker or other lender involved in considering a small business loan for his client will, more likely, reveal his interest that the shareholder(s)' respective business are also injecting or contribute with some advances to the business, even on a temporary basis. Such a contribution should be reasonable in relation to the existing or newly created debt. In this respect, the so-called gearing or the ratio of debt to shareholder(s)' funds or contributory advances, is an important tool used by a lender, in his analysis of a firm's accounts. Certain current ratios and related calculations are performed with the purpose to establish as to whether or not losses have been incurred or profits have been made during certain selected periods of time; if purchases or sales of fixed assets took place, and the length of time borrowed funds are to be repayed.

COMPANY'S ABILITY TO REPAY THE DEBT. In this line of thought, it is expected that the banker will show his interest to look into the firm's forecasts of its projected future targets. He will also look into such trends like sales growth and eventual fluctuations in gross margins. These will serve him as a useful purpose in assessing the likelihood of company's future profitability and its potential ability for further development and/or expansion.

In assessing a company's balance sheet accounts, as part of its yearly set of official and formal financial statements prepared for government reporting and fiscal purposes, a lender will, normally, deduct intangible assets, in particular goodwill, from the shareholders advances of funds, before any calculations using major ratios.

Certain accounting principles and standards, as used in certain countries, require that purchased goodwill be eliminated from accounts, against reserves, after the time of their acquisition. But as an alternative, it can be amortized over its useful economic life.

It can also be stressed that a lender will concentrate his judgement on certain important categories or group of accounts, according to their recognized significance, like the following ones:

INVENTORIES OF GOODS FOR RE-SALE. The acknowledged difficulties in this respect, as far as their assessment is concerned, has to do with the company's tendency to make unusual or wider provisions in order to manipulate the figures and cover certain items that are either slow moving stock or have to be treated as discontinued articles for sale. This fact may lead to the distortion, to a certain degree and extent, of the interpretation of the existing or reporting profits of the respective business enterprise.

As in respect to inventories of goods of various categories, useful information are needed, like the following:

— if stock increased or decreased and in relation to such items like slow-moving ones, obsolete or unsaleable items. Precious information should be obtained regarding the soundness of inventories control and the turnover rate during a certain particular period under consideration.

ESTIMATING PROVISIONS AND RESERVES OF VARIOUS KINDS. This especially, in respect to guarantees. Again, here, the tendency shown by certain companies may be in the direction of making excessively large estimates and put them forward to the lender.

PLANT EQUIPMENT, FIXTURES AND MACHINERY. Here, the negative aspect of influence on any assessment performed by the lender, may arise from certain methods of depreciation calculations used by a given company under consideration for a loan. But most of all, the distortion may appear from sale of certain assets, in significant amounts, above the recorded accounting figure of their book stated value.

DEBTORS. Depending on the volume of transactions or credit sales operation of a certain firm under consideration for a business loan, the relative amounts shown in the list of debtors (ageing list) may appear to have a significance of material importance).

The company's picture of debtors or accounts receivable from trade, mainly, will indicate the state of efficiency in debt collection, eventual bad debts to be considered following an analysis of the accounts according to their 'age', the discounts given or allowed in order to increase the size of collection funds and eventual, as the case may be, the increase of the level of cash sale.

An analysis of the state of Creditors of the business, may indicate if cash-flow problems were experienced by the business during the period. This may be revealed when the business asked and obtained longer credit time needed to make the due payments on accounts and loans payable. Conversely, if better or less favourable conditions have been granted by suppliers of goods and services, to the respective business.

PROPERTY. This account, in respect to its assessment, may reveal that the amount is affected due to a subsequent depreciation value.

Learning to manage funds is a matter of necessity for anyone involved in the process of running a business in general, and in the area of financial management in particular.

As there is no one best way of handling the financial matters, and due to the complexity of various factors involved in the business operations, it is advisable that one will seek the guidance of a professional or expert in the field, especially during the first stage of a business development.

THE FINANCIAL ANALYSIS: CERTAIN USEFUL RATIOS AND RELATED CALCULATIONS

IMPORTANT FINANCIAL RATIOS AND RELATED CALCULATIONS

Certain financial ratios are used with the scope of measuring the impact of management business decision-making process and its results, on the financial outcomes of the business activities and its ending operations.

Such ratios are considered to be an effective method in this respect.

When used properly, financial ratios help to depict a certain pattern of trend of business behaviour of its performances. They also serve a special need and usefulness when used in the areas of cash flow and profit categories in order to determine, especially, the impact upon the return of capital investment and the level of profitability.

EXAMPLES OF IMPORTANT FINANCIAL RATIOS IN USE.

THE FINANCIAL RATIO IN USE   **THE RELATED APPLIED FORMULA**

1. Return on Capital Employed Ratio

$$\frac{\text{Net Profit for the Period}}{\substack{\text{Capital Employed} \\ \text{(total assets)}}}$$

This ratio measures the return on amount injected into a business and it will assist one in the work of comparing this trend against the available alternatives to choose from.

2. Net Profit Ratio

$$\frac{\text{Net Profit after taxes}}{\text{Sales}} \times 100$$

Such a ratio will reveal the amount of net profit earned from sales. It helps analysing and finding out if a satisfactorily level of sales was achieved during the period under consideration by using a certain level of overhead costs.

3. Capital Turnover Ratio

$$\frac{\text{Sales}}{\text{Capital Employed}} \times 100$$

It depicts the value of sales resulted from every monetary unit contributed through the capital employed in a business. It shows if the prices generated enough value of sales or whether or not the level of sales can be considered satisfactorily for a given business, or it should be increased to a certain point.

4. Inventory Turnover

$$\frac{\text{Costs of Goods Sold}}{\text{Average Inventory}}$$

It shows the number of times the inventory of goods available for sale by a certain business enterprise, turns over during a certain selected period of time. It also indicates if the level of inventory is too low or too high.

The ratio is meaningful only when analysed on a comparative basis with that of other enterprises in the same industry or to the company's past performance in this respect.

5. Average Credit Granted to Clients

$$\frac{\text{Accounts Receivable — Trade}}{\text{Amount of Sales}}$$
$$360$$

The ratio is meaningful only in relation to the company's credit terms.
This ratio will reveal how fast the collection of cash from accounts receivable took place, and helps to analyse and find out one best way to deal with certain accounts in respect to doubtful collectable amounts and bad debts, if any, and slow-moving amounts collectable, etc . .

6. Average Payment Period
Average Credit Obtained from Suppliers

$$\frac{\text{Accounts Payable — Trade}}{\text{Amount of Purchases}}$$
$$360$$

It indicates how fast payments are made to suppliers, for example, and can assist one in analysing various accounts involved regarding creditors, so that certain beneficial steps may be taken in order to improve or seek better and longer terms based on negotiation with company's active creditors.

This ratio is meaningful only in relation to the average credit terms extended to the firm.

7. Gross Margin (Profit) Percentage

$$\frac{\text{Gross Margin (Profit)}}{\text{Sales}} \times 100$$

Such a ratio will reveal the amount of gross margin earned from the sales of the period under treatment for analysis. The respective ratio it will more likely be affected when new products are introduced in the market by the company, eventually, or/and buying conditions or terms are changing.

8. Current Ratio

$$\frac{\text{Current Assets}}{\text{Current Liabilities}}$$

In this respect it has to be mentioned that any level above the resulting ratio of number 1, will indicate that some amount of working capital is available to be put to use from converting the inventory of goods in stock and the accounts receivable, plus other current assets, if any, into cash. The acceptability of the resulting ratio depends normally on the industry in which a firm operates.

9. The Quick Ratio or 'Acid Test' Ratio

$$\frac{\text{Current Assets — Inventory}}{\text{Current Liabilities}}$$

Usually a quick ratio of 1.0 or greater is desirable, but it also depends on the industry in which a firm operates.

Liquid assets will include only those current assets of a business that are considered to be of quick capability to be converted into cash. And this, in a short period of time, for example, one month. It has to be stressed that the same treatment should be applied for current liabilities of the same business, when using this formula.

10. Break-Even Turnover

$$\frac{\text{Overhead Costs} \times 100}{\text{Gross Profit (Margin) percentage}}$$

This kind of ratio will indicate what turnover is required in order to cover all the existing costs of overhead available to be spent by the business in question, when margin is maintained at the same level.

11. 'Break-Even' Gross Profit Margin

$$\frac{\text{Overhead Costs} \times 100}{\text{Sales}}$$

This ratio will indicate how much the margin can be lowered while still using the same available costs.

12. Fixed Asset Turnover

$$\frac{\text{Sales}}{\text{Net Fixed Assets}}$$

This ratio measures the efficiency with which the business has been using its fixed assets to guarantee sales.

13. Total Asset Turnover

$$\frac{\text{Sales}}{\text{Total Assets}}$$

Such a ratio will reveal the efficiency with which the firm is capable to use all its assets to create sales.

14. Debt Ratio

$$\frac{\text{Total Liabilities}}{\text{Total Assets}}$$

It indicates the proportion of total assets provided by the company's creditors.

15. Times Interest Earned $$\frac{\text{Earnings Before Interest and Taxes}}{\text{Interest}}$$

It indicates the firm's capability to honour its contractual interest payments.

16 Price/Earnings (P/E) Ratio $$\frac{\text{Market Price per share of common stock}}{\text{Earnings per Share}}$$

Detailed business data and suitable or adequate related information or documentation can only be of help and may constitute a decisive factor, especially during a business' difficult stages of development or at the start of its foundation or establishment.

APPROVAL OR REJECTION:

The Leading Factors for Success

As one may, correctly or rightly assume, there are certain factors which will, undoubtedly, exercise influence on the lender's judgement and assessment leading towards approval or rejection of a client's application for a small business loan.

We shall enlist a series of such factors that may influence favourably the lender, towards an approval of an application for a loan. The factors presented below are not necessarily in their order of priority in any assessment. They may have a different weight in the overall assessment made by a lender, depending on the particular client and specific elements involved in the case under consideration.

— Good credit standing as verified by lender;

— The lender's flexible rules, policies and guidance giving its manager the latitude to overcome certain negative aspects in a case, which otherwise would have been taken into account and bring the application to a complete refusal or rejection;

— Good economic and financial climate in a particular country where the client resides, making possible for the lender to lower its conditions or higher demands for security, otherwise required during harsh economic and financial circumstances, the same country might experience;

— Good quality of financial reporting together with sound figures presented by the client in the documentation submitted in support to his application for a loan;

— Good financial strength of the business applying for a loan;

— Good prospective cash-flow projected by the business that will make possible the repayment of the borrowed funds, under the agreed terms suggested or required by the lender;

— Enough assets of substantial value, with good title by the firm;

— Good prospect for growth and development revealed through the information submitted by the company;

— Key people in the company and the management working team of the firm have the needed skills, knowledge and abilities to carry on successfully, the business various activities — its operations;

— Trust in the company's capabilities to attain its stated aims, goals and objectives;

— Lender is satisfied with his verification and the results and information of the business state of affairs, as disclosed by the firm's representative(s);

— The references and the reports presented by the professionals involved on client's behalf, are good and acceptable by the lender;

— There is enough coverage in the insurance policies regarding the key people managing the business, the contemplated undesirable circumstances that may result from accident, sickness and business interruption;

— The purpose of obtaining the loan is considered legal;

— The past record of the client's business performance is good, its system of internal control is soundly in place and the personnel who is fulfilling the company's various tasks are seen as capable in the eye of the lender;

— The degree of management needed expertise, the age and the strength of health, are considered good by the lender or his representative;

— There are enough securities and/or guarantees to support the applicant request for a loan of a certain size.

It has to be emphasized that other factors may be added on to such a list, as a particular case may require.

Conversely, lack of one or more of the factors of influence, as listed above, may lead to refusal or rejection of a client's application for a loan.

It has to be emphasized that it is through perseverance, diligence, hard work and good experience on the job and this primarily in a healthy interrelationship milieu, that one's work can stand the test of time while overcoming the unexpected or undesirable business circumstances or events.

A SUGGESTIVE MANAGEMENT QUESTIONNAIRE
FOR
EFFECTIVE FINANCIAL PLANNING

— What are your new ideas for growth and development, if any, for your business?

— Do you know how to build up a business plan for your business, a budget, cash flow projections and other necessary forecasts, as may be required from time to time by lenders, especially? If not, are you ready to consider and seek assistance from outsiders, like your prospective bank manager, your accountant, your solicitor, and others?

— Can you formulate in writing your aims, goals, and objectives?

— What are your existing or available sources of financial assistance in order to be able to pursue such aims, goals and objectives?

— Are you aware of all the kinds of risks involved in your business venture and ready to accept them with determination and confidence in your abilities to overcome all the eventual arising financial difficulties?

— What are your traits of personality that characterize you and can help you in your endeavour towards progress and development and affect your business activities in the future?

— What are your knowledge, technical skills and abilities needed to carry on your business operations in their various aspects, in your occupational area? But most of all, what is your level of specific experience in the field of your business?

— Did you perform a marketing investigation project and analyse your business environment with its prevailing conditions and marketing forces at work, within the framework or context of the existing competition?

— Do you know how to, rightly, price your products and conduct, properly, the advertisements and business promotional activities so that the right clientele will be drawn from your immediate environment, and from a larger audience beyond your sector of operation?

— What is your level of knowledge and experience in handling the various financial matters and related business transactions needed for your business?

— Do you have the right staff and management assistants to support your needed tasks, on a continuous basis?

— Do you have the necessary or adequate premises to carry on your business activities, its various operations?

— What are your available assets and/or available finance to acquire the needed machinery and equipment, for example, during the short and long-term in support to your planned business activities?

— What are your financial needs and requirements to pursue and translate your business plan into practice?

— Do you know how to search for the right financial institutions?

— Do you know how to search for the right financial products offered or made available by the existing financial institutions?

— What is your level of knowledge into various business subjects, like record-keeping, accounting, finance, economics, marketing, salesmanship, business law, use of business machines and other office equipment within a computerized environment?

Note: Many other useful questions can be created that will assist you during your process of self-assessment of your business ability to carry on your proposed tasks.

As one experienced writer in the field once stated, one of management's main responsibilities lies in the decision-making process and it has to do, mainly, with the balancing of risks and rewards. Such an important and interesting process constitutes one of the most delicate tasks that confronts the modern manager in today's complex and demanding world.

PART NINE

OTHER RELEVANT ISSUES

The present practical and detailed knowledge as revealed in the related parts of this useful Manual is supplemented by some selective and relevant issues in the field of much needed business education.

Considered as a whole, this Manual of universal application is designed to be used for self-instruction purposes on one hand, and for 'classroom' teaching-learning situations, on the other.

The various exhibits included in this practical Manual and represented by selective illustrations, diagrams, and tables are presented in order to support the various relevant topics. However, the respective patterns should be used while keeping in mind the specificity of a business operation and should be adapted to suit one's particular needs or interests.

As such, the entire work of this practical study should also be seen as merely a guide and not as a substitute for one's need to complement the already acquired knowledge in the field.

CONTENTS

Useful Knowledge of Certain Business Matters 377

Running the Business for Profits and the Role of Managers 382

Company's Aims, Goals and Objectives 383

Management Functions...384

Motivating and Stimulating People at Work 386

Manager's Timing: Its Improvement 387

Planning 388

Influencing Factors at Work 389

Certain Aspects of Communication
     Brief Considerations 391

Important Aspects and Problems of Delegation 393

A Self-Testing Questionnaire 394

The Character and Personality of the Manager 396

The elaborated or detailed collection of useful descriptions and illustrations as presented in this practical business education Manual, will, undoubtedly, enlarge one's horizon in the field and at the same time assist him to make a better technical or professional adjustment at the place of work, while making a noticeable progress in the field.

USEFUL KNOWLEDGE OF CERTAIN BUSINESS MATTERS

One of the main priorities of a modern business manager is to progress through learning, not only at the place of work but also through active participation in various technical, professional and business seminars, workshops, lectures and business-trade shows. This on one hand. And on the other, to be exposed to various technological and updated machinery and equipment.

In the process of his personal and professional development, it is useful for the manager to accumulate certain basic knowledge of certain known business matters. This will enhance and also facilitate his process of business communication, both in his interrelationship at the place of work and with the outside parties, like banks, professional accountants, governmental agencies, brokers, insurance agencies, etc.

Some of these subjects can be enlisted below:

— Basic Bookkeeping-Accounting;

— Payroll and Payroll Related Matters;

— Budgeting and Cash-Flow Projections;

— Inventories: Control and Management;

— Business Letters and Writing Skills;

— Business Finance;

— Business Mathematics;

— Marketing Strategies;

— Salesmanship;

— Data Processing, etc.

It is mainly in this way that his capabilities and professional development will reach a better and higher level of progress and success, and his image as a skillful manager will also be placed in a better light.

It is for this reason also that many companies around the world, in order to prepare a solid force of good personnel at work, provide numerous training programs, in a coordinated manner, technical libraries at the place of work, with updated material needed by the various firm's departments, incentives for taking related professional and technical courses, and many other avenues to stimulate learning and professional development.

It is undeniable that certain characteristics are essential and can exercise a positive impact on a manager's success and progress at work, like his drive, thinking and communication abilities, his technical knowledge and human resources skill.

Sooner or later, during his professional development, the manager will find himself involved in analyzing financial statements and the related business' state of affairs, the firm programme and proposed financing, forecasting, cash-flow projections, etc.

Successful operation and management of a business enterprise can also be associated with maintenance of adequate business records and business specific documentation and related relevant information for both internal and external use. Such information is to be found in a company s books of accounts like ledgers, journals and subsidiary records, in support of the business financial statements issued yearly, at the minimum, for taxation purposes, as well.

Practically speaking, good and proper records of a business, with adequate specific business forms and documentation of the daily business transactions of a firm, will make possible to measure the performances in progress, depict faults and any eventual irregularities, so that corrective steps can be taken before it is too late.

In this line of thought, the following statements can be advanced:

– Simple records will permit accurate measurement of performances;

– It will also allow analytical review by management and make possible better business decisions;

– It will facilitate to depict the strong and weak points within the various existing units or departments.

As the main objective of a business is to make a profit from its operations, the following categories should be under the attention for analysis by the management, namely:

– Sales Volume;

– Cost of Goods Sold;

– Costs of Operating the Business Enterprise, and

– Other Income than that resulting from the normal course of business activities.

A Manager should become familiar with the company's type and structure of financial statements, the various budgets, business plans, cash flow projections and forecasting, various working -time schedules, etc.

Any manager or prospective manager, occupying the position at any level, should strive and become familiar with the various existing kinds of auditor's reports related to a firm's financial statements, their usefulness and advantages and limitations to various users.

Furthermore, a manager should take interest in learning the meanings of the various categories, most commonly found in the financial statements and the notions and terminology of accounts listed in the firm's chart of accounts and/or the business 'books'.

Needless to say, the financial statements of a firm constitute the best instrument, in its final form, to be used for assessing the end results of the business — its operations, for a given period under consideration, namely to tell how the company fares into the future, based on its past accomplishments.

There is an unquestionable need by any manager to be able to understand and interpret the figures and notes of such statements. Thus, he will learn if the company will likely stand the test of time, in the light of the present situation along its financial lines and based on its aims, goals and stated objectives to be attained.

An analytical review of the company's figures, as presented by the auditor or company's controller, should include the study and application of the following yardsticks, on a comparative basis:

– Ratios of various kinds;

– Analysis of eventual trends, both internally and externally. This will bring to light any eventual fluctuation(s) of earnings per share. One should also learn the various advantages and disadvantages before making use of trend ratios.

– Regarding Balance Sheet Ratios, the following are some of the ones most commonly in use:
  – Funded debt/working capital;
  – Working capital ratio (or net current asset ratio);
  – Quick asset ratio (the 'acid' test ratio);
  – Net tangible assets per 1000 long-term debt;
  – Equity value (or book value) per preferred share and per common share;
  – Capital structure or invested capital ratio;
  – Current assets/current liabilities;
  – Fixed assets/net worth;
  – Inventory/working capital;
  – Total debt/net worth;
  – Current liabilities/net worth;
  – Common equity/capital funds;

- In respect to Earnings Statement Ratios, the following are normally in use:
  - Interest Coverage, by using the basic method and the alternative method;
  - Preferred Dividend Coverage, by using the simple method and the prior charges method;
  - Cash Flow; the analysis of cash flow will provide a better insight into the firm's earning power and as a 'signal' of the firm's ability to pay dividends and utilize funds for eventual expansion, if planned;
  - Percentage Dividend Payout Ratios in respect to savings.

- Value Ratios; Here, the following can be included:
  - Rate of return on common stock holders equity;
  - Price earnings ratio;
  - Bond yield ratio, etc.

- Other Useful Ratios and relations using the information from the statements, may include the following ones:
  - Pre-tax return on invested capital;
  - Net (or after-tax) return on invested capital;
  - Net (after-tax) return on common equity;
  - Earnings per common share;
  - Inventory turnover ratio;
  - Capital contribution of owners and creditors;
  - Pledged plant assets to long term liabilities;
  - Times fixed interest charges were earned;
  - Rate of return on total assets employed / return on investment;
  - Rate of return on common stock holders equity;
  - Price / earnings ratio;
  - Price level changes;
  - Sales / capital funds;
  - Sales / common equity;
  - Profit margin / sales;
  - Sales / working capital;
  - Profit margin / capital funds;

- Profit margin/net worth;
- Operating profit/capital funds;
- Sales/inventory;
- Sales/fixed assets;
- Average collection period.

Normally, it is expected that financial statements will be presented and analysed on a comparative basis.

It has to be stressed that when someone is making use of ratios and other relations in order to analyse and interpret the results presented in the firm's financial statements, one best way to follow is to compare the figures against the information in the same industry and of similar size of company, if possible. Such information can be found, for comparison purposes, in the various existing publications made available by specialized agencies.

By learning to apply such ratios and relations and making use of them, whenever applicable and necessary or possible, the manager will, on one hand, gain insight into the company's state of affairs and the results of operations for a given or selected period and, on the other, make a noticeable progress on his path of successful performance of his tasks and duties, as assigned to him by the upper echelon. This will enhance his level of communication with others, both internally and externally, and increase his chances of making better or wiser decisions during his daily business life.

Seeking assistance from others who have specialized training in the field, like accountants, business consultants, brokers, etc., can only be of help on the manager's road to success.

RUNNING THE BUSINESS FOR PROFITS
AND
THE ROLE OF MANAGERS

The profit motive is much alive and it can be found thriving everywhere around the world and in any type of industry. Profits constitute the main motivation for many to establish a business enterprise, to consider and making investments and create jobs for others. Profit plays an important role in promoting economic efficiency in any nation and, as a known economist once stated, 'Nothing contributes so much to the prosperity and happiness of a country as high profits'. Yet, another expert on the topic stressed that 'Profit is the return to owners of businesses for innovating and for taking risk'. Some consider profit as the 'superstar' of the annual meeting. In its simplest terms, profit is the difference between revenues and costs in a business activity (after deducting taxes and royalties to the government).

Management of any business enterprise will be asked always to have employees work in an efficient manner, keep costs of all kinds as low as possible, increase the revenue in all possible ways, thereby making the gap between revenue and costs, as high as possible, favouring profits.

Under a manager's attention should come a series of factors affecting revenue and costs, like the ones listed below:

REGARDING REVENUE:

- size of the market;
- advertising and promotions;
- strength of the existing competition;
- ability to forecast market conditions and to adapt to market changes;
- management ability;
- etc.

REGARDING COSTS:

- efficiency at work;
- productivity;
- innovation, research and technology;
- management ability;
- etc.

Profitability and growth become necessary for any business enterprise and determine how to consider strategies of both Marketing and Financial Management. It is through strategic planning that profit goals of a business is set up and how to go about it, in attaining it.

COMPANY'S AIMS, GOALS AND OBJECTIVES

In this respect we can enumerate the following:

- More profits resulting from increase in revenue(s) or decrease(s) in cost or both;

- To bring the firm on a higher level of dynamics and integration;

- To increase the quality of production to the best existing standards required in the field;

- Wise marketing of the company's products while maintaining fairness and competitiveness;

- To increase public confidence and trust for the firm's products and services;

- To reveal one best way of co-operation with outsiders like suppliers, subcontractors, agencies, etc.;

- To attract investors and offer greater incentives to stimulate injection of more capital into the business;

- To create public acceptance and goodwill for the company's services and products;

- To increase the number of good jobs, increase wages and job satisfaction and create more opportunities for advancement in return for more earnest contributions by employees, their increase initiative and innovation at work.

- To make a noticeable contribution to the entire national economy by meeting the social, civic and economic requirements and responsibilities as a sound corporate entity.

It has to be mentioned that various firms will have different goals and objectives based on owners/ managers or management stated needs and/or interests.

MANAGEMENT FUNCTIONS

Quite often, managers are confronted with the need to perform certain expected functions, during the performance of their duties, like the following:

Setting-up Objectives – These are related to the scope and purpose of the established enterprise, namely the results towards which all firms' activities and the outlined plans are directed. The objectives must be clearly stated or identified, expressed in a specific and concise way. It has to be indicated, for example, how much profit the company desires to attain, sales volume, target dates, and the like, during a certain given period. Objectives should be stated realistically and related to the available resources, in terms of money, skills, people, etc..

Analyzing the available resources – These resources – the availability and suitability of each – consist of money, materials, machinery, manpower, methods, markets and time, to mention only a few, for example.

Planning – It means selecting and using facts and assumptions to plan the activities necessary to reach objectives. Simply stated, planning means making decisions about a future course of action. A business should have a specific plan of where the business should reach in the short term and a detailed plan for the longer term (three or five years, for example). The plan should be revised from time to time, as the need may arise, depending on the new information and developments that may arise. It is only in this way, by revision, that decisions of various kinds, taken at different times, can be improved.

Organizing – 'This function consists of arranging human and other resources in an orderly pattern to effectively accomplish planned activities.' At the minimum, there is a need in any type of business enterprise to consider some of the basic principles of organization. Organizing, includes also the decisions or the establishment of various positions to be held within the firm, the related duties of each position involved, and the interrelationship amongst them.

Staffing – It means 'Recruiting, selecting, planning, training, developing, appraising and compensation of manpower to fill the positions in the organizational structure'.

Directing – It refers to 'Directing staff regarding their performances of planned activities, in a manner which encourages them to support the achievement of corporate activities and objectives'. It also includes giving orders to and motivating personnel (subordinates).

Controlling – The term stands for 'Measuring performances, comparing them to the expected standards, and correcting any deviation from standards'. This function is exercised by means of budgets, reports, visits, for example. This is in order to ensure that orders given are being carried out and various objectives are met.

Coordinating – It simply means getting the employees to work harmoniously together.

Innovating – It consists of developing new profit opportunities.

Motivating – It has to do with persuading people to work enthusiastically.

Representing – It means representing the firm outside the organizational framework.

Policies – the very purpose of policies in various companies is to guide employees in their day-to-day performances of their duties. The policies must be specific and clearly stated. They affect all the firm's employees.

Procedures – In certain companies, written procedures come to light that specify the sequence of steps to be taken in order to reach an objective. This becomes necessary, especially when the tasks employees have to perform, are of a complex nature.

Delegation – It represents the ability to delegate authority to others. This is in order to ensure the successful operation of a business. Employees should be trusted in performances of their duties.

Departmentation – Activities of a business can be grouped by function, e.g., sales, personnel, production, accounting departments. Also, the extent and authority for each function should be clearly defined in order to ensure a smooth operation of the business under consideration.

The basic managerial functions constitute the framework of any kind of learning in the art of management. The concept of management as a continuing process is an important one, and it must be performed effectively by supervisors at any level and in any type of business enterprise.

The successful performance of any supervisor may depend, mainly, upon his or her ability to manage well, the technical skills and/or other requirements.

Nevertheless, one should strive, constantly, toward an improved level of performance, and this in turn can be attained through learning. In order for an effective management to take place, the total managerial process should be integrated and properly coordinated.

The concept of authority is an integral part of any supervisory job. A supervisor equipped with basic authority will have also the right to expect good performance of his employees.

The managerial functions, including the ones mentioned above, should be considered, basically, of a universal character, in almost any type of business endeavour

MOTIVATING AND STIMULATING PEOPLE AT WORK

The manager should be able to reach a good and solid level of understanding of the activities take place in the business enterprise and explain how and why, at certain times, the motivation does not meet his expectations and/or of his subordinates-employees.

In this line of thought, the manager should be equipped with the necessary ability and knowledge to construe a Plan of Action in order to eliminate the eventual motivational shortcomings.

Motivation is a complex matter and a difficult issue to grasp with. It has to do with the psychology of human nature, styles of leadership, human relations, business performances, etc.

Motivation is what makes people to act, and it is a response to a pyschological drive.

The following can be enlisted as important internal and external factors that can exercise effect on an individual's motivation or lack of it:

— The desire to succeed;

— Recognition;

— Company policies, rules and regulations;

— Working conditions and the related psychological climate;

— Compensation and rewards provided;

— Interrelationship among people at the place of work;

— Status;

— Job security;

— Etc.

Motivation can be increased by broadening and enriching a task, and in various ways, like the ones mentioned below.

— New tasks added to the existing ones;

— Removing the difficult tasks;

— Increasing the volume of work;

— Removing certain controls;

— Stimulating people's initiative at work;

— Conferring or delegating more authority to the subordinates;

— Increasing specialization at work;

— Introducing more complex tasks;

— Etc.

MANAGER'S TIMING: ITS IMPROVEMENT

Any manager should try and learn how to make use of his time effectively. It is in this way also, that efficiency and productivity at work can be increased.

A few tentative suggestions, in this line of thought, can be made:

— Making use of the so-called Time-and-Motion studies that will increase efficiency and productivity at work. This method will make use of charts, graphs and analysis of other factors, in order to depict the areas where management can make improvements.

— Keeping a diary of the activities that take place and, subsequently, performing an analysis of what should not have been done, which part of work should be delegated and what should be avoided in order not to waste others precious time of work.

— Reviewing manager's job description and identity the work objectives and priorities.

— If a job description is not in existence, then an analysis as to what assignments or tasks as expected, should be drawn. Also an assessment of the inter-relationship amongst the various incumbents within the organization should be made, by drawing a company's diagram to indicate 'Who is Who' and who is reporting to whom, within the framework of the firm.

There are many factors responsible for manager's waste of time, like the following ones:

— unexpected visitors;
— clientele;
— colleagues;
— involved in sorting mail;
— telephone discussions;
— socializing during the business time;
— poor planning and poor organization, etc.

Whatever the cause may be, a manager should always be concerned with slashing time-wasters and boost his efficiency and productivity at work.

A basic criteria analysis program should be developed and put to use in a business enterprise.

Undoubtedly, it has to be adjusted in order to become suitable to the specificity of the company's operations in question, and based on its needs and interests.

All the related questions of a check list for improvements should be phrased in an objective manner and answered with the highest degree of accuracy.

After the so-called diagnostic program is accomplished and properly analysed and problems of deficiency depicted, they should be scaled down in their order of importance to be dealt with by the management.

PLANNING

As we are living in an increasingly complex society and within an interdependent world, with rapid technological and marketing changes, businesses of various sizes are confronted with the imperative need to do strategic planning for growth. Effective planning requires also effective means necessary to start the planning process. Owners and managers must be constantly preoccupied not only with solving problems but also look for opportunities for growth, be more flexible and more responsive to the impact of marketing changes in customers needs and general conditions prevailing in the market place. In this respect, certain things can assist managers plan effectively:

- Effective planing has to be designed to suit the firm's particular needs and specific interest, capabilities and opportunities.

- Good and effective planning has to lead to create new ideas and make the capital and human resources more productive.

- The company's situation should be under constant review and realistic appraisal regarding its objectives, plans for attaining the goals, estimating the cost for implementing such plans, and the like.

- Specific results should be sought and clearly stated, with dates outlined for attainment of the planned targets.

- An information system should be in place in order to sense any changes occurring in the marketing conditions, customers needs, new products, the state of competition, etc..

There is a consensus amongst the experts on management, that planning, as the first function of management, is one of the most important and crucial ones. This simply because managers are responsible to take care that things are done according to the plans.

How the manager thinks becomes very important and in a sense a crucial factor in order to reach an effective planning. The policies of any firm are continuing plans which lead the firm in certain directions. Good managerial judgement is always needed, especially when firm's policies, procedures, methods and rules, cannot fit a certain particular situation or a newly arising circumstance. Better planning can make better use of available resources. In this respect, the time factor can serve as a useful illustration and it must be used in an efficient manner, based on a structural plan of activity for the future terms.

Planning should also be related to motivation of subordinates in the process of performing their tasks. It is always expected by the employees that their manager is well organized and well planned. It is for all these mentioned reasons above, that the planning function is a paramount one in the context of the total managerial process. Simply stated, planning means deciding ahead of time what is to be done. Adequate amount of time and careful attention should be conferred to the function of planning. It is only in this way that a manager will find himself on the road of improvement, toward progress and success.

All kinds of plans regarding various periods of time should be coordinated and integrated and consensus reached, and related knowledge shared among various levels of management. By accomplishing this, beneficial outcomes will be recorded, based on good organizational planning. Timing is considered a critical factor in planning. Undoubtedly, good experience and good judgement, can only help a manager's action for selecting a strategy for implementation.

INFLUENCING FACTORS AT WORK

Referring to the management responsibility in this respect, one of the leading critics on productivity said that 'Much of the responsibility for increasing productivity rests with management to ensure that technological change is taking place, new markets are developed, the workplace is organized to achieve the most efficient level of output, labour management relations are well managed, programs exist to improve the skills of workers and the level of managerial know-how is constantly improving'.

There are certain interacting influences affecting feelings and behavior on the job, at the place of work, in almost any type of business and in any field of work. Such influencing factors include also the management methods used in organization, like leadership style, company policy and wage and promotion. These in turn, are related to the feelings and sentiments revealed by the people at work, like job satisfaction attitudes and morale that determine their behavior of performance, absenteeism, turnover, grievances, strikes, accidents, spoilage, the quantity and quality of production, for example. All these, will again, reinforce people's feelings and sentiments.

There are a certain number of factors found to characterize events on the jobs that led to either satisfaction or dissatisfaction and affecting job attitudes, like the following:

> Achievement
> Work Itself
> Advancement
> Recognition
> Responsibility
> Growth
> Security
> Relationship with subordinates
> Relationship with Peers
> Work Conditions
> Supervision
> Status
> Personal Life
> Salary
> Relationship with Supervisor
> Company Policy and Administration
> Hygiene

How people are doing in any given time is dependent, sooner or later, on the Country's productivity gains. Increased productivity means getting more output from the same inputs – and is the basic source of rising standards of living. Productivity is calculated as the real gross national product per employed person. 'When real wages are rising faster than productivity, it has a number of adverse effects. First, it creates inflationary pressures; second, it increases unit labor costs to the detriment of competition with the trading partners; and third, it depresses capital investment because there is less money left over for profits.' It is this that causes the need for productivity to increase to an acceptable or desirable level.

Optimum productivity is attained by the best use of all inputs (labor, energy, machinery, materials) and that is determined mainly by price. The formula for productivity growth requires far more than simply extra effort by 'workers'. There is no consensus amongst economists on how to define or measure productivity. However, it can be found at the heart of a country's economic performance. His/her productivity is associated with increased wages and/or profits, without the need for related price increases. Conversely, lower productivity is related to forcing cutbacks or fuelling the 'inflation cycle'.

A good manager should reveal ability in making timely and useful suggestions for improvements and express them clearly down the line, amongst his subordinates-employees, monitor how his messages are perceived, received and 'translated' into action, towards more efficiency and more effectiveness and productivity that will, further, lead to an increased level of output of goods or better services and increased profits.

It is also assumed that the management at the top will, more likely have a profit-sharing plan in place or will contemplate having one. This can only have a beneficial impact on the company's employees, increase their motivation and enthusiasm at work.

It is in such a working spirit that the firm's aims, goals and objectives can be met and higher standards of performance attained.

As an over-all company policy, along this line of thought, a system of good incentives and bonuses should be instituted within the firm. This will have a reinforcing effect amongst the good performers.

People of every kind of occupation and in various industries around the world, look always for appreciation and understanding of their efforts and endeavours, that will come from the upper echellons within the business organization. It is in this way that the manager, will, more likely, find himself surrounded by a good team of performers who are ready to give more of their time, efforts and skills, with minimum of control and supervision.

It is also recommended that managers will organize, from time to time, short communication sessions with his employees-subordinates in order to discuss their progress at work, their concerns and needs and interests, and make use of such occasions in order to encourage them to speak out and make constructive suggestions related to higher standards of performance, improve their working conditions or increase available means on hand to execute their tasks.

As one expert in the field of communication once stated, certain useful principles should be highlighted for managerial improvement, and adopted widely, namely:

– The worst communication is no communication;

– Communication is a transfer of meaning;

– Put the other person first;

– Mutual respect and consideration for other people's good knowledge and experience constitute the key to continuing and effective communication;

– The receiver is the more important person, and

– Communication is human.

In connection with these stated principles of communication. a good manager always trys to know the minds of his subordinates-employees or do research on them in order to favour a better and mutual understanding at the place of work.

— A manager should always recognize and allow for weak points, but focus on the good ones;

— While learning to receive a message, a manager will also learn how to send it soundly and effectively within the reasonable expected time of transmission along the known communication lines;

— The receiver is an active communciator and the feedback necessary to him implies always a two-way communication;

— The approach used by managers should be a personalized one. He will know his subordinates-employees by their name and make use of them and of their attitudes.

CERTAIN ASPECTS OF COMMUNICATION

Brief Considerations

The object of any kind of communication is to transmit a message or transfer its meaning; It is mind to mind intended.

The 'avenues' of communication comprises three major elements:

- The sender
- The message, and
- The receiver.

THE SENDER

The message ready for transmission should be formulated clearly, briefly, concisely, namely the message alone. It has to be passed on in its entirety, accurately.

The receiver should know the source of the message transmitted to him, or researches its sources. He will frame the message for him, and it will affect (it is assumed) how he will react to the message.

The 'tools' of communication can be either ORAL, using words to give expression to the message, and/or visual-words, graphs, charts, etc.

THE MESSAGE

The language of communication should be common to both the receiver and the transmitter, namely they should agree as to the meaning and perception of the terms. However, the transmitter should have in mind the receiver's interpretation of the terms.

THE RECEIVER

It is assumed that the receiver understand that it is his duty and responsibility to concentrate on the message, at the point of receiving it, will try and understand the message and also respond to it within reasonable or expected time, namely he will supply the feedback and follow-up on it.

THE BARRIERS OR OBSTACLES IN THE COMMUNICATION LINES

The obstacles can be of a general nature related to the situation or circumstances involved. This may be created either due to outside distractions or due to the fact that the message was received indirectly or **second-hand;**

Other obstacles or barriers may be generated at the point of receiving the message, by the receiver, due to some undesirable attitudes or habits. For example, jumping to conclusions while missing the relevant facts, being illogical, etc. It also may happen that the receiver is in a habit of making pre-judgements or lacking the needed or relevant knowledge contained in the message or related to its implementation, if performance of some sort is implied or required expressly.

IMPORTANT ASPECTS AND PROBLEMS OF DELEGATION

– **MOTIVATIONAL ASPECTS**

Managers at all levels will try always to motivate people through rewards and punishment devices and methods.

– **PERCEPTION PROBLEMS**

As managers have a well-developed system of attitudes and values which determine how the managers regard themselves, in particular, and others in general, so the employees have theirs, differently than those of managers. This fact should be taken into account and managers should get feedback as to how their employees consider delegation, learn about it and then make changes during the working process.

– **COMMUNICATION**

Most of the communication the employees engage in with managers is receiving information about the work. But managers should not rely on one-way communication systems in order to find out how well the delegated authority is being carried out. Instead, a free, easy and open relationship with the company's employees should be developed. This can be simply accomplished by increasing the frequency with which the managers see and talk to their subordinates.

– **TRUST BUILT-UP**

It has to be emphasized again in this respect, that delegation is a two-way process of communication, reciprocity, interrelationship and interdependence, mutual respect for one another's feelings (superior vs subordinate), values, attitudes, aims, objectives, aspirations, ideas, and the like; in other words, the building of a solid and fair or sound interrelationship based on trust. In this way, the managers will transfer to their subordinates, to a certain degree and extent, certain delegated authority, based on trust.

– **THE NEED TO INTRODUCE CHANGES**

Managers should reveal readiness to accept new ideas, even when these ideas are coming from 'below' their level. Wise management has also to do with unleashing creativity, potential for creativity, through delegation. In this line of thought, it has to be stressed that employees – subordinates will accept changes if they are presented to them on their terms. This means participation, involvement and trial-and-error experimentation by employees.

– **GROUP METHODS**

Practical findings in various places of work indicate that the working group can become a solid force for creativity, moral and acceptance of decisions, for example in setting goals, standards, planning details, etc...

THE MANAGER'S BENEFITS FROM DELEGATION

– The manager's tasks become easier.
– It facilitates a better job done by manager.
– It allows manager more time for thinking.
– It is conducive to an improved relationship with subordinates.
– It assists managers to unleash the employees' creativity and potential capabilities.
– It prepares managers for more complex and responsible tasks.
– It assists managers to reach high levels within the organizational structure, based on promotability.

A SELF-TESTING QUESTIONNAIRE

- What are your general management capabilities?

- What is your background in business in general, and in your chosen field of occupation in particular?

- Do you know how your business is doing?

- Do you have a firm programme of financing or a proposed plan?

- Will such a plan favorably affect your business?

- Are you aware of the risk(s) you are taking? What is your degree of feeling of security?

- What is the extent of your market knowledge with respect to cycles, product and competition?

- How strong is your cash flow standing and your working capital?

- Is your business strong enough to cope with eventual economic cycles?

- Are you doing forecasting to know where you are going?

- But, above all, what are your attributes or essential characteristics related to your business, prospective growth and development, like the following:

    - Drive: responsibility, acting, taking risks, etc.
    - Thinking ability: both creative and analytical
    - Human relations: ability gained through good and wide experience in dealing with people of various occupations and different backgrounds
    - Communications ability: both verbal and written
    - Technical knowledge of the business, etc.

- Are you self-motivated?

- To what extent are you independent in knowing what to do?

- What are your feelings about other people?

- To what extent are you able to get along with them?

- Are you capable of undertaking responsibility?

- Would you rather delegate tasks to others?

- How good are you at organizing?

- Do you like planning in advance?

- How good are you as a worker?

- Would you rather be a manager?

- How good are you at decision-making?

- Do you like making independent judgements?

- Are you trustworthy?

- How important is it to you to know what people think about you?

- How persistent are you in getting things done?

- What is your state of health?

- Are you an energetic person?

THE CHARACTER AND PERSONALITY OF THE MANAGER

The character and personality of the manager can strongly influence the success of the business operations, its aims and objectives. The manager's character, habits, instincts, background, drives and motivations have a direct and paramount bearing of his success. A good manager should be fully aware of his personal strengths and weaknesses. Ambition, strong will, determination, patience and understanding, self-confidence and solid common sense can only be of help, on the road to success and progress. Good business communication, both orally and in writing, ability in dealing with people like employees, customers, suppliers, outside agencies, will have a positive impact on manager's accomplishments during his daily business life. The ability to cope with stress in a positive and productive manner is a much needed characteristic of a modern manager. The ability to, analytically analyse a situation, a problem or a certain data of information is, yet, another useful characteristic of a good manager. In fact, the kind of person you are, is the keystone for your success, and the message suggested by many experienced people on their job in managerial positions is that one should look inward before looking outward.

There are certain ingredients of success that must exist and be revealed constantly during the manager's performance of his duties. In their absence, there is doubt that a manager will accomplish much in his relationship with other people, both inside and outside the organization. Let us mention only a few of such elements of success:

COURTESY

Essentially, it means concern about people. If one does not respect something or someone, he is likely to respect nothing or no one at all.

The real motive behind an existing state of courtesy is that making other people feel good will in turn make one feel good too. As differences may arise amongst human beings, courtesy, if it exists, it will ease such differences. Courtesy has benevolence built in and it is easily recognized in a person who has a genuine regard for the feelings of another person. True courtesy is universal and it implies keeping some thoughts to yourself in order not to offend or hurt other people.

NOTES

NOTES

A FINAL WORD

It is highly recommended that any prospective business education learner or interested reader who may be involved in his or her practical business operations, either directly or indirectly, make use of the services of a professional consultant knowledgeable in the specific field of operations. This, especially during the first stage of progress and development in the process of learning, both along the theoretical and practical lines.

Needless to say, one's potential capabilities and technical abilities and skilful training, together with one's innate drive for better accomplishments at the place of work, will make it possible to attain fruitful results, on the road to success.

I would like to stress again that, as there is not a royal road to reach the sea of knowledge, it is my strong belief that with perseverance, sound will and determination, while having the right consideration for other people's good experience, one may reach its splendid shores.